NANNY 911

NANNY 911

EXPERT ADVICE FOR ALL YOUR PARENTING EMERGENCIES

DEBORAH CARROLL AND STELLA REID

WITH KAREN MOLINE

10 ReganBooks
Celebrating Ten Bestselling Years
An Imprint of HarperCollins*Publishers*

All photographs courtesy of Granada Entertainment USA. G

HarperCollins books may be purchased for educational, business, or sales promotional use. For information please write: Special Markets Department, HarperCollins Publishers Inc., 10 East 53rd Street, New York, NY 10022.

FIRST EDITION

Designer: Nancy Singer Olaguera/ISPN Publishing Services

Printed on acid-free paper

Library of Congress Cataloging-in-Publication Data has been applied for.

ISBN 0-06-085295-X

06 07 08 09 WBC/RRD 10 9 8 7 6 5 4

Nanny Deb

This is for all my babies. So many of you are grown now! You captured me with your smiles, and my heart has expanded with the love I have for all of you. I couldn't have done this without you. You really are my true reward.

And to my Grandfather Howell. In life you were my rock; now you are my shining star, lighting my way and guiding me along. Thank you for always believing in me.

Nanny Stella

To my mother, Anne Reid. You gave my brother Billy and me an amazing upbringing. There was a time in our lives where you worked three jobs to provide for us and for that I am eternally grateful. I love you heaps . . . and I miss you more!

To my husband, Mike, because he is my life. If you pricked a vein, nothing but goodness would spill out. You listen to me when I know you would love to gag me. The day you called the wrong number was the luckiest day of my life.

CONTENTS

FOREWORD

. . . .

by **Head Nanny Lilian Sperling**

I've always loved children. In 1958, after my own three youngsters were no longer little children, I decided that I'd like to share some of the things I'd learned as a parent with other families. Before long, I was hired by a London agency that immediately placed me with families from the British upper crust.

When I used to care for newborns and toddlers, it was a great thrill to watch human life develop from its earliest days. After all these years, you'd think that I'd be used to that or even have become bored with it. But I'm not. In fact, I'm just as amazed and thrilled watching how a newborn grows into a toddler, and how toddlers grow up, become teenagers, and finally adults.

Some of my job placements were wonderful. The parents were lovely, receptive individuals who easily integrated my suggestions into their own child-rearing ideas. They were open to new ideas, eager to learn, and fully involved in their children's lives. And their children were full members of the family. Often, they took me traveling with them and their youngsters. We were all focused on developing healthy bodies and inquisitive young minds. Of course, there were other family situations that were less than ideal, either because the parents quarreled, were closed-minded, or had disorganized homes and lives. In some instances, it seemed as if the children were afterthoughts, and that mom and dad couldn't be bothered or weren't interested in doing their jobs as parents. Still, what made each position enjoyable was caring for the children. I must have done a good job because I was always getting recommended by the families with whom I worked to their friends. By the time I left England for the United States in 1986, I had worked for about two hundred families.

Initially I came to the United States because I was working for a British family that had moved to America, but before long, I realized that I wanted to live here permanently. I love it here—especially the openness of American society, the warmth of its people, its toleration of differences, and its casual lifestyle. Soon I was working again as a nanny. I was working through an agency, and once the managers realized that I was British—although it was plainly obvious to anyone speaking with me—it was decided to take advantage of this fact and mention it to all prospective employers. Once they found out I'd worked for some members of the aristocracy, American families clamored to hire me.

Parents and their children in every country have similar needs—to be respected, to be treated fairly, and to be well cared for, and it quickly became clear that working as a nanny for an American family was really not much different from working for an English family. Some of the parents I was now working for were marvelous, others inevitably less so. But for me the thrill was in caring for the children and in teaching nervous and frustrated parents how to become effective caregivers.

Today, even though I'm almost eighty years of age, I still love taking care of newborns and toddlers and I still occasionally work as a nanny. Little did I dream that the job I love so much would result in my appearance on a hit television show. It has been a thrill to lend the knowledge I've gathered through forty-seven years of experience to the people who watch *Nanny 911* each week.

To work with these special families on *Nanny 911* and to

reach out to so many people in similar circumstances is a wonderful opportunity and a blessing for me and my fellow nannies on the show.

What can be more important than giving your child the right start in life? Chances are that during pregnancy the mother-to-be ate carefully, made sure to get enough rest, and observed all those other healthy habits that would help her child to develop safely and strongly. And once that baby has arrived, the mother will want as much expert help as she can find to raise the little one into a happy, well-adjusted adult. Bear in mind that no one is more crucial to a baby's growth and development than the parents. And parents rely on family, friends, and books written by experts. But as you've seen on *Nanny 911*, a sensitive and seasoned child-care professional can go a long way toward helping you become a more effective and relaxed parent.

In this book, two really excellent professional nannies offer advice and guidance to a wider public on how to deal with many of the questions and issues that face parents all over the world—issues that are by turn infuriating, potentially dangerous, and even quite comical. We have paid particular attention to examples that have arisen whilst we have been working on the television series.

One of the reasons I think *Nanny 911* is unique is that the producers understood from the start that different nannies have different skills, insights, and experiences to draw on. Nanny Deb is strong and confident, but at the same time she has an intuitive ability to understand families, which endears her both to young ones and adults. She is so sensitive, in fact, that I've observed tears in her eyes at times when she is faced with moving family situations.

Nanny Stella is also very strong and understanding. Her specialty is establishing orderly routines and systems for families. Although Nanny Stella is known for her tough love, she's also caring and demonstrative and instantly wins over children. And she's not afraid to confront parents who aren't as easily won over. This book brings together their combined wisdom in an easily readable, highly accessible guide to parenting.

I hope that you enjoy reading *Nanny 911: Expert Advice for All Your Parenting Emergencies* and that its wise tips about child rearing will help smooth the exciting, often challenging, but ultimately rewarding journey known as parenthood. With your love and this book's expertise, you are on your way to raising happy and well-adjusted children.

With love and best wishes,
Head Nanny Lilian

INTRODUCTION

. . . .

> *"They're every parent's worst nightmare . . . Kids completely out of control and taking over the household. . . . These families have reached the end of their rope[s]. . . . They're in desperate need of help. . . . Can these families be saved? They have only one alternative left. . . . It's time to dial Nanny 911."*

Take heart, America. When your family's in trouble, *Nanny 911* is there on the double.

Millions of you tune in to our show every week to see what out-of-control family has begged us to take charge and transform their chaos into serenity . . . in only seven short days. No matter how loud the tantrums, how clueless the parents, and how unwilling these families may be at first to making the kind of sweeping changes we know they need, pretty soon they come to realize that we can help them turn it around. We teach them that their mistake is often to look only at what's going on *today* without thinking ahead to what will develop into far more complicated repercussions *tomorrow*.

Parents, you need to learn that you can nurture and love your children, but you must also be teachers and role models for good behavior. After all, children learn what they live.

When you yell and scream, your kids yell and scream.

When parents don't work together and undermine each other's parenting styles, your kids don't work together.

When there are no consequences for naughty behavior, your kids realize there's no reason for the naughtiness to stop.

When you indulge your kids because you feel guilty for working so much, kids turn into spoiled little princes and divas.

When you just don't know what to do, your kids take over.

Time and time again, we tell parents that it is their responsibility to parent. In one family, four-year-old Jamie announced, "I'm the boss of this family!" He thought he was. He acted like he was. Because his mother let him.

After a week with Nanny Stella, his mother doesn't let him

anymore. Jamie was relieved that he could be a four-year-old, and Mom was thrilled to feel like she was finally in charge. She learned that good parenting doesn't mean children have their every whim catered to or that they never get upset. She also realized that she had to give up some of her need to control all the parenting and let her husband in. She and her husband learned to work together as a team; to be consistent. Before we arrived, they weren't on the same page—they weren't even reading the same book! As a side effect, their marriage was in serious trouble.

We wish we could tell you there's some magic parenting pill that makes children instantly behave 24/7. But the truth is that there is no magic pill. There's only consistency, determination, discipline, and an end to lazy behavior. If you want to have a happy household, you've got to confront the problems as soon as you can, with conviction and consistency. If the problem is small, deal with it now. It's easier to take a pacifier away from a baby than it is to take it away from a three-year-old.

All the parents who called *Nanny 911*, begging us for help, were so used to choosing the easy way out that they didn't know how to get around it. Frankly, we believe that every parent knows in their hearts that if you do choose the easy way out—"Yes, Alexander, you can have that candy bar before dinner if only you stop screaming in the supermarket so everyone will stop looking at me and thinking I'm a terrible mom"—you'll be paying for it and not just at the supermarket checkout.

The Nanny 911 philosophy is simple: Brats are not born; they're made—shaped by parents who can't say no, formed by parents who never follow bad behavior with swift consequences, and enhanced by parents who can't communicate.

We believe in the No Nonsense School of Parenting.

When we're on the job, this means the parents learn to *grow up* and be *parents*.

Coming from the No Nonsense School of Parenting doesn't mean we're cruel or harsh or unkind or not loving—on the contrary. What parents come to realize is that being strict does not mean being a tyrant. Far more damage is caused because they've let their kids walk all over them, instead of establishing clear-cut boundaries and order in the house.

Nanny Deb once worked for a family whose dad let his daughter practice her gymnastic flips off the chaise, raid her older stepsister's hidden stash of M&M's, and watch his beloved Hong Kong kung fu videos—at the same time and at the tender age of three. Well, Nanny Deb told dad that practicing her flips and eating her sister's chocolate at the same time was unacceptable and that Dad's violent videos were entirely inappropriate viewing for a three-year-old.

Dad snapped, "Don't talk to me about my child like that."

Nanny Deb's reply was short and to the point: "Until your daughter can tell you, *I'm* telling you. Right now, *I'm* her voice. And my voice is saying, "*Cut it out*."

So if you want advice that's sweet and fuzzy and cuddly, this book is not for you. If you do want answers that *work*, then we're here to help.

We believe that children need lots of love, but they also need lots of House Rules, giving structure to their days. This means strict limits tailored to children's personalities, and lots and lots of positive reinforcement rather than constant nagging and negativity. We'll show you how to confront your family problems head-on, with firm but loving discipline, clear and effective communication, and the implementation of family rules. We'll teach you how to stop making excuses, avoid tackling problems that may seem insurmountable, and how to stop giving in when your children are whining and crying.

Paradoxically, imposing *more* order on children allows them the freedom to thrive and stretch their wings and to grow up to be happy, healthy, and loved.

Parents often tell us that they don't have time to deal with House Rules, and we tell them, fine, just watch the show. It isn't staged. It isn't scripted. It is possible to undo years of deeply entrenched behavior and stubborn problems in only a few short days. We do it all the time—because we have the experience to zoom right into the essence of what's going wrong. We know how to sweat the big stuff and let the small stuff go. Only a limited number of families can be chosen to appear on episodes of *Nanny 911,* but we've had such an overwhelming response to the show that we decided to share our system with overwhelmed parents—parents who we know are desperate for parenting advice that's foolproof. Advice that really and truly *works.*

You'll see some of the same phrases repeated over and over again. That's because we need to drill them into your heads so they become as much a part of your daily routine as brushing your teeth and sending your kids off to school.

We've formatted *Nanny 911* in a unique way as a parenting crisis manual, so you can think of it as the at-home replacement for a trip to the parenting E.R.—not only for babies and toddlers but also for all your children.

Part I deals with communication. Without effective communication, none of our advice in Part III will work. So parents, read the first three chapters right away. Chapter 2 lists different parenting styles of communication and teaches couples how to get on the same page. Chapter 3 has vital information teaching parents how, precisely, to talk to their children. Chapter 4 gives you tools to help your children be able to express themselves effectively—and that means no more whining, crying, screaming, tantrums, and fits.

Part II tackles House Rules. In chapter 5, you'll read about how to figure out and set up your own House Rules. Chapter 6 explains the Nanny Rule that actions have consequences, and how to turn that into House Rules of time-outs as well as a reward system like the marble jar. Chapter 7 delves into how to set up routines and be consistent, especially with the crucial concept of a family dinner. Chapter 8 deals with the all-important topic of cleaning up and getting rid of clutter and how that means chores for the children. Chapter 9 leaves you with information about the most essential of House Rules—those dealing with love and respect.

Part III is a reference guide to specific problems, listed alphabetically. If you have a problem, feel free to turn to this section first, then go back and read the earlier parts for more detailed information. Chapter 10 includes problems inside the house, chapter 11 includes problems outside the house, and chapter 12 deals with tough issues.

You, too, can learn how to pinpoint what's gone wrong in your household, see what's not working, and devise a plan. Do this and your family can make amazing progress in a relatively short time. Our quick fixes will give permanent results—if you follow our plan.

And if you have to take a week of your vacation time to set new House Rules in motion, then do it. What are you waiting for? Drastic problems need drastic measures.

Parenting isn't rocket science, but it *is* hard work. It will probably be the hardest work you'll ever do in your lifetime but also the most rewarding. We firmly believe that it is the *parents'* responsibility to create a happy home.

Most of all, every child deserves respect, order, consistency, and love. We hope this book helps you to establish House Rules that work for you and allow your family to grow and thrive so you can be the family you always dreamed of being.

Love,
Nanny Deb
Nanny Stella

THE 11 COMMANDMENTS OF *NANNY 911*

BE CONSISTENT
No means no. Yes means yes.

ACTIONS HAVE CONSEQUENCES
Good behavior is rewarded. Bad behavior comes with penalties.

SAY WHAT YOU MEAN AND MEAN IT
Think before you speak—or you'll pay the price.

PARENTS WORK TOGETHER AS A TEAM
If you can't be on the same page, your children are not going to know who to listen to—and they'll end up not listening to anyone.

DON'T MAKE PROMISES YOU CAN'T KEEP
If you tell the kids you're going to Disneyland, better get ready to pack your bag.

LISTEN TO YOUR CHILDREN
Acknowledge their feelings. Say "I understand" and "I am listening"—then take the time to understand and take the time to listen.

ESTABLISH A ROUTINE
Routines make children feel safe and give structure to their time.

RESPECT IS A TWO-WAY STREET
If you don't respect your children, they are not going to respect you.

POSITIVE REINFORCEMENT WORKS MUCH BETTER THAN NEGATIVE REINFORCEMENT
Praise, pleasure, and pride accomplish far more than nagging, negatives, and nay-saying.

MANNERS ARE UNIVERSAL
Good behavior goes everywhere.

DEFINE YOUR ROLES AS PARENTS
It is not your job to keep your children attached to you. It's your job to prepare them for the outside world—and let them be who they are.

COMMUNICATION

1 CAN THIS FAMILY BE SAVED?

DAY 1

The McCray family had a problem—seven problems, actually. Two parents, and five rambunctious, overwhelmed, inconsistently disciplined boys, ranging in age from three to ten.

Dad Craig was a New York City cop, tough as nails at work, but unable to lay down the law at home. Stay-at-home mom Tracy was so overwhelmed that she just about gave up completely when it came to disciplining the boys. The boys hit one another, screamed, and yelled all day. Tracy yelled back. They didn't listen. Eventually, she simply tuned them out, then collapsed, even as her boys were climbing the walls—literally. It was a miracle no one had gotten seriously hurt scampering up the bookshelves or using Mom's heavy candlesticks for batting practice!

"I'm at work a lot, so when I'm home with the boys I kind of let certain things go because I feel guilty," said Craig, as he leaned over to his son Jack. "Don't tell Mommy I gave you coffee," he told the seven-year-old. "If you tell her I gave you coffee I'll get in trouble. Mommy doesn't want you with the bikes in the house. Jojo, you want to try on your bike?"

Luckily, Mom didn't hear that conversation, but she had her own headaches to deal with. "Disciplining the boys, that's an issue.

Hey—quit it!" she yelled to CJ. "I'm going to pull you by the hair. Go inside and stay there! Why are you hitting Mommy?"

"'Cause I want to," her charming little boy replied.

Tracy threw up her hands. "Oh, don't bite me!" she shrieked.

Every evening the boys screamed for their dinner, and then, after eating a few bites, dumped it on the floor under the kitchen table. By then, Tracy was too frazzled to care. Craig yelled some more. No one listened. Eventually, they all collapsed into bed.

And then the chaos started brewing all over again the next morning.

No one in the family was happy about this situation. Everyone woke up grumpy and out of control.

Has any of this happened in your family? Perhaps not in such an extreme manner, but at some point every parent wants to just give up and let the craziness take over.

Let's see what happens when Nanny Stella arrives. She's going to assess the situation, sit down with Tracy and Craig, and set up a plan. Take a look at what **Nanny Rules** she chose to use, and how quickly they being to work.

DAY 2

After spending a day observing the craziness in the McCray house, Nanny Stella had the big talk with Tracy and Craig.

"I've been in your house making some observations," Nanny Stella said. "One of them being there is absolutely no discipline in this house whatsoever. There's no consistency. There are no consequences. There's no what's right and what's wrong.

"The good news is I'm going to come up with a plan, and if you put that plan into effect and you follow it through, then I guarantee you a much more normal family life. The bad news is I think you're in total denial, and I'm not convinced that you're going to be receptive to anything I've got to say!"

Tracy looked bemused, but agreed to try it. So did Craig. But then he admitted he was so sure the nanny's plan wouldn't work that he was willing to stake his pension on it.

At a family meeting, the looks on everyone's faces were priceless when Nanny Stella went through the list of **Nanny Rules** that this family needed the most.

- The first thing you need to do is **establish order**. Introduce a timetable, and keep the boys informed.
- What you need to do is **say what you mean and mean it**. I hear a lot of "Don't do that," but nothing follows.
- There is absolutely no discipline in this house. **Actions have consequences.** So, there must be consequences for bad behavior.
- What I would like to introduce is the **time-out**.
- You've got to be firm, not angry. **Don't yell.** Believe me, yelling never works.
- You've got to treat your family and others as you would like to be treated. You're a family, yet you're fighting all the time and shouting and yelling. **Respect is a two-way street.**

Parents

1. Establish order
- Introduce time table.
- Keep them informed.

2. Consistency.
- Say what you mean and mean it.
- If you make a promise, see it through.

3. Discipline.
- Reward good behavior.
- Consequences for bad behav...
- Time out.
- When disciplining chang...
- Be firm, not angry. I...

- Absolutely under no circumstances is anybody going to hit anybody anymore. **Hands are not for hitting.** Hands are for praying or for playing but not for hitting.
- You are brothers; you are family; and families love one another. All of you are **brothers for life.**
- Just as important, mom and dad, remember that **parents work together as a team.**
- I would really love to see some good manners. **Manners are universal.** I don't honestly think that I've heard a please or a thank-you.
- I'm going to show you your schedule timetable. **Establish a routine.** This is your board from this time forward. At 7:00 A.M. we wake up, then 11:00 to 12:00 we have lunchtime and nap time.
- You're going to eat dinner together because **family time is essential for communicating.**

The room was silent for a moment as the family digested this long list. Craig did not seem to be happy at all. "You're looking a little horrified there, Craig," Nanny Stella told him.

"The problem is when you throw a woman into it," he replied.

"Whoa!" exclaimed Nanny Stella.

"What is that supposed to mean?" an indignant Tracy asked.

"Well, you know what I mean," Craig said, throwing up his hands. "When you put your touch into it as mom, everything gets thrown apart.

"So it's my fault," Tracy said, with some anger.

"Well, let me see you follow this schedule," Craig said.

"It's not just for Tracy. Craig, it's for you, too. Parents are supposed to work together as a team. This is your family's schedule. It will make everyone's life far better." Craig looked even more skeptical. "Well, we're willing to try it," he said dubiously.

THE TIME-OUT

Before anything else could happen, the boys needed to understand the Nanny Rule that actions have consequences. The way to do this was by going back to basics—the Nanny staple of the time-out, an effective disciplining technique that seems incredibly simple, yet is incredibly effective. Time-out was not a word that existed at the McCray house before Nanny Stella arrived.

We'll go into this in much more detail in chapter 6, but here are the basics. A child who is naughty goes into time-out, which is a cooling-off period, after a warning is given that the time-out is imminent if the misbehavior doesn't stop. The rule is one minute for every year of age. A timer is set, and the child is the taken to the specified time-out spot. If your child starts misbehaving in any way during the time-out—acting up, talking, trying to leave the time-out area, and so on—the clock gets started all over again.

A few minutes might seem like nothing to adults, but is an eternity to a child.

Which is why time-outs work.

In the McCray house, the eldest child, nine-year-old CJ, was the ringleader. Agile and sassy, he was a real smarty-pants—and he knew it. He often egged his younger brothers on to start fights and to pummel one another like crazy. Then he'd sit back with a lazy smile, pretend he was the innocent victim, and enjoy the ensuing chaos. He had a unique ability to let everybody else take the blame for his naughtiness.

Worse, because he was the oldest, he was the one who got his younger brothers going. This is pretty typical. The oldest child often sets the pace for the rest of the brood. The trick is to turn the oldest child around—take out the general, as it were—and then the rest will follow.

So CJ was the first to go into the time-out. Nine minutes of pure torture!

Nanny Stella set the timer, and CJ had to sit on the sofa in the brightly lit living room, with his brothers nearby and Nanny Stella watching from the next room. He was astonished that he was being

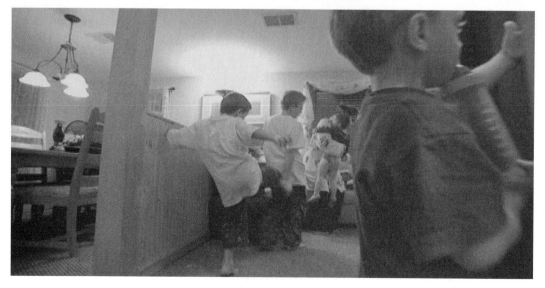

disciplined. He turned on the theatrics, and no one paid any attention. Then he got up and tried to stop the timer, but that just made
matters worse for him.

"Every time you come out of time-out, it starts again," Nanny
Stella told CJ as she reset the timer. "So you're going to be in time-
out for the rest of your life unless you want to behave."

"You don't mean that!" CJ retorted with a laugh.

"How old are you?" Nanny Stella asked. "Every time you're in
trouble, you're going in time-out. So listen the first time, and do
what your parents ask you."

CJ pouted. He flipped and flopped on the sofa.

"Time-out is like sitting in a cage," he said. "A dark, scary cage."

Finally, after what seemed like an eternity to CJ, the timer
dinged.

"Four, three, two, one . . . oh, yeah! Freedom!" CJ exclaimed.
"The world's back to normal!"

"I'm very proud of you," Nanny Stella told him.

"He was screaming, shouting, and kicking," Nanny Stella explained. "That didn't bother me—my philosophy is consistency no
matter what you're applying. If you get up and keep putting children back in the time-out, in their seats, eventually they're going to
get the message that you mean business, and stay in their seats."

"After the time-out was over, CJ actually seemed to be a little
more relaxed," his dad said with some amazement.

CJ was also in shock from actually being disciplined.

Time-outs are an effective way to calm children down, make
them realize they are responsible for their actions, and teach them
that naughtiness is not to be tolerated

DAY 3

Time to go to the park. The car was still in the driveway after
twenty minutes because three of the boys refused to get into their

car seats. It was a struggle to get them in, to strap them down, and to keep them from unbuckling the belts. There was so much screaming, shouting, and yelling that Tracy gave up.

Aside from the fact that it's illegal to not have children restrained in either car seats or booster seats in many states until they reach eight years and eighty pounds, it's also extremely dangerous and potentially lethal. Nanny Stella's first priority to any family in her charge is safety. (Of course it's a parent's first priority, too.) She wasn't about to let Tracy drive off with the kids crawling out of their car seats. The kids had to learn that sitting quietly in their car seats is nonnegotiable if they want to go anywhere in the car.

So Nanny Stella suggested that Craig bring the car seats into the house. Let the boys play with them, crawl all over them, and get used to being buckled up in them.

Tracy immediately scoffed at the idea, but after Craig brought in all the seats and plunked them down in the living room, she was astonished when the boys went right to their seats, playing in them happily.

By bringing the car seats into the house, the kids got used to them, so that took away the fear factor. Plus, each child could identify his or her own seat, which made them feel proud and careful.

After Craig was able to take the kids for a nice, long afternoon outing to the park, it was time for dinner.

"Mom, can we go out to dinner?" asked Francis.

"That's a really good question," Nanny Stella told him. "Do you know what Mom's answer *should* be?"

"No," he said.

"Her answer should be, 'If you behave yourselves.'" Nanny Stella replied.

Meals at the McCray house were typically like feeding time at the zoo. Because there were no fixed mealtimes, the family rarely sat down at the table together. The boys ate either in the living room as they watched TV, or they grabbed their plates off the kitchen table, gobbled some of their food under the kitchen table, then threw the rest of it at one another, leaving a stinking mess on the floor for their mother to clean up in despair.

Because Nanny Stella was in the house, Tracy and Craig tried to get the boys to eat at the table with them. At first, it worked well, but as soon as CJ got up and went under the table, the rest of his brothers crawled over the top, then grabbed food off their plates and disappeared under the table. When they were done eating and throwing food, they simply got up and went to watch TV, leaving an incredible mess and a frustrated mother.

Nanny Stella had a talk with Tracy. "Family time at the table is essential for communicating," she explained. "To make it work well your boys have to stay in their seats, and everybody needs to say please and thank you. What applies at home applies in a restau-

rant and vice versa. But when your boys started climbing out of their seats, you and Craig didn't do anything."

"I was eating," Tracy protested. "I couldn't go anywhere. I'm tired. I've had enough. We start off at the table, and it always winds up like this."

"Because it's a habit," Nanny Stella replied. "It's just a bad one."

"I mean, it's just ridiculous for me to grab all of them and put them back in their chairs," Tracy went on, not knowing that her whining didn't faze Nanny Stella in the slightest. "My dinner would be ruined."

"Everyone's dinner is ruined when the kids eat on the floor," Nanny Stella calmly said. "You're hoping for a miracle to happen overnight to make your kids start sitting in their seats, when you're not willing to do anything about it."

By the end of the day, Tracy had become so fed up with all the chaos that she simply stopped caring. Naturally, the boys' behavior became even worse.

Nanny Stella had another talk with mom and dad. Craig seemed receptive to her suggestions. Tracy did not.

"Nanny has some good rules," she admitted, "but I don't think we're going to follow them."

Clearly someone had to get on the same page as her husband, or this family could *not* be saved.

DAY 4

After a visit from Tracy's mother, Nanny Stella began to understand quite a lot more about the family dynamic. Tracy is so used to being criticized that she has simply stopped listening. She had no idea that she was doing the exact same thing to her children—and they had tuned her out completely. Tracy seemed unable to show

that actions have consequences, to put the kids in time-out, or to do anything, frankly, except raise her voice.

Worse, her attempts to become a disciplinarian were constantly undermined by Craig. Parents must work together as a team for any kind of discipline to work. This is absolutely critical. When kids chronically get contradictory messages from mom and dad, they don't know whom to believe. Or they quickly learn how to play off one parent against the other.

Tracy finally reached the end of her rope when her two-and-a-half-year-old son Jack misbehaved. See how dad contradicted mom.

> MOM: Oh my God, he drew all over my couch. Oh, I feel sick. Jack wrote on my new leather couch with a pen.
>
> DAD: Jackie, who did that? He didn't mean to do it. It was probably someone else.
>
> MOM: He meant to do it. He took the pen and drew on it.

NANNY: Why do you think he did it? For attention?

MOM: No, because he's just a brat. You're going to get time-out for writing on my couch.

DAD: Who?

MOM: Jack.

DAD: No, no, I already gave him a warning.

MOM: Jack, you're going in time-out. Because you start ruining my furniture . . .

DAD: No, stop fussing.

MOM: No, he's going to sit right here. You get time-out, Jack. You don't write on Mama's couch!

NANNY: Tracy, I'm so impressed I could cry. Because of your couch this is the most firm I've ever seen you. Good job.

MOM: He gets six minutes—two minutes for each line.

DAD: How do you know it was him with the pen? The boys said it was Francis.

MOM: I saw him with it. Jack had the pen in his mouth.

NANNY: I know this is killing you, Craig, but you've got to support her. Jack drew on the couch.

MOM: Jack, did you draw on the couch?

CHILD: [crying] Yes.

After Craig realized what he was doing, he quickly stopped siding with his son, and helped Tracy make it clear to Jack that drawing on the furniture wasn't acceptable. He even told Jack to get the cleanser and clean up the couch himself—which Jack did with alacrity.

That night, as the family sat down at the dinner table, Tracy and Craig were firm about the new rules. They were a family, and they were all going to eat together, at the same table. No questions asked, and no sitting under the table allowed.

The meal started well, but after a few minutes, the boys were screaming and shouting and trying to crawl down into their usual spot. This time, Tracy and Craig acted as a team. Whoever acted out was put back in his seat and told to behave.

Eventually, the boys got the message. It wasn't easy, but Tracy and Craig stuck to their guns.

Amazingly, the boys finished their meals at the table. Then, without prompting, they picked up their plates from the table and put them in the sink and the dishwasher. All the brothers were working as a team.

Tracy and Craig had learned that mealtimes are very important. Family time at the table is essential. It's not only about bonding as a family but also about socialization. It's about everything that children need to know.

DAY 6

CJ, the eldest son, has made an astonishing transformation. Formerly the ringleader of the circus of naughtiness, he is now thoroughly relishing his role of older brother and has taken the younger boys under his wing. When he behaves, they behave. They look up to him for advice and guidance, and he positively beams with pride. Instead of the eldest sibling's bad behavior setting a bad example for the younger kids, it was encouraging a sense of pride and responsibility in them.

Dinnertime is now fun and relaxing for the entire family. The kids talk about their days. They mind their manners. They help to set the table, clear the table, load the dishwasher, and wash up some of the dishes.

Tracy and Craig can't believe it, but the kids have proven that if they're trusted with a little responsibility, they will be eager to help and prove themselves.

Tracy and Craig shower their boys with well-deserved praise.

They finally realized that good parenting equals consistency and teamwork.

DAY 7

A long-awaited family gathering at a posh Italian restaurant has been making Tracy a nervous wreck. Craig, too, was worried about how the kids will behave out in public with a roomful of hypercritical relatives.

Before they leave, Tracy and Craig get down on the floor, at their kids' level—this is a crucial way to effectively communicate (which we'll discuss in much more detail in chapter 3)—and have a heartfelt talk with each of the boys before they leave, telling them what an important occasion this is and how they know their boys can behave. The kids listen carefully. They want to please their parents.

By respecting their kids' intelligence and talking about their feelings, Tracy and Craig are able to work with their boys as a

team. Children often don't know what's expected from them, especially during a special occasion. But even little kids are smart enough to understand what they're meant to do, if their parents prepare them in advance. The McCrays were now able to trust their boys to be able to listen to them and to help them when they need it most.

At the restaurant, Tracy's mom began crying with joy. She'd never seen her grandsons behave so well, especially in public. Tracy and Craig got teary, too.

They finally felt like a family.

They finally acted as one, as well. When Nanny Stella arrived, the children had no boundaries whatsoever. They could do anything they wanted without any consequences at all. But in one short week the children have learned to be polite and respectful. The time-outs worked. Setting up a routine worked. Manners worked. Tracy and Craig, and all their boys can be proud of their hard work—their *teamwork*.

2 COMMUNICATION: PARENTS WORKING TOGETHER AS A TEAM

On each episode of *Nanny 911*, we spend a day observing families, then devise a plan to help turn these families around. We sit down with the parents, and we have a talk.

We *communicate*.

So now, we're talking—and just to you, moms and dads. This chapter is all about you, about how your style of communicating *with each other* is absolutely critical to raising happy children.

Without good communication, no family can thrive. Without parents working together as a team, discipline is impossible. Without effective conversation, none of the ideas in this book will work. Sounds dramatic, but it's true.

This is why you'll often hear us say that parents aren't even on the same page with each other. One parent is the disciplinarian and another is the softie. One is the good cop and the other the bad cop. One does all the yelling and one gives all the hugs and soothing.

This problem can start with only a few simple words:

Mom says "Yes" and Dad says "No."

Mom says, "That's okay, sweetie," and Dad says, "Go to your room."

Mom screams, "Wait till your father gets home," and when Dad comes home, the incident is forgotten.

Mom says, "No more yelling," and Dad starts yelling the minute he walks in the door.

This has simply got to stop.

KIDS WILL NEVER LEARN TO USE THEIR WORDS UNLESS THEIR PARENTS DO

NANNY RULE

Remember that kids are sponges. They learn what they live. You're playing to the audience, whether you realize it or not—and whether you believe they're listening or not. They're soaking up every single thing you say. They're mimicking your body language. They're going to emulate your behavior.

So when parents are divisive and inconsistent, kids quickly learn how to get their way by playing mom and dad against each other. Since little kids are by nature egocentric, this isn't difficult to do. They want their own way, and they're going to find the easiest way to get it.

· ·

PARENTS WORK TOGETHER AS A TEAM

NANNY RULE

Mom and Dad, you are a team. No matter how difficult you find this, you must get over your differences, and find a quiet time and place to work out what it is you want for your children.

You must—and we mean MUST—figure out some way to meld your parenting styles into a coherent whole. This means having some tough talks with each other. More often than not, the families who hire us have a mom and dad who are at odds with each other. Or worse, moms and dads undermine each other. Not surprisingly, this can lead to a real strain on the marriage. It is a terrible thing when two people who love each other allow their family to disintegrate because they cannot learn how to open up and talk candidly to each other about what works and what doesn't.

We know it's tough. We know it's scary. But couples have got to get communicating if families can not only survive but also thrive.

NANNY RULE

TEAMWORK STARTS WITH THIS.
- compromising
- sharing the parenting duties

NANNY RULE

TEAMWORK STOPS WITH THIS.
- undermining each other
- contradicting each other
- fighting, especially in front of the kids

NANNY RULE

ACTIONS HAVE CONSEQUENCES
You'll see this in every chapter because it's such an important rule. Whatever mom and dad do, it has repercussions for their family, good and bad.

INEFFECTIVE PARENTING STYLES

Let's take a look at the different parenting styles we never like to see or hear.

Most parents are a mix of styles. Let's be realistic, of course. Everyone loses their temper, or nags once in a while, or yells, or makes excuses, or whatever. That's not what we're talking about here.

If you're brutally honest with yourself, you'll admit that you in-

THE PARENTING-ON-DIFFERENT-PAGES GAME

The object of this game is for children to push as many buttons as possible so they win (and get what they want).

WHAT HAPPENS	THE RESULT
Dad yells that it's time to go.	Yelling
Mom says give three-year-old Amelia another minute.	Contradicting Dad
Amelia throws a fit because she wants to wear her pink tutu.	Tantrum
Dad yells some more.	More yelling
Mom digs through the hamper for the tutu.	Giving in to child
Amelia gets what she wants.	More attention from Mommy and to wear her tutu.
Amelia running the household	She wins!

The only way for parents to win this game is if they work together on their disciplining techniques so their children don't play mom and dad against each other.

stinctively tend to fall into one of these main categories when your buttons get pushed. Even if you're a single parent. (When it comes to compromising, single parents are spared the arguments about what's wrong and what's right, but problems really arise when mom or dad feels as if she or he is like a single parent, doing all of the parenting with no input from the spouse.) For instance, angry parents are almost always loud. Clueless parents usually make excuses, too.

We've divided this list into eight different styles.

1. Angry/frustrated
2. Avoidance
3. Clueless

4. Disorganized

5. Excusing

6. Loud

7. Nagging/hypercritical

8. Undermining

Take a look at these parenting styles, the fallout, and how you can make it better.

The Angry/frustrated Parent

WHAT HAPPENS:	You can't control your temper You have a very short fuse Anything sets you off You can resort to corporal punishment
WHAT YOU TYPICALLY SAY:	"Do what I say and do it now!" "Because I said so, that's why!" "Get in your room and stay there!" "I told you to stop complaining and go to sleep!"
WHAT YOUR PARTNER DOES:	Tunes it out Gets angry and frustrated at you for being angry and frustrated Undermines your behavior behind your back
WHAT YOUR CHILD DOES:	Tunes it out Becomes afraid of parent Feels disrespected Thinks anger is a solution to problems

How to Manage Your Anger

Anger is one of the most destructive emotions. (It can also be appropriate, as you'll see on in chapter 3.) Parents who can't manage their rage send a terrible, soul-destroying message to their children.

There are many techniques for managing anger. One is breath control. You may want to look into taking yoga classes or watching yoga DVDs, which teach effective breathing. If you are in the process of conscious breathing, it becomes impossible to yell.

If you don't want to do that, try the simple counting technique. Aloud, count backward from twenty. This takes more concentration that simply counting from one to ten. It is also impossible to yell when counting.

Keep a small squishy ball handy—the kind you can hold in the palm of your hand. Squish it fiercely instead of yelling.

Whisper instead of yelling.

Start vacuuming, washing the floors, or cleaning the toilets.

Doing an intense, pain-in-the-neck activity in the house will redirect the physical symptoms and clean your house at the same time.

Ask your kids to help you stop yelling when they see your mad face!

If you are aware that your anger is out of control, we suggest

you speak to a professional who will help you get to the bottom of your rage and help identify triggers that you can then conquer.

The Avoidance Parent

WHAT HAPPENS:	Parents avoid being around their children
WHAT YOU TYPICALLY SAY:	"Sometimes I don't even want to come home. I'd rather be at work because I know it's more stressful to be at home with all the yelling and screaming."
WHAT YOUR PARTNER DOES:	Gets angry and upset at your absence Feels discounted and ignored Looks elsewhere for comfort
WHAT YOUR CHILD DOES:	Longs for the absent parent Resents the parent's avoidance Ignores the absent parent's discipline

TIME-OUT FOR PARENTS

Parents who are prone to anger can put themselves in time-out, just as they put their children in one. It is an excellent way to show your children how to use self-control in emotional situations.

A parental time-out takes discipline and split-second timing, but removing yourself from the situation is often the only way to stop from blowing a gasket in front of your kids.

Tell your kids that you are putting yourself in time-out. This is pretty much guaranteed to leave them in awe.

Then leave the room. Take some deep breaths. Recite a poem. Whack a pillow. Try to not be critical about yourself or your kids.

Most of all, calm down.

When you're marginally more calm, ask yourself: Why am I so mad? What started it this time? What were my expectations? What if they aren't realistic?

Time-outs for parents are not about communicating, but about evaluating your behavior. Time-outs for parents are about chilling out.

After time-out is over, when you've wound down and are more relaxed, then you can think things through. Clear your head, and you'll be able to talk about what you were feeling or whatever had happened.

Without anger!

We'll discuss how to talk to your children about a parental time-out in the next chapter.

Instead: Stop Avoiding Your Parenting

We've found that the avoidance parent is most often the dad. He works hard. He has a tough job. He wants to come home to peace and quiet.

But he's not willing to do anything to help create that peace and quiet.

He often feels that because he's the primary if not sole bread-winner, he can call the shots, parenting when he feels like it—or not at all.

Like this dad, who spent more time in the backyard, attending to his hobby of racing pigeons, than with his wife and children.

DAD: I don't think there's a huge problem with this family.

CHILD: Do you love the pigeons more than us?

Being married to an avoidance dad can be especially difficult for working moms, who have jobs and then find themselves managing the children and household, too.

Avoidance parents not only ignore their children but also their marriages. We always ask them: What about the person you've left at home? What are you doing to alleviate his/her stress? How can you pay any attention to him/her when you're never at home?

Both moms and dads must be equal participants in their marriages and with their children.

For parents who admit they don't even want to come home to face the chaos or recriminations, we suggest you look at this situation as if it were a work problem. You're good at your job. Parenting is a job. Just as you'd sit down at work and figure out the task at hand, sit down at home and figure it out. Decide that *you* are going to be the solution. Face it head on. You can flip yourself, and put yourself in your children's shoes and see how you feel being yelled at or talked to that way by your boss.

Sometimes dad has become an avoidance parent because mom literally won't let him do anything. See the supermom syndrome section later in this chapter.

The Clueless Parent

WHAT HAPPENS:	Parents give up doing anything
WHAT YOU TYPICALLY SAY:	"It's like we don't know what we're doing, so we don't do anything." "The kids know how to manipulate both of us and get their way."
WHAT YOUR PARTNER DOES:	Agrees with you to keep the peace Thinks that admitting incompetence is okay
WHAT YOUR CHILD DOES:	Takes advantage Rules the household

Instead: Stop Being Clueless

Parents who say they're clueless and that they "don't know how to do anything" actually do plenty. They just do it wrong!

First off, stop abdicating responsibility for your role as a parent. Saying you're clueless is just an excuse for not wanting to do the hard work of raising children. Don't sit there complaining about what you supposedly don't know.

Second, sit down together and figure out what you want for your children, and how to do it together. You've already taken a big step by buying and reading this book. Take the time to think and plan. Talk to other parents you trust and respect.

Admitting you don't know what you're doing is not a viable excuse for a grownup.

The Disorganized Parent

WHAT HAPPENS:	You have no routine so nothing gets done
WHAT YOU TYPICALLY SAY:	"Why is this floor soaking wet? All right. Get out. Good, now you're done." "Why is this room such a mess? Oh, I give up." "Oh no, we missed the bus again."
WHAT YOUR PARTNER DOES:	Makes excuses Pretends the situation isn't happening Gets mad and casts blame
WHAT YOUR CHILD DOES:	Tunes out due to inconsistency Avoids chores because parents don't delegate Is chronically late and disorganized, too

Instead: Get Organized

Read chapters 5 and 6 for advice about setting up routines, chores, and cleaning up your clutter.

The Excusing Parent

WHAT HAPPENS:	You make excuses for all kinds of bad behavior and rarely discipline the children
WHAT YOU TYPICALLY SAY:	"It's not such a big deal." "I was like that when I was a kid." "He didn't hurt anybody."
WHAT YOUR PARTNER DOES:	Makes excuses, too Thinks you're a clueless parent Feels undermined when trying to discipline the children
WHAT YOUR CHILD DOES:	Gets away with anything he or she wants Learns how to play the parents off against each other Feels entitled to act naughty Cries/whines till parents cave in

Instead: Stop Making Excuses

Parents who make excuses for their kids' naughtiness need a time-out.

We guarantee that if you continue to make excuses, your children will soon be completely out of control. This is a real problem that can escalate from the "cute" to the truly problematic—such as violent, threatening, out-of-control bullies. Becoming violent because there are no boundaries in a household run by excusing parents is downright dangerous, as in this family.

NANNY: You make excuses for him. He doesn't just tell tall tales. He hits girls in school. He blatantly lies to people.

DAD: Well, I guess he got caught up in the moment.

NANNY: Then he has to lose a privilege or be removed from the situation.

DAD: Yes, he does a lot of things he shouldn't be doing, but . . .

NANNY: He lies. He hurts his brothers. He's a juvenile delinquent in the making, and he's only eight years old.

DAD: Yeah, but you don't see the good side of him, either.

NANNY: There aren't enough times when he's nice. He's going to end up in juvenile hall.

DAD: If that's the way you think, then maybe he deserves to be there.

NANNY: I don't believe what I just heard. Either this dad is so busy yelling that he didn't hear me, or he's more clueless than I thought.

This eight-year-old didn't get caught up in the moment. The "moment" was a culmination of years of such "moments." Not being disciplined coupled with being yelled at all the time and indulged by his parents created a bully.

Thankfully, dad did come around and realize his son needed direction and started treating the naughtiness and outbursts with appropriate discipline.

But take this peerless example of dad trying to do the right thing, and mom making excuses.

MOM: I wish Matt would help me get them ready and just take a more active role.

DAD: (*To nearly three-year-old daughter Natalie, who put her feet on the dinner table*) No feet where we eat.

CHILD: Yes I can.

DAD: No feet where we eat. If you want to put your feet where we eat, you can go to your bedroom.

CHILD: Me do it anyway.

DAD:	Natalie, okay, I'm warning you. No more feet.
MOM:	You know what?
DAD:	No feet where we eat.
MOM:	Of course, surprise, surprise, I think we should just kind of let her do it because I think she really doesn't feel well, as long as she's not against the major rules.
DAD:	That means this behavior is acceptable to you.
MOM:	I mean it's choosing my battles, and I think that she really doesn't feel well today.

Naturally, Natalie felt just fine. Mom just couldn't stand having her fuss for more than five seconds. Dad was justifiably frustrated and humiliated. And for what? There should never be feet where you eat anyway.

When one parent constantly made excuses for a naughty child's behavior, it can cause a huge rift in a marriage. If dad says "Gina, don't do this," and mom says, "Oh, let her," dad feels insulted and belittled. His authority is being undermined. (And vice versa, of course.)

Plus, hearing parents contradict each other is very confusing to children.

Try to avoid making the, "Well, he's only a baby . . ." or "Well, she's only two . . ." excuses. Nanny Deb once worked for a woman with a six-month-old baby, who liked to put her hand roughly on Deb's face. Deb would say, "That's not nice" and then gently took the baby's hand away.

Mom would say, "Well, she's only a baby."

Flash to a year later and this baby is now eighteen months old and whacking everyone in the house in the face.

Except Nanny Deb.

Once you devise House Rules that both mom and dad agree upon, it's much easier to stick to them. There is no reason to break them—and then there's no reason to make excuses. Your children

will learn that good behavior is rewarded, and bad behavior comes with penalties.

The Loud Parent

WHAT HAPPENS:	You scream, shout, and yell
WHAT YOU TYPICALLY SAY:	"Shut up! I SAID SHUT UP!!" "Turn that TV off right this minute!"
WHAT YOUR PARTNER DOES:	Tunes you out Gets angry at all the shouting
WHAT YOUR CHILD DOES:	Tunes you out Becomes afraid of the parent who yells Thinks shouting is a solution to problems

Instead: Stop Screaming Now

One dad came up with a real corker when he said, "I'm not yelling. I'm just talking loud."

Trust us. He was hollering his head off.

Some families are by nature loud. They tend to be the families who have the television on all the time, with the volume on high and the kids screaming just to make themselves heard. These families are honestly unaware of just how noisy they are until it's pointed out to them, usually when they're driving everyone crazy in a restaurant or playground.

For most parents, however, by the time they're shouting, the situation has already gone too far.

Stopping the yelling takes a conscious effort. But it can be done. Try putting yourself in a time-out. Or instead of yelling, try whispering. Then no one can hear you if you're swearing.

The Nagging/Hypercritical Parent

WHAT HAPPENS:	You nag, criticize, and set impossible standards
WHAT YOU TYPICALLY SAY:	"Why aren't your shoes on? Where's your backpack? Clean your room! Why didn't you get an A?"
WHAT YOUR PARTNER DOES:	Tunes you out Thinks you're a nag and loses respect Overcompensates to undo the criticism
WHAT YOUR CHILD DOES:	Tunes you out Is deeply hurt by the criticism Shuts down in the face of all the criticism Starts failing on purpose rather than live up to impossible ideals

Instead: Stop Nagging

Nagging parents are incredibly common. Half of the time they don't even hear what they're saying. They just go on and on, like the Energizer bunny, till everyone is worn out and fed up. Because after the big nag comes the old yeller.

Take this scene with the mother of three children: She'd already confessed to Nanny Deb that she never used to yell and that she doesn't want to yell anymore. See what happens.

MOM: Dana, get up and go in your room, now.

Dana doesn't move.

MOM: You know what? Then you sit there. And you can wait there until your father comes home. I'm going to call him.

Next, Mom lit into her other two children.

MOM: Lauren, why are your shoes still not on? Get in your room. Dana, are you even listening to me? Tyler, I don't need you in here. Go in your room. Stop it. SHUT YOUR MOUTH, and quit yelling at me!

She took a break for a moment, then lit into her eldest son, Tyler.

MOM: Here, let me be very specific for you. Finish eating, take out the trash, and wash your hands. Then get your homework started.

CHILD: Why should I listen to you?

MOM: Why should you listen to me? Because I gave birth to you, and without me, you wouldn't be here.

Way to go, mom! You've just made your child feel guilty for being born!

Not only did this mom nag all her kids to the point of them tuning her out completely, she also completely discounted her son's very real feelings when he said she never listened to him. He wasn't making that up. She was too busy nagging to listen (we'll discuss this in detail in the next chapter).

What compounds the problem is that naggers tend to go hand in hand with being overly critical and demanding. Parents like this often have immaculate homes. Not a pillow out of place. They spend so much energy keeping up appearances that they forget that the kids who live there would rather have a mom who ignores a few dust balls and plays with them or helps them with their homework instead.

So how can you stop nagging? Try putting on a tape recorder one day. Then, after the kids are asleep, play it back and listen to yourself shred your kids to bits. It's like putting a mirror up to yourself so you can see (or in this case, hear) a reflection of what you're saying to your children. Trust us, they hear what you're saying, *especially* the bad stuff, whether they acknowledge you or not.

Ask yourself: What am I doing to my child when I nag or criticize?

Remember: You don't give anything up for your children. You are there for your children because you wanted them and you love them.

If that doesn't help you, stop, read the rest of this book, set up some effective House Rules, work together as a family, delegate chores and activities, listen to your children, acknowledge their needs, accentuate the positive, and concentrate on what makes these kids happy.

The Undermining Parent

WHAT HAPPENS:	Constant contradiction
WHAT YOU TYPICALLY SAY:	"She's not capable of change. It's not going to happen."
WHAT YOUR PARTNER DOES:	Feels belittled and diminished Doubts his or her parenting ability Becomes increasingly frustrated Withdraws and shuts down
WHAT YOUR CHILD DOES:	Feels confused by the conflicting messages Learns how to push parental buttons Acts out to get attention from the withdrawing parent

Instead: Stop Undermining

Here's a typical example of an undermining dad who is also an avoidance parent. Mom is in the middle of cooking dinner and supervising the kids, who are engrossed in their homework.

MOM: You don't realize how much I do.
DAD: We getting close to eating?
MOM: Um, no.
DAD: What are you doing out there?

Another family was a textbook example of how a dad undermines the mom. Dad had his home office in the basement. He gave mom no help at all in the morning with the six kids (three sets of twins!), he made an appearance at lunchtime and then criticized what she cooked without offering to help, then went back to work, demanding peace and quiet. He gave her no support at all, yet criticized everything she tried to do.

After Nanny Deb had a stern talk with them about their children's behavior, dad admitted he hadn't been helping at all with the kids, and went with the program. But he automatically assumed his wife was incapable of coming on board.

DAD: We need to do this for them and for each other, but I'm not sure she can be consistent.

MOM: He doesn't give me a chance to try. Like today, I hung up the phone when I was having a conversation.

DAD: So big deal, you hung up.

MOM: It *is* a big deal because I *did* it! I never did it before!

NANNY: Every little step is a big one. The message you're giving her, dad, is that she's incapable of doing anything.

MOM: It's negative in, negative out.

NANNY: Your negativity makes her shut down. And then the kids shut down.

MOM: Just give me a chance!

Once dad swallowed his pride and learned not to be so bossy and sure in his superiority, he was able to acknowledge the huge role his wife has in taking care of these children.

Then, they set up House Rules, and worked on not only listening to each other, but also listening to their kids. When the kids felt acknowledged, they started working together as a family and taking responsibility for themselves.

House Rules are essential so parents agree about how to treat their children. Once they agree, there no longer is any need to undermine each other.

They can also easily trade off the parenting tasks.

Let's say the House Rule for bedtime is ten minutes of story time, then talking about what happened that day for five minutes, then kisses and hugs and prayers, then lights out and leaving the room. Mom and dad can alternate this routine with all the kids. The kids will get to know the drill. It will be the same every night. It will reassure the kids. It reassures the parents. End of nightly tantrums. Mom and dad can reclaim their evenings.

All because they stopped undermining each other.

THE MARTYR MOM AND THE SUPER-MOM SYNDROME

One phrase we never like to hear is: "I gave up everything for you."

Our response: "Who asked you to?"

Martyr moms (and dads, let's not forget) need to feel the pull of sacrifice to bolster their own self-esteem. They tend to crave a lot of control—which allows them to "give up" their own needs and become their own sacrificial lamb. Parents like this are afraid to let go of control because they think it means that someone has won the thing they've given up.

Martyr parents must try to unlearn this damaging behavior and realize that they, not their children, are responsible for fulfilling their needs.

Martyr moms usually also fall into the dreaded category of super-mom. Super-moms have to be the sweet and tender nurturers—never mind that they're screaming at their kids half the time. They don't want to relinquish control. They crave the smooches and attention from their kids, even as they secretly despair about tantrums and fighting.

Super-moms usually cut the dads out completely. Like this couple.

DAD: The kids both want her and then she gets frustrated with it, and then she yells, Matt, Matt I need your help. And it's like, I'd like to help but they want to be with her, especially our three-year-old, Dylan.

MOM: I still need your support, though. Dylan, I'm the boss, remember, buddy.

Dylan ignores his father completely. He's not yet able to articulate how this push/pull from mom is very confusing. To him, and to all kids who hear it.

Dad's role has been reduced to doing what mom tells him to do, instead of being the strong, assertive, involved parent he wants to be. And if he tries, she can't help stepping in every time dad exercises his authority, undermining everything he says.

Then she can complain that he never does anything.

Martyr and super-mom, all in one!

Obviously, this behavior has to stop if marriages are to survive.

CONFLICTING PARENTING STYLES

Now that you've been brutally honest with yourself about your parenting style, let's take a look at what happens when mom acts one way and dad acts another.

In this family, dad is a marine and he's too strict. Mom is a former nanny who's forgotten all her training and is too soft. Here, dad is talking sternly to his children. Mom immediately comes to their aid, using baby talk.

DAD: Leave your sister alone. Or else your sister is going to mess with you. Got it?

MOM: Mommy will fix it, Mommy will make it better.

Daddy gets the children all riled up, then heads to work, leaving mom with two kids who are bouncing off the walls and don't respect her authority. They do what they want because they know they can get away with it. But until Nanny Stella laid down the law, mom was totally unwilling to be firm with her children.

Often, some of the biggest problems with communication arise because opposites attract. What made mom fall in love with dad could have been that he was totally different from mom's domineering dad. This can work brilliantly in a marriage.

But it can fall to pieces when the kids arrive.

When opposites attract, they can also clash. This is especially true with the different parenting styles listed here. Some of the most difficult situations we've worked with have come from moms and dads who were polar opposites in parenting styles.

Because they were such opposites, they could not find a way to talk to each other about it. They just kept pushing each other's buttons until somebody snapped.

Take the mom who was a compulsive chatterbox who monopolized the conversation. Dad, however, didn't mind this so much before the kids came along, but because he was of the "kids should be seen and not heard" school, the endless talk at mealtime drove him crazy.

Both of them were making mealtime a living hell for their kids—mom talking as if she didn't have a care in the world while dad seethed.

Dad needed to stop bottling up his rage. Mom needed to let other people talk. They had to sit down and really communicate with each other about how to find a middle ground and resolve what should never have become a problem in the first place.

Another mom had a husband who was angry and loud. She didn't know how to ask him to stop. She was having panic attacks from pure anxiety and couldn't manage the unhappiness in her house.

NANNY: I'm laying bets that there's a lot of time that you are crying.

MOM: Sometimes I just break down and cry for no reason.

NANNY: It's not "no reason." It's living a lie. But do you know the seriousness of the anxiety you're having with your family? Your panic attacks are not going to go away with the house in continual, utter chaos.

MOM: I want it to go back to the way it used to be, when we used to have fun all the time. Things were happy.

DAD: Right.

MOM: And most of it's because when you come home I really want to leave the room.

Dad was really shocked that his meek wife finally came out and spilled her guts about the horrible effect his behavior had on her and the kids. But he's not the only one at fault. Because she didn't confide in him, he had no idea about the extent of her anxiety.

FINDING A HAPPY MEDIUM, OR POTTY TRAINING FOR PARENTS

One of the most common elements on our show is parents who can't compromise. Mom walks around with the baby attached to her hip 24/7, and she's killing her marriage (and her back). Dad has abdicated all responsibility for the parenting, while simmering with resentment.

An unhappy couple cannot raise happy children. Having children will never improve a bad marriage. They'll make it even more difficult for parents to reach the level of loving intimacy needed to overcome different parenting styles and beliefs.

When it comes to communicating with each other, parents simply have to find a way to get out of mental diapers and train themselves to overcome entrenched bad habits. Parents who cannot communicate will not be able to establish the House Rules that will literally put their home in order.

One mom was particularly stuck in a deep trough of complete denial.

NANNY: You have to deal with the problems in this house. And you have to deal with them now.

MOM: You'll have to excuse me. I have to go outside.

Mom literally could not hear any comment, and she literally could not talk about her problems and worries. Her children had been taught to mirror her response to any unpleasant situation— by repressing their feelings, shutting down, and walking away as if nothing was wrong. So when Nanny Deb initiated this tough conversation, mom had to be practically forced back inside. It was extremely painful for everyone, but once Nanny Deb encouraged this mom to talk, the floodgates opened and mom was able to begin to come to grips with her pattern of denial.

You should take heart, as this mom did. Once you recognize and acknowledge your parenting style, you *can* change. Cycles of familial behavior and patterns *can* be broken. Just because you were raised a certain way and automatically click into a certain mode of parenting doesn't mean that that's always going to be the only way. We see amazing results every day from parents motivated to make changes in behavior they know doesn't work.

Accepting your faults isn't easy. Raising children isn't easy.

And raising children without parents who can talk to each other is *impossible*.

Parents simply must find a happy medium—or middle ground, or way to compromise—to open channels of communication.

Ideally, the happy medium should be established *before* the kids arrive. You both agree on what you're going to name your child, where you're going to give birth, and what kind of crib to buy, right? Of course, if you started fighting about this sort of thing during the pregnancy, wouldn't you expect that the writing is on the wall in terms of how you'll both deal with the kids?

Here are a few suggestions.

- If you find it difficult to talk calmly, try making lists of the goals you have for your kids. Then compare notes. This should give you something to talk about without shouting.
- If you have trouble talking to each other without getting defensive or interrupting, set a timer. Allow mom to talk uninterrupted for two minutes. Or five. Then dad.
- Most of all, try to avoid making judgments.
- Don't exclude each other from making important, fundamental decisions.
- Don't make promises you can't keep. Couples often don't realize how much they break each other's word. This can escalate into a huge, marriage-ending problem when the "You said we were going to do this and we're not" types of situations arise.
- Remember what you most love about each other. Then say it.
- And then tell yourselves that you're a team, and teams work together.
- Once you set up the House Rules, be consistent. Pick your battles within the confines of those rules.
- Most of all, talk to each other. Every day. Just as you ask your child about his or her day, ask your spouse. And then, listen. Really and truly listen.

NOT IN FRONT OF THE CHILDREN

There is an old saying. Little pitchers have big ears!

When you have important issues or problems to discuss, *never* talk about them in front of the children. Getting on the same page has to be negotiated outside of the hearing of the children.

Wait until you're both either out of the house or the kids have gone to bed. Then, talk about it.

Quietly.

Children worry about everything. They stress out about *everything*. They internalize *everything*. When mom and dad fight, they blame themselves. They can start to act out in really destructive ways when they hear arguments. One family Nanny Deb worked for had children in a permanent state of anxiety, because mom kept threatening to leave dad, in front of them. Sometimes she'd actually haul them into the car and stay at her mother's for a few hours. Then drive them all home and start fighting with dad again. No one was happy, and the kids really suffered.

So keep it down, please, and keep it to yourselves.

IF YOU HAVE TROUBLE FINDING A HAPPY MEDIUM, USE A NEUTRAL PARTY TO HELP YOU OPEN UP

Because we've remained neutral, we've been able to deal with parents who can't communicate.

Finding a neutral party to help a couple confront their problems can be incredibly helpful. For many couples, a pastor or a trusted friend could be there to listen. Often, therapy is not needed—you can find family counselors who are trained in mediation to give you the tools to figure out how to get on the same page.

However, don't be afraid of different forms of professional help, such as conflict resolution, mediation, or short-term cognitive

therapy. They should help you zoom right in to the nub of problems, saving your sanity and your marriage.

If you seriously have anger management problems, however, especially if you've found yourself getting violent during a fit of anger, then please seek professional help.

KEEP YOUR MARRIAGE HAPPY: HAVE A DATE NIGHT EVERY WEEK

All couples need to have regular date night.

Date nights keep couples happy. They give moms and dads grown-up time together with something to do other than coming home and talking about the baby. They allow you to nurture your loving relationship and reaffirm your devotion to each other.

Yet, we can't tell you how many times we hear "We don't leave our children."

Sometimes mom's idea of fun would be to say, "Okay, let's do something for the whole family tonight. Let's have the kids sleep in our bed!" Without asking dad first.

That's not our idea of date night!

For one thing, it's good for any child to establish relationships with other people besides you. A child who is used to gentle, caring babysitters is going to have a much easier time with teachers. It's unbelievably scary for a three-year-old to go to preschool and be dropped off with a bunch of other children and two teachers who they've never met before if they've never been left with anyone other than their mothers.

It's also very selfish. It's about mom's and dad's need to keep their little ones little, dependent, and unexposed to other people, personalities, and ideas.

The most common excuse we hear is that both parents work, so they feel guilty if they go out because they haven't spent that much time with their kids all week.

But you should *not* feel guilty because you're trying to have a healthy relationship as a couple.

Remember: An unhappy couple cannot raise happy children.

If you find that babysitters are too expensive when money is tight, try the barter system. Babysit for another family while the parents go on date night. Then have them babysit for you. Or try using a trusted teenager or a local college student. They're usually less expensive than older babysitters and can be wonderful with children.

3 USE YOUR WORDS:
LEARN HOW TO
COMMUNICATE WITH
YOUR CHILDREN

QUESTION: What's the biggest problem we see on *Nanny 911*?

ANSWER: Communication. If you can communicate, you can solve any problem that you have.

QUESTION: What can we do about our communication problems?

ANSWER: Learn how to talk to your children! Talk, talk, and then talk some more—not *at* your kids, but *with* them. Realize that there's a *huge* difference between talking for the sake of talking—and honest, necessary conversation. We're going to give you lots of specific techniques to help.

Communication truly defines your role as a parent.

We don't believe that it's your job to keep your children attached to you forever. We tell parents that when they bring their children to preschool, they aren't getting their children back. Their children will have teachers, and classmates, and new experiences every day that are outside your control. They'll pick up on everything. They'll also probably learn lots of things you wish they'd never have learned from other kids.

But at the end of the day, your children are not your possessions. You are blessed with them and given charge of them, but your truest role is to prepare them for the outside world.

The best way to prepare them is to teach them how to communicate.

BE CONSISTENT

Consistency is the essence of good communication.

Be consistent is the single most important Nanny Rule. It makes your children feel safe. It gives them secure boundaries. It lets them know they can count on you.

But—and this is a big but!—be consistent is the hardest rule any parent has to follow.

We're not kidding!

If you don't want Johnny jumping on the couch, and you tell him to stop jumping, then that means stop jumping today, tomorrow, next week, and next month—until you decide he can jump on the couch. (Not something we recommend!)

If you're not prepared to be consistent, your kids won't listen to you or believe you, and you might as well just throw this book out right now. (Something else we don't recommend!)

· ·

NANNY RULE

SAY WHAT YOU MEAN AND MEAN IT

This concept goes hand in hand with be consistent. Your children have to know you're trustworthy.

When we say something, we mean it—good and bad. It doesn't matter what you say, it's that the intention is true. If you tell your kids, "I'm taking you to Disneyland," come hell or high water, you better be ready for Mickey Mouse and "It's a Small World After All" reverberating in your head for the next twenty years. If you say, "If you don't stop that right now, you're going into time-out for six minutes," and the bad behavior does not end immediately, somebody better be going into time-out. For six minutes.

We've gone into houses on the show, and the kids are climbing the walls. The parents will shout, "No, get down, get down, get down" and guess what? No one gets down. Mom and dad keep nagging. Actually, half the time they're not even looking at their little monkeys. They're just spouting the words. The kids ignore them because with parents who don't have the rule that actions have consequences, they know they're not going to get punished.

Like this ten-year-old: He's egging one of his younger brothers to whack the other one, right in front of his mother.

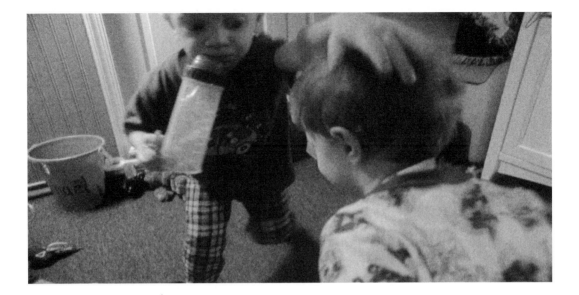

CHILD: Punch him. Kick him.

MOM: Hey, don't tell him that.

CHILD: Come on, punch him in the face.

This boy not only told his brother to do something awful, but also his mom's noncommittal response and, worse, inability to do anything let the situation deteriorate. The message to these boys is that mom really didn't care if the brothers punched and kicked the life out of each other.

Trust us. The kids knew this, too. So they'll keep testing and testing, punching and kicking, until someone gets hurt. Or until mom and dad get with the program!

NANNY RULE

MOM AND DAD ARE RESPONSIBLE FOR TEACHING THEIR CHILDREN HOW TO COMMUNICATE

This sounds so simple, like be consistent, but it really isn't.

It's your responsibility as parents to establish a safe home—not only in terms of physical safety, but also in terms of emotional safety. An emotionally safe home is one in which kids and parents talk freely to one another about everything; one where kids feel comfortable confiding their innermost fears and worries without fear of being judged or criticized; and one where love, pride, and encouragement are clearly and regularly stated.

We know how difficult this can be, especially if you grew up in a house that discouraged or inhibited frank conversation.

Parents who aren't good at talking to each other aren't good at talking to their children. And you know what? It's often difficult for *anyone* to talk about feelings.

Still, you need to realize that if you're the kinds of parents who by nature are loud or angry, there might be a real possibility that your children will be too scared by your booming voice and your anger to talk to you. Additionally, if you aren't comfortable with you own emotions and tend to shut down into denial, chances are pretty high that you will have shut-down kids too. No one will talk about anything important at all. But repressed kids can still be seething inside—and eventually, their repressed feelings are going to blow. So if you haven't read the previous chapter, please do so now.

So please don't go blaming your kids' day care providers, babysitters, nannies, siblings, friends, your mom, your relatives, the TV, or their video games if your children feel that they can't talk to you! Take a good hard look at how you talk, how often you do, and what you feel comfortable talking about.

DON'T LABEL YOUR CHILDREN

Some children are shy, some are outgoing, some are rambunctious, and some are bookworms. It's their nature. And their nature is fixed at birth.

Embrace each child's unique personality. Love it. Cherish it. Never try to change it.

Let's say you were a painfully shy child who grew up to still be uncomfortable at big parties or other social occasions. But you've learned that your shyness doesn't mean that you're never going to go out or have a successful career. You have to be able to talk to people to function.

If your child is shy, try not to label him or her as such. Many kids are shy at two but not shy at five. If you continually reinforce the label, however, you child is going to hear it so much that after a while he or she will believe it's true and start acting that way.

Nanny Stella has a friend who took her three-year-old daughter to birthday party. In walked Patricia without a care in the world, surveying the room full of strangers, and then she put her hands on her hips and announced, "Hi, I'm Patricia, and I'm SHY!"

She actually wasn't shy at all. She'd just overhead her mother talking about her and using that label.

Parents often label their children because the parental style of communication is pretty much going to be based on the parents' own personalities. It's what they're comfortable with, so attaching a label to a child makes it easier to deal with who they are and how they act. (It also serves to differentiate siblings—the quiet one, the noisy one, the peacemakers, the troublemaker, and so on.)

If you are a calm, passive person, you no doubt feel most comfortable talking to your child in your usual calm, passive manner. If you are strong-willed, your children will undoubtedly know that, too. If your child is very much different, you'll have noticed those differences early on. It can be tough when you're a calm, passive person and your child is a strong willed, outgoing, determined little spitfire. These kids can completely take over the house—if you let them.

Successful parenting is about blending your unique personality/form of communication with your child's own unique personality/form of communication. Some of the biggest problems we've tackled are in families where the child and parents are very much alike. Boy, do they butt heads. Kids who are very similar to you in personality and mannerisms tend to push your own buttons before you've even realized it. Then, it's easy to just give up and say, "Oh, Timmy is just like me. What can I do?"

What you can do is remove the label, look at your kids' personalities, be consistent with your expectations, and allow them the freedom to discover who they really are.

Most of all, don't expect your kids to be like you, or to fulfill any frustrated dreams and ambitions you wish you'd fulfilled. Dragging your reluctant kids to auditions or signing them up for choir when they're tone-deaf is not going to make anyone happy.

Let's take a look at the do's and don'ts of communicating to your children. This means speaking politely and respectfully. It means no more yelling and screaming, pleading, and nagging.

We're going to divide this section into four parts.

1. How to Talk to Your Child: Basic Technique
2. The Do's of Communication
3. The Don'ts of Communication
4. What to Talk About When You're Talking

HOW TO TALK TO YOUR CHILD

Effective communication begins right after your baby is born, when you're gazing into his or her eyes, brimming with love and happiness, and cooing endearments. Babies can barely focus their tiny eyes, but from the sound of your voice and the soft touch of your hands, they know you're head over heels in love already.

FIRST, TALK TO YOUR BABY

We believe that babies are far more intelligent than they're given credit for simply because they're preverbal and, well, they're babies! This is why we suggest you start talking to your child in full, complete sentences, as if they were much older. That doesn't mean there isn't a place for baby talk, but that the earlier you speak clearly to a child, the earlier your child will understand your words and begin to process language.

The sooner you start talking to your baby, the easier it will be to use our effective techniques to redirect naughtiness and stop normal behavior from escalating into uncontrollable problems.

Be sure to praise children who use new words, and especially grown-up words, to express themselves.

HOW TO DISCIPLINE A BABY WITHOUT GOING CRAZY

Tabitha is a darling baby with curly brown hair, and big brown eyes. She's seven months old, and her nickname is "Slugger." Even at this age, she likes to hit. This is perfectly normal. Tabitha isn't hitting because she's angry—she's merely exploring her space and learning about how the world works.

Let's say she whacks you on the face. What you can do is gently take her hitting hand away, hold it lightly, and say, "That's not okay."

Then put her hand back on your face, and stroke it. Say: "Gentle, gentle—that's nice."

If you have to do this over and over again—and chances are about 100 percent that you will—realize that this technique is *not* discipline. It's redirection. It's education. It's communication.

Fast-forward to another family. This mom thought that her little darling Daphne's penchant for throwing her food on the floor was funny. (Actually, Daphne had so much fun making a mess, it was pretty hilarious. At first.) She also thought that her little darling Daphne's penchant for thumping mom on the rear was funny, too.

When Daphne turned two, however, it wasn't funny anymore. Mealtimes were a disaster because Daphne threw not only her food but also her plate, her cup, and her silverware. Mom's rear was now constantly covered with bruises, because when Daphne thumped her, it really hurt. Daphne was turning into a world-class brat—because her mother hadn't learned how to tell her to stop, that her food and body needed to be respected, and that when Mom said Stop, she meant it.

Let babies know what's acceptable and what's not.

Trust us, they'll learn to listen.

BASIC TECHNIQUE FOR TALKING TO A CHILD

When we're working with families on the show, parents are always incredulous when their out-of-control kids instantly quiet down once we arrive during a screaming match. Why do their children listen to us and not to their parents?

Because we take these simple steps to make children feel safe, and when they feel safe, they can talk freely and honestly.

Follow these steps and you will find your child responding to you right away. Use this technique to calm down any child who is upset.

1. Get down to the child's level. Sit or kneel, whatever's comfortable.
2. Make eye contact. This is essential. If you have to, turn the child's head—gently—so he is looking directly at you.
3. If a child is very upset, **it's okay to touch them gently** on the

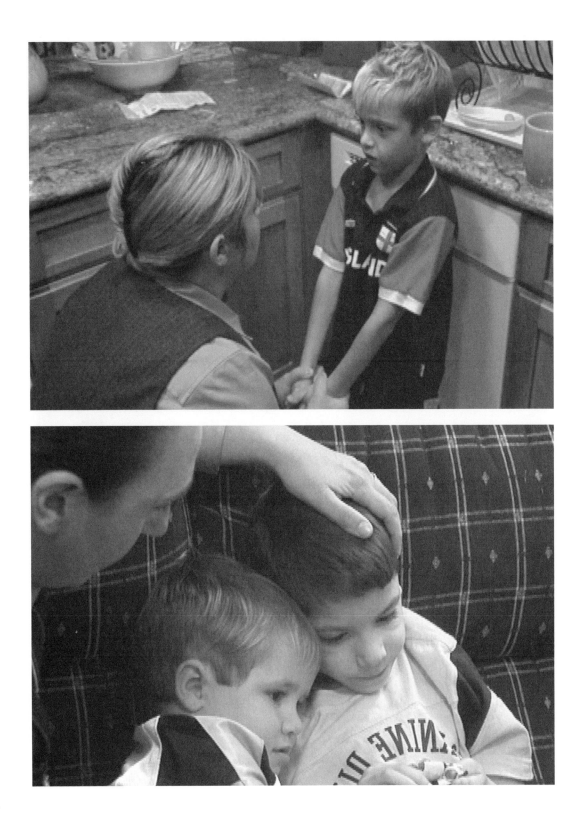

back or on the belly. This is simply an acknowledging touch. You don't need to hug or pull a child close when you're talking unless the child is clearly hysterical and in need of comfort. (In that case, let the child calm down before proceeding with any conversation. Telling them to breathe and helping them do so is usually very helpful.)

4. Change the timbre of your voice. **Speak in a firm, low tone.** Your voice naturally rises when you're happy or having fun. A serious voice is a low voice. Once, Nanny Deb walked into a house where the seven-year-old was literally belting his mother while she sat frozen on the couch. Without missing a beat, Nanny Deb took the boy by the arm, and said, "You are gone, right now. Never do that to your mother again." Then off he went to time-out without a

backward glance. Nanny Deb hadn't yelled or fussed. Her tone of voice said it all: No nonsense will be tolerated.

5. **Give the child words** to help the conversation along. See the examples below.

For very young children, say, "Use your words" and prompt them along. For older children, it's okay to initiate the conversation by stating the obvious, such as the following:

"You look really upset."

"Would you like to tell me what's getting you upset?"

"Is there something bothering you?"

"Are you angry about something?"

6. **Repeat what the child is saying.** This shows them that you are absolutely listening. It also gives you time to organize your own thoughts.

7. **Don't interrupt.** Let the child speak his mind. Say that you understand. Then, when it's your turn, they will stop talking (because they've said it already!) and listen to you. If they do interrupt when you're talking, say, "I understand, but you need to let me finish, and then it's your turn."

8. **Stay calm.** No matter how riled up inside you might be!

Here are some sample conversations.

WITH A TWO-YEAR-OLD

NANNY: Did you get angry? You got mad and threw your toy at your sister?

CHILD: [Nods]

NANNY: Your sister started playing with your favorite dolly and she made you mad?

CHILD: [Nods again]

NANNY:	Use your words.
CHILD:	Me mad.
NANNY:	I see that you're mad. I understand. You don't want your sister to play with your dolly without your permission, right?
CHILD:	Yes.
NANNY:	I understand that, but it doesn't mean you throw your own toy at her.
CHILD:	Okay.

WITH A TWO-YEAR-OLD WHO IS HAVING A TANTRUM

Natalie is nearly three, and her Mom has not yet learned the Nanny Rule that good parenting doesn't mean your children never get upset. Mom does everything for these kids. So when Nanny Deb came to the house, she realized that mom's spoiling the kids had to stop.

Naturally, the children, four-year-old Dylan and Natalie, were not thrilled with this development!

Here, Nanny Deb has given the children chores, explaining to them what needs to be done. She knows they aren't unrealistic expectations for kids of this age, and that Dylan and Natalie are fully capable of understanding the rules and doing what they're told. Dylan needs to make his bed, and Natalie is sitting on the blanket and doesn't want to budge.

NANNY:	Natalie, Dylan's going to make the bed. Come on down, please.
CHILD:	No, big.
NANNY:	Yes, I see you're big. Dylan is going to make the bed.
CHILD:	Go away.

NANNY: No, I'm not going to go away. If you don't choose to listen, you're going to go to your own room.

CHILD: I'm not!

NANNY: One, two, three. [Removes her from the bed] You need to sit on your bed now.

CHILD: [Screaming, crying, and flailing]

MOM: Okay, am I going to sit with her?

NANNY: No, you leave her.

MOM: Oh my God. I feel like I'm abusing her.

NANNY: No, by doing this you're teaching her that if you get angry, you take time to cool off.

CHILD: [Screaming louder]

MOM: Is this going to get better?

NANNY: You can go back in there in a minute, and you can say to her, "I know you're angry. When you're ready to talk about it, you can come out." See, she's calming down already.

MOM: *I'm* not!

NANNY: Go in there and talk to her. Just go over and get down to her level. See if you can get her to look at you.

MOM: Natalie, will you look at Mama?

NANNY: No, not "will you."

MOM: Natalie, look at Mama.

NANNY: No, your voice has to be the right tone. You're telling her you mean business. You need to use a business tone because you mean business here. She needs to be told.

MOM: She just wanted to play.

NANNY: Maybe so, but I had asked her to get off the bed because we were going to make it, and she did not listen. That is not respectful.

MOM: Can she understand at this age?

NANNY:	She can understand. You understand, don't you?
CHILD:	No.
NANNY:	Did you say you didn't want to get off the bed?
CHILD:	No.
NANNY:	No, you wanted to stay on the bed.
CHILD:	I stay with Mama.
NANNY:	And now you want to stay with Mama, but you need to use your words. Natalie, Natalie, look at Mama and tell her you need to use your words.
CHILD:	No.
NANNY:	Yes, you need to use your words.
MOM:	Can you look me in the eyes, Natalie?
CHILD:	No.
NANNY:	Are you ready to come back now?
CHILD:	No.
NANNY:	Okay, so we're going to leave her.
CHILD:	I want to go, too.
MOM:	Are you going to listen?
CHILD:	Yes.

Natalie clearly had understood everything that had gone on. When her tantrum was ignored, it stopped. When she was properly prompted, she used her words.

Mom needed to learn that she had to get down to Natalie's level, be firm, and get over her own unrealistic fears about disciplining her children. Leaving a child who is throwing a tantrum alone for a minute is not child abuse. She had to make the rules and enforce them, even if that meant seeing her children temporarily unhappy.

And we do mean temporarily.

A minute after this scene, Natalie had gotten off the bed and was happily playing with her dolls.

WITH A FOUR- OR FIVE-YEAR-OLD

This mom used to yell at her children and had a difficult time believing they were capable of listening to her without mouthing back or getting violent. Nanny Deb suggested they have a talk, in private, about all the new House Rules, and coached them along.

> **MOM:** Okay, tell me what the problem is. Why are you so angry? Why did you throw water at me?
>
> **CHILD:** I don't know.
>
> **MOM:** And kick and hit and spit. You don't know why?
>
> **CHILD:** I was mad.

MOM: Why were you mad?

CHILD: Because my brother—he cut me on the Candyland game.

MOM: He cut you, I know. But remember what I said?

NANNY: Okay wait, wait one second. When she's talking about her feelings, and she said she was mad, I'd like you to praise her because it's great that she's able to talk about these feelings. Every time she says something, you say that's great. You said you were mad. Good. [to child] It's good to tell her you're mad.

MOM: If you want to talk to me because you're angry, use your words and talk to me. Are you still angry or you want to talk some more?

CHILD: I want to use my own rules.

MOM: Your own rules.

CHILD: It's too hard.

MOM: I know. You don't like the rules. Are you having a hard time?

CHILD: I don't like the rules.

MOM: Do you like the rules in school?

CHILD: Yes, but I hate rules at home.

MOM: What do you think would happen at school if you threw a glass of water at somebody?

CHILD: I'd get sent to the principal.

MOM: I bet you the principal would send you home.

NANNY: The rules are going to be very similar to the rules at school. And I know it's different and it's hard, but the only thing I'm asking you to do right now is when you're mad I want you to say—like you just said to mommy—I'm mad.

MOM: Right. You can tell me when you're mad.

NANNY: And then mommy will say to you, now let's go talk about it for a couple of minutes.

MOM: Are you ready to come downstairs?

CHILD: I'm going downstairs.

NANNY: I think this has been an eye-opening experience for you, mom. To realize that four-year-olds are actually capable of taking the time to talk about their feelings. That was great. You did really well talking to her. And you really made a breakthrough and got through to her. My only pointer is when she's telling you her feelings make sure you reward her for being able to do that. Her feelings need to be validated.

MOM: They probably were expressing their feelings all along. And I think the most important thing that I've learned is to listen. I'm sorry I haven't listened to them before.

WITH A SIX-YEAR-OLD

In this situation, Dana was upset because she'd forgotten a family rule and was told she had to lose a marble from the marble jar (see page 155 for more about the marble jar). As a result, she sat screaming and crying on the couch. Her mother tried to talk to her, but Dana put her hands over her ears so she wouldn't have to listen. Her mom snapped at her, then gave up trying.

MOM: I'm sorry you forgot, but maybe you'll remember from now on.

CHILD: Noooooooo!

Nanny Deb came in, sat down right next to Dana, put her arm gently on Dana's back, and initiated this conversation.

NANNY: First of all, I understand that you forgot. Everybody forgets some time. And it's hard to remember when something new has become a family rule.

CHILD: I don't want to lose the marble.

NANNY: I know you don't. You're obviously very, very upset about it. Because you feel like nobody's really listening or understanding what you want to say. Am I right?

CHILD: [stops crying, nods]

NANNY: You told me yesterday that you wanted to save your marbles because there was something special you wanted to buy for somebody in the family. Is that part of why you are so upset about losing a marble?

CHILD: Yes.

NANNY: I understand that. I understand that.

CHILD: Yes. [blows her nose]

NANNY: Why did you feel daddy wasn't being fair? It's important when you feel it isn't being fair to talk about it. Do you want to talk to daddy about it?

CHILD: Yes. [smiles]

Afterward, Nanny Deb explained to mom why her technique worked and mom's didn't.

MOM: I *did* try to talk to her.

NANNY: I know you did, but you were talking to her from across the room.

MOM: Well, her hands were over her ears, so I feel like that she doesn't want to listen.

NANNY: That is only her body language. Her body language really meant: "Stop telling me what to feel, please try to understand me. *Listen* to me." Dana calmed down and told me what was going on because she knew I was listening to her. I sat down right next to her, I was down at her level, I acknowledged the situation, and I

told her I understood that she was upset. And then she felt safe enough to talk about it.

WITH A NINE-YEAR-OLD

Nine-year-old Connor was having real trouble with Nanny Deb setting up rules in his home. He was used to being the boss and getting his own way. His mother yelled at him and his brothers so often that he tuned it out. His dad either yelled or spent little time with him. Plus his parents were simmering with unspoken resentment, so the atmosphere in the house was tense and filled with anger and chaos.

Nanny Deb knew that Connor had put up some pretty intense defenses to deal with his worries about his parents and the constant yelling. Instead of lashing out at him, as his parents did, Deb crouched down to his level, and started talking about the issue she knew was bothering him. She initiated the talk by confessing that her life had been similar to his, as her family had moved a lot, too. She realized that the moves had not been a positive thing for him, and she wanted to make it clear that she understood where he coming from.

NANNY: I want to talk you about when I was a kid. When I was little, my family moved a lot. By the time I was twelve, we moved sixteen times.

CHILD: I moved four times in the last couple of years to four different houses. And to seven different schools.

NANNY: Sometimes I remember it being kind of scary for me. And I thought you being oldest, may be able to help me figure out how you think people in this family deal with the changes. You know, if you think they're feeling what you're feeling.

CHILD: And now our parents are thinking of moving again.

NANNY: Well, how do you feel about that?

CHILD: I don't want to move.

NANNY: Do you like this house?

CHILD: It's not that I like it. I just don't want to move.

NANNY: Right, you don't like the moving part.

CHILD: Because I have to go to new schools and make new friends. I just want to stay here. (His eyes filled with tears.)

NANNY: I really want your dad and your mom to hear what you have to say about when you have to move.

CHILD: They don't listen.

NANNY: So, you know what I think we should do?

CHILD: What?

NANNY: I think we should have a family meeting.

Nanny Deb organized a family meeting right away, as the constant moves were obviously a major issue for these children, and their parents needed to realize how troubling it was for all of them. Once the feelings were aired, mom and dad decided not to move again.

Notice how Nanny Deb gently steered the conversation from being about her to being about Connor's feelings. She acknowledged his distress, and she also used the word "we" to emphasize that he wasn't in this alone.

Because Nanny Deb was so kind and empathetic, Connor opened up. He finished this talk in tears. Instead of being seen as a nasty, naughty brat, he revealed the truth—that he was a scared and hurt little boy, bearing his worries in silence because his parents had never asked him how he was feeling.

As we've seen all along, brats are not born. They're made. Connor was acting out because it was the only way to get his parents' attention. Even negative attention was better than none.

THE DO'S OF COMMUNICATION

Now that you know the basics of how to talk to your children, let's take a look at some of the ways you can improve your communication skills.

Do Say "I Love You" Every Day

One of the easiest ways to open up channels of communication is to state the obvious. We can't tell you how often we've gone into homes where the parents, who love their children, rarely tell them so.

Children do not need to be fussed over and overpraised for doing simple things that should be done every day or told they are geniuses for putting a cup in the dishwasher. They do not need to be made into the center of the universe and spoiled rotten because it's easier for you to give in rather than put the brakes on.

But they do need to be encouraged. They do need a hug and a kiss every day. They do need to feel that they are important to you.

Every day your children should hear the following:

- I love you.
- Please.
- Thank you.
- Thank you for being my child.
- I'm proud of you.
- I believe in you.
- I trust you.

Also try to take the time to slip a little note into a lunch box or a backpack. A little acknowledgment can go a very long way during the day.

Do Prove That You Are Listening

It is very easy to show your children that you are listening to them.

1. Say, "I'm listening."
2. Say, " I understand."
3. Repeat what they've said.

This lets your children know you have acknowledged them and validated their feelings. You haven't said yes, no, good, bad, or anything of the kind. You are simply there to hear them.

Repeating whatever they've said not only shows that you really listened, but also helps buy you a minute or two to collect your thoughts if a child is very upset about something and you want to be sure to say the right thing.

Do Teach Your Children How to Breathe

When small children are clearly upset, we tell them to take a breath. And they do.

Taking a breath distracts them in a flash. It helps calm down crying, as it's impossible to cry and do conscious breathing at the same time.

Conscious breathing is a great tool for parents, too. Just as kids can't cry and breathe, adults can't yell and breathe.

Here's how to do it.

1. Say, "Breathe. Breathe in. Relax."
2. Inhale long, deep, and visibly. Have the child do the same.
3. Say, "Breathe out."
4. Purse your lips and exhale long, steady, and loud.

You can also do conscious breathing by saying, "Breathe, 1, 2, 3." You can also find some other pattern that works for you.

Keep on breathing slowly and steadily for a while until the child is in a better state of mind.

Saying words such as "relax" and "calm" can help. You can also find a special word that works for you.

Do Give Your Children Words to Use

Whining usually starts when kids are preverbal. Whining often continues because it's easier for kids to make noise than it is to speak.

Children need to be taught that words are the only effective form of communication. Just as you teach your baby and toddlers to learn how to speak, you'll want to give them words so they can express their feelings.

If you don't teach them, the words don't become an essential part of their regular vocabulary.

After all, children have feelings all the time. They're going to be happy, sad, frustrated, angry, worried, ecstatic, overwhelmed—you name it—every day and all the time. That's life.

Unfortunately for everyone, kids often tend to lose their words when they're frustrated and angry.

Help them along. When your children are babies and toddlers, tell them to use their words so they can express themselves. Praise them when they use these words, and especially when they add new words to their vocabulary. As you saw with the example of Natalie on p. 62, she was perfectly capable of using her words at age two. She just didn't have to use them until Nanny Deb told her to.

See it as a major accomplishment when your kids feel secure enough to say, "I'm really angry!" instead of yelling, crying, and whining.

A few years ago, Nanny Stella was with one of her young charges, and she heard one of their five-year-old friends say, "I'm stressing out." He didn't yell it. He simply stated the truth in a very positive way. Something was going on, and he said how he felt.

And then prompt action was taken to find out what was stressing him.

Do Really Listen to Your Children

No child wants to talk to anybody who isn't listening to what they have to say. Adults don't like to talk to people who don't listen to them either.

DAD: The kids weren't listening so I yelled at them.

NANNY: What do you think yelling is going to prove?

DAD: What do you know? You've been here a few days. I've been doing this for years.

And he had the miserable, noisy kids to prove it.

Learning how to listen establishes a true bond of trust. Kids who know their parents will always listen to them—and especially, who will listen to them while suspending judgment about the conversation—are kids who grow up knowing that their parents respect their feelings.

This is an absolutely crucial part of positive parenting.

Once, when Nanny Deb was working with one of the families on the show, an eight-year-old girl was very upset with her mother. The little girl said, "My mom punched me. She kicked me and she hit me."

Nanny Deb had been watching on the monitor in the other room, and this mom did not punch or kick her daughter. But when Nanny Deb did come in to talk to this child, she didn't immediately sit down and ask, "Why are you lying about your mom?"

Instead, Nanny Deb got down to the little girl's level, talked to her about her feelings, saying, "I hear what you're saying. I can tell that you're very upset. Tell me what's wrong. I hear what you're saying. Tell me what happened."

A few minutes later, the truth came out.

Later, the *Nanny 911* producers were amazed that she had ignored the fact that this little girl had lied. Nanny Deb explained it to them: The little girl felt as though her mother *had* punched her—she was that upset. Although lying usually needs to be addressed, in this case it wasn't the essence of the little girl's pain. It wasn't anywhere as important as the fact that she had *felt* attacked.

In the previous chapter, we used an example of a hypercritical mom. Let's take a look the full conversation she had with her son, Tyler.

CHILD: Why should I listen to you?

MOM: Why should you listen to me? Because I gave birth to you, and without me, you wouldn't be here.

CHILD: You never listen to me.

MOM: I don't want to hear that.

CHILD: You don't care.

MOM: That's what you think, right? Now go to your room!

This example bears repeating in its entirety because it's such a breathtakingly painful example of how *not* to listen to your child. When Tyler said, "You never listen to me," Mom's response was, "I don't want to hear that." Amazing! She literally confirmed what he'd just told her. She *didn't* want to listen to him.

After he said, "You don't care," she sent him away. Again, her actions confirmed what he'd said. The message was: You're right. I don't care. Because if I did care, I would acknowledge your distress and want to comfort you, talk to you, and figure out a way to deal with the situation.

Of course, there will always be times when your children will want to speak to you and it's just not a good moment. Admit that it isn't. Apologize if you lose your temper. The key is always to acknowledge the moment.

The better you are at listening to your kids, the better they will become at listening to you.

It's a gift you give each other that will last a lifetime.

Do Respect Your Children's Feelings

The Nanny Rule is simple. Respect is a two-way street.

Respect your children's feelings. Whether you agree with them isn't the point. They are not your feelings. They belong to your child.

A child's feelings deserve validation, just as yours do. Don't tell children not to feel a certain way. They *will* feel that way, whether you're there to listen and believe in them or not.

Do Learn How to Manage Your Frustration

The kids have been screaming for the last twenty minutes, and you've had it.

So you start screaming, too.

Frustration comes with parenting. No one's perfect. We all lose it at some point or another. And frustration is usually what brings everything to a noisy, messy, screaming head.

One mom went crazy over her kids' annoying habit of dropping wet towels on the easily stained and ruined hardwood floors in the living room. It drove her crazy. She never knew what was clean or dirty. She told her kids over and over again not to leave wet towels on the floor. They didn't listen. She yelled. . . . they finally picked them up. The next day, bang, back on the floor.

What should this mom do?

Parents either give in (in this case by picking up the towels and getting mad about it), or they let it go so that the situation festers (mom is still so mad about the towels she blows up about something else entirely). Letting a bad situation go never works. It just means that nothing gets done.

Go back to basics.

When talking doesn't work, it's time to go back to basics. Sit down, ask yourself what the problem is, and how you want to talk about it. Rehearse what you need to say, if necessary, or write it down to keep it clear in your head. (You probably won't have to do that when it comes to wet towels getting picked up, but you may have to do it with more serious behavior issues, such as siblings fighting with one another.)

Then, sit down with your child, be at their level, look him or her in the eye, speak in a low, firm tone, and speak your mind. If he or she looks away, turn their heads gently back so you make eye contact. Don't allow your child to interrupt. Accept no excuses. Lay down the law—but do so calmly and firmly. Respect your child.

Even if she never picks up her towels.

Do Modify Your Expectations

Kids make messes, act out, and don't do what they're told. So what else is new?

When it comes to communication, it helps to modify your expectation for what is age-appropriate behavior.

In other words, squawking at a toddler for spilling his juice is counterproductive. Don't get mad; don't say, "See, now you spilled your juice."

Say, "Oops, all right, let's clean it up."

Clean up the mess, then say, "I'm going to wait to give you more juice until you sit still."

When he's sitting still, say, "Remember what happened the last time when you were wiggling around near your juice? It spilled everywhere. So, this time, let's try to remember where your cup is so it doesn't spill."

This is an effective technique for little kids. You aren't blaming them for doing something that is annoying. You're addressing the situation without any change in the tone of your voice, which makes it a nonissue. It happened. It's over. No big deal. Next time can be different.

This is the AMMO technique: Acknowledge and Move On.

Besides, we're sure you already know that screaming and yelling about mess to toddlers only makes them want to make more mess. Hey, it worked. They got your attention.

As your kids get older, your expectations for their good behavior will increase, of course. Read the section on manners in chapter 10 to see what we mean.

Do Use Humor—Make 'Em Laugh!

One way to defuse a tense situation where children are feeling grumbly is to use humor.

This is a tactic that works incredibly well with babies and toddlers—they love when you do the unexpected, especially when it's funny, and it makes them laugh. Anything from funny faces to silly walks to just acting goofy will do.

Older kids always love a good joke, too. If you find that you're about to blow, try to use a joke to calm yourself down. Instead of screaming "Go to your room!" say "Knock, knock" instead. Your child will say "Who's there?" and you will have to answer, instead of yelling.

Don't use humor in a sarcastic way, however, as it can result in some very hurt feelings. Telling jokes when somebody is obviously upset may make a child feel that you're ignoring the situation by trying to laugh it away.

Use your best judgment to know when to insert a joke.

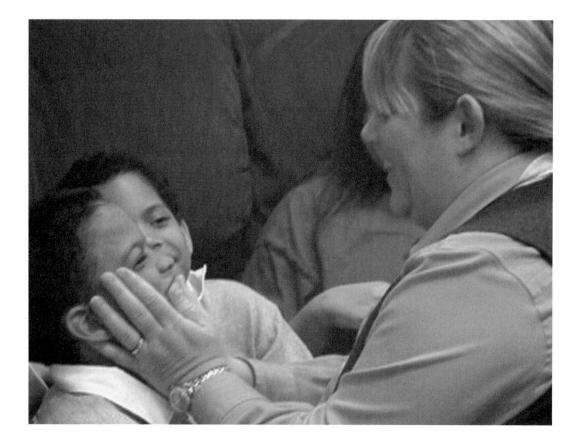

Do Keep It Simple

One of the things that drives parents really crazy is kids who can't make up their minds. We're going to talk about this more in the next chapter, but remember this: If you keep it simple when you're talking, then the result should be simple too. Don't make conversations complicated if you don't have to.

To do that, be specific. Don't ask questions that have answers you don't want to hear. Do offer the choices *you* want. Do offer the choices *you* can follow up on.

Here's a successful conversation between a mom and her three-year-old.

MOM: "Would you like eggs or pancakes for breakfast?"

CHILD: Ummm . . .

MOM: You have one minute to decide, and if you can't decide, I'll pick for you.

CHILD: How about eggs *and* pancakes?

MOM: That's a great idea. I'll cook you both.

CHILD: Good. I'm hungry!

If the mom had said, "What do you want for breakfast?" her son would probably still be trying to make up his mind. "What do you want for breakfast" is not specific enough.

Do Negotiate—It's Fine as Long as the Parent Wins

Parents who aren't specific with the questions they ask their kids can feel like they're negotiating their life away. Sometime it's okay to negotiate. It's fine as long as you win.

The way you win is by only offering *your* choices. The choice of A and B. And that's it. Not C and D and Z.

By offering a choice, when the kids choose they think they've won.

Samantha says, "I want ice cream before dinner."

Instead of the usual fight about no sweets before dinner, try it this way.

"You can have your ice cream with dinner, and that's it for your dessert, or you can have it for dessert. You choose."

Then follow through. Don't make a big deal out of a scoop of ice cream on the plate with the meat loaf and mashed potatoes. Chances are very high that Samantha won't eat her ice cream with dinner again.

Don't give in when the kids say that they don't want either A or B.

Say, "Fine. That's your choice, too. My offer still stands if you'd like to change your mind later."

AMMO: Acknowledge and Move On!

Do Allow Your Kids to Get Mad—It's Okay to Blow Off Steam

Babies cry. Children cry.

Message to parents: It isn't going to kill them.

What we find rather ironic is that parents understand that babies cry, so it doesn't bother them. They take appropriate steps to find out what's causing the crying so that it can be soothed.

But then these same parents somehow believe that their toddlers or preschoolers shouldn't cry at all. They will do anything to stop the crying. They get overprotective. They think their children will be emotionally stunted for life. They can't bear to see a few minutes of tears rolling down sweet chubby cheeks. They will do anything to prevent tantrums for erupting. So parents will beg, wheedle, plead, buy toys, stuff faces full of candy, cajole, and tear their hair out to make the little ones turn off the waterworks.

And we'll bet that the kids who are stopped from crying aren't any better behaved than the kids who do cry. In fact, the kids who are stopped from crying are more likely turned into spoiled brats, thanks to moms and dads.

Children absolutely must learn how to deal with their feelings of anger and frustration—but that's impossible to do if their parents won't let them cry and work out their feelings.

This is one of the most important issues we tackle on the show. Over and over again, we see naughty, overindulged children whose parents think crying is tantamount to child abuse. In the meantime, however, these parents don't teach their children how to deal with anger or frustration, which can become a really serious problem when children go off to school and have to deal with the daily frustrations of school work and classmates.

With this family, the mom is so overprotective that she can't let go of her need to baby her children. Not surprisingly, they act like babies. Mom also undermines dad's attempts at being an active parent. Here, Natalie is crying because her father is helping her get dressed, and she wants mommy to do it all for her.

NANNY: It's okay for her to have a tantrum. It's a normal two-year-old emotion.

MOM: I know, but do they need to go through all this? I mean, isn't it also normal for a mother to hug her children and comfort them? I want to hug and kiss them all the time.

NANNY: Yes, but you already know how to hug and kiss your child. I'm trying to teach you how to set limitations for your child and how to work with your husband as a team.

MOM: But she's only two and a half.

NANNY: Her dad comforted her. He handled it appropriately. There was no reason for you to be in there. He knows what he's doing. She is used to you rescuing her. He's her father. He needs to be part of the picture.

MOM: I don't want her to have a tantrum.

NANNY: Why not? Why can't she be upset? Why can't she be angry? *You* get upset. *You* get angry. How is she going to learn to cope with her own emotions if they're repressed?

MOM: It doesn't have to be this extreme.

NANNY: She's with her father. It won't be extreme if you allow him to comfort her and to be in there.

This mom's notion of "extreme" was actually what was extreme—as extremely distorted. Luckily, as soon as she saw her daughter calming down with no damage done, she realized that she hadn't been doing her any favors by coddling her.

Parents also don't want their older children to say, "I'm angry. I'm really mad." Well, what is a child who is angry or really mad supposed to say?

A parent saying, "Don't be angry and upset" both invalidates the feelings, and discourages open channels of communication.

If your child says, "I'm angry," it's your responsibility to not deny the anger, but to calmly ask what's causing it.

Use the techniques we've discussed already. Repeat what's been said. Acknowledge the situation. Breathe.

Nanny Deb worked in a family with a mom who was in deep denial about her feelings, so her kids never talked about theirs. Instead, they communicated with violence—hitting, kicking, choking, and biting each other.

Because they needed a lot of help to learn how to use words to express feelings of anger and frustration, Nanny Deb set up a magnet board (see chapter 6) to reward the children when they *said* they were angry instead of acting on this anger. She would say, "I know you're upset. Okay! Good. Let's work on it," and then reward them for it.

The magnet board (you can use a marble jar, too) became a sensible way for these kids to fight the anger when they wanted to lash out. Instead, they could control their behavior by identifying it.

Do Learn How to Show Pleasure, Too

Communicating is not just about *how* you say it. It's also about *what* you say, too.

We've found that even the most loving parents don't know how to be happy when they speak. They don't know how or when to give praise and encouragement. Positive reinforcement applauds children for their good behavior. It should become a habit as necessary to their well-being as you saying "I love you."

Showing your children pleasure isn't conveyed by the low, firm tone you use when you're disciplining or having a serious talk. When you're happy, sound happy. You don't have to go over the top. Simply change your demeanor and your voice—it tends to get naturally higher when you're pleased.

We like to use a lot of energy in our voices and bodies when we've complimenting children. If Bryan says, "I did this," we say "Great job—give me five!" Put a "Wow!" in your tone.

Children love to be rewarded, and simple praise is often the best reward a child can receive. But this doesn't mean you should go overboard with your praise—only that if something makes you feel good, you can easily show it with your tone as much as with your words.

THE DON'TS OF COMMUNICATION

Take a look at this list and see how many don'ts you've done. But don't beat yourself up too much because everyone acts like this eventually (hopefully not all at once!). It's not possible to communicate perfectly all the time. One you're aware of these don'ts, however, it'll be easier to put a stop to them.

Don't Make a Promise You Can't Keep

Parents tend to use the word "promise" like they use the word "no." Either way, it doesn't work.

Don't make a promise you can't keep. Don't say, "I promise

you that if you do that you're grounded," and then not ground the misbehaving child. Otherwise you're like the little boy who cried wolf. And you're about to get eaten alive.

With this situation, dad had promised his oldest son, eight-year-old Joe, that he would spend a precious hour of alone time with him before dinner, but he was running late. Dad had to get dinner ready instead. Joe, in his frustration, began to bother his sister. She began chasing and yelling at him. Dad's response was to blow his stack.

> **DAD:**   I just had enough. Give it back! Shut up! Why are you taking her book?
>
> **CHILD:**   Because I didn't get to—
>
> **DAD:**   Shut up. Cool off. You want me to hit you?
>
> **CHILD:**   No.

Dad honestly didn't mean to break his promise, but he didn't take the time to explain to Joe what had happened or that he'd make it up to him. Joe was upset by the broken promise, and he was so desperate for some of his father's attention—even if it was negative and punitive—that he acted out to get it. Instead of spending a happy hour together, everyone ended up yelling, threatening, and miserable.

Really think about the consequences before you make a promise.

Don't Think White Lies Will Always Work

Children have incredibly sensitive radar for lying. It's practically uncanny how much they know when mom and dad aren't being truthful.

Let's say you promise to take the kids to play miniature golf, but something else comes up instead that needs to be taken care of.

You don't want disappoint them, so you tell the kids that the golf course is closed for the day to repair the fountains. Then your kids are out with you in the car later, and they see that it is open.

You're busted!

And they're upset—with good reason.

If you did make a promise and it has to be broken, don't lie about it. Respect your children and your own integrity and tell the truth.

Don't wallow in your mistake and promise your kids the moon for having messed up. Use the AMMO technique: Acknowledge and move on.

If there's a tough situation to deal with, use age-appropriate language. Nanny Stella had a situation where a mom told her little girl that her father was going to be away for a few months on a new job, when in truth he was in rehab. Even though her daughter was four, she shouldn't have been lied to. Mom should have said, "Daddy's not well at the moment. He's in the hospital that will make him feel better."

However, if you're having a talk with your spouse about a topic that is inappropriate for your children to hear, and your children burst into the room and overhear part of the conversation, it may be wise to make something up to change the topic. This is not the same thing as you making up white lies to cover your own behavior.

Don't Make Children Talk When They're Still Too Angry to Do So

Kids often need to calm down and collect their thoughts before they can talk rationally. So do grown-ups.

If your child is very upset and not able to calm down with controlled breathing, acknowledge the situation and show that you are ready to listen when the time is right. Try saying the following:

"You are angry right now, and I can see that you're not ready to talk. You need to take time to calm down. Please go to your room and calm down, and I'll be here when you're ready to talk."

Do not say, "What's the matter now?" or "What are you so mad about?" Hearing that is pretty much guaranteed to shut a child down and make the situation worse.

Don't Say "No" All the Time

We'll deal with this is in more detail in the next chapter. Just remember that "No" is most effective when used the least. Save "No" for extreme situations, such as physical danger (such as if your child runs across the street or reaches for a hot saucepan on the stove), and it will be a much more useful part of your vocabulary.

If you can't accept no as an answer, don't ask the question, "Do you want to go to time-out?" We never ask questions like that. We never ask, "Do you want to go to the store with me today?" If they have to come with me, I don't ask them. I tell them that we have to go to the store.

Don't Say "If You Just Listened"

Whenever we hear parents saying, "If you just listened . . ." or "You never listen to me." we say, *Stop right there! Start again.*

Children do listen. If you have something to say, know how to say it. Don't dump the responsibility for listening on a child when you haven't mastered the art of communication.

Don't Yell

We all yell. We all lose it. No one is ever going to get through parenting without yelling bloody murder. But that doesn't mean it's okay.

Yelling is just about the most useless form of communication between parents and children. All it does is raise adrenaline levels, get people upset, and make the situation worse.

With this family, dad's chronic yelling had given mom such a case of anxiety she would leave the room as soon as he got home. And his children only became more aggressive as soon as he lit into them. Here, dad is trying to defend his yelling and his having spanked his oldest son.

NANNY: Mom seemed optimistic, but I'm not convinced dad really believes that his yelling is tearing this family apart.

DAD: What am I going to do? I can't *not* yell. I can't not grab him because, you know what, so far he's not listening and behaving. I'm not a person who's just going to sit there and let him act the way he's been acting and not do anything.

NANNY: So you scream and then he screams.

DAD: To me, it's not screaming. To me, it's talking loud.

This dad soon realized that his "talking loud" was loudly tearing his family apart.

NANNY: You need to spend more time with Joseph, and I'm nervous you're not seeing the big picture. I'm telling you the real home truth. If you don't get tougher in your discipline—as opposed to your yelling—and make Joseph aware of the consequences, there are going to be serious repercussions in the future. I mean it. You need to tell him that you are going to spend more time with him and that he doesn't have to be badly behaved to get your attention. He has to stop.

Joe sat down and had a heart-to-heart with Joseph.

DAD: Joe, Joe, can I talk to you a minute? Come over here. I need to talk to you. No, turn around and look at me. I expect you to behave. I expect you to listen, okay? Don't you want to have a nice relationship with daddy?

CHILD: Yes.

DAD: All right, look at me. Don't you want to have fun?

CHILD: Yes.

DAD: Do you want to get in trouble when you get older?

CHILD: No.

DAD: Okay, come here, okay. I love you very much, Joe, but you got to start learning how to behave better. Okay? You act better, and I'll act better. Good deal?

CHILD: Yeah.

DAD: Give me a kiss. Okay? I love you, Joe.

Overnight, incredibly enough, dad found a way to stop himself from yelling. It was pretty amazing and pretty wonderful to watch this man go from screaming and shouting to gently talking to his children. He finally showed that he could discipline Joseph without yelling. There was a lot of love in this house, but it just got lost amid the screaming and shouting.

Don't Nag

Nagging is like yelling. It's mental noise.

Forget about it. Nagging never works.

One mom who Nanny Stella worked with kept saying, "I swear to God, CJ, I swear to God," over and over again. *What* exactly was she swearing about? She never said. Nanny Stella did, however, get a bit fed up with her swearing to God and started wishing this mom would start *praying* to God for guidance because her nagging certainly wasn't working.

As soon as nagging starts, little ears miraculously close. When you say the same thing every day—"Get off the couch, no jumping, get off the couch, no jumping"—and do nothing to stop the jumping, obviously what you are saying doesn't mean anything.

Unless you're prepared to live with the Nanny Rule of actions have consequences, curb your nagging.

Nanny Deb had this tough talk with a nagging Mom.

NANNY: All day long, all I heard you say was do it, do it, do it, do it, do it. Oh, you didn't do it right. Do it again. Do it this way. These children are constantly striving to meet your standards. But every day a child needs to be praised for something, too. Not once did these children get praised.

MOM: I do. That's not fair because I do say thank you. You can ask them.

Nanny Deb didn't need to ask them. Mom didn't either. She knew she was wrong.

And remember another rule: Respect is a two-way street. Nagging doesn't exactly engender respect, does it?

If you don't think you're a nag, even when your children or

spouse tell you that you are, try leaving on a tape recorder during the time you are most prone to nag, such as after school and before dinner. Then replay it at your own risk. You may be very surprised at just how awful you sound.

Don't Belittle Your Children

Belittling makes kids shut down. Even parents who dearly love their children have no idea of how often they belittle their kids, or the damage it does. Some of the nastiness that parents spew at their children is well and truly shocking to us.

Belittling really has to stop if you want your children to trust you. No child can trust an adult who consistently discounts his or her feelings.

Take this dad who was putting his seven-year-old daughter to bed.

CHILD: Are we really going to bed?

DAD: Yes, we're really going to bed.

CHILD: Please leave the light on.

DAD: Don't start. Close your eyes and go to sleep.

CHILD: I'm scared of the dark. [crying]

DAD: Enough, already.

CHILD: [Screaming and crying]

DAD: Nobody has light. You happy? Now put your head down and go to sleep. I told you to stop complaining and go to sleep.

CHILD: I don't like it.

DAD: Good, now cry.

Let's take a look at what this conversation was really about. Haley admitted she was scared of the dark. Dad's immediate reaction was to dismiss her fears. She felts belittled and more scared. When she started to cry, dad continued to dismiss her. Her fears escalated into a full-blown panic attack. Dad not only refused to acknowledge her fears, but also compounded her terror by punishing her.

This was a *terrible* way for any adult to treat a child. Haley cried herself to sleep. Her fears of the dark deepened. Dad's rage intensified.

If dad doesn't believe that kids should have a light on when they go to sleep, he could easily have compromised with a dimmer switch, that gradually—and the key word here is *gradually*—could be turned down to darken the room.

Instead of belittling and dismissing Haley's fears, the very least dad should have done was to acknowledge them. It is incredibly common for kids to be scared of the dark. This dad just didn't want to be bothered trying to understand what triggered Haley's fears. It was easier to make her feel bad about it.

After he left Haley sobbing in bed, dad went on to belittle her sister.

DAD: What's the matter?

CHILD: I want Mommy.

DAD: Oh, I'm gonna be here. What do you need Mommy for?

CHILD: I want Mommy.

DAD: Cut it out. Enough.

Dad hid his anxieties about his parenting skills under a brusque mask of bullying and belittling. Once he realized that he was a capable father, his approach softened, and he was better able to accept and deal with his children's fears and desires without hurting their feelings.

In another family, mom was determined that her kids were going to be stars, even though they weren't at all interested in acting. Determined to fulfill her own thwarted dreams through her hapless brood, mom schlepped her kids to auditions they didn't want to go to. Since the children would never be able to meet Roxanne's unreasonable demands, she tended to work herself into a lather.

After one such dismal day, her eight-year-old daughter Dana was desperate to please her mother anyway. She took it upon herself to creatively decorate her room and was justifiably proud of her special little art project. Then, mom walked in.

CHILD: Look.

MOM: What did you do?

CHILD: My decoration, of course.

MOM: How long are you planning on keeping it up there? You don't want to make marks on the bed.

Dana was devastated. Nanny Deb was furious with mom's hurtful negativity.

NANNY: What did you say when you walked in?

MOM: I don't remember my exact words.

NANNY: You said, "How long are you planning on keeping it up there?"

MOM: That wasn't the first thing I said.

NANNY: Then you told her it better not make marks on the bed.

MOM: Well, I don't want them to make marks on the bed.

NANNY: It was all negative. You didn't walk in and say, wow, that's very creative. Wow, that's a great job. You're upset because you know deep down that I'm right. Look at me. I'm not saying that you're bad. You are a good mother. You love your children. But your two older children bottle everything inside because they're afraid.

These kids need to go through life normally. They need to make mistakes, and they need to know that they can come to you with anything because no matter what, you're not going to turn around and say, see, I told you, you didn't do it right.

I know you're trying to do this because you want the perfect life for your children. But in trying to achieve the perfect life for your children, you're making them unhappy. There's no such thing as a perfect life. And as a nanny who's been doing this for twenty-two years, I can tell you what the outcome for your children is going to be if you carry on nagging and belittling. And it's not pretty. Okay? I'm telling you, you need to change. And I know you can do it.

And she did do it. It took Nanny Deb's stern wake-up call, but it worked. Mom replaced her chronic negativity with positive reinforcement, and her children blossomed in the gentle praise that was long overdue.

Don't Compare Siblings

When you say, "Why can't you act more like your sister?" a child will never want to communicate with you.

Instead, it's a good way to alienate, hurt, and belittle your child. We know how hard it is not to compare siblings. Please just try not to.

Don't Pretend It'll Just Go Away

Taking the easy way out is one of the main reasons desperate parents call the *Nanny 911* hotline.

One mom was so overwhelmed by the constant noise and shrieking in her house that she literally tuned it out. "All of a sudden I start zoning out and I get this headache and I can't even process simple questions," she confessed. "And I eventually start going crazy."

In this separate case, mom gets mad at her daughter and drops the whole thing.

MOM: It's like I'm talking to a wall. Do you understand when I say stop, what that means?

CHILD: Yeah, stop.

MOM: Then why did you do it again?

CHILD: I don't know.

MOM: You need to get ready now.

CHILD: No, I don't.

Well, that was productive, wasn't it?

Don't Put Ideas in Their Heads

This is a tough one because ideas can easily slip out before you've even noticed it. For example, this mom is comforting her child, who woke up from a bad dream.

MOM: Oh, honey, did you have a bad dream?

CHILD: Uh-huh.

MOM: Did you see a monster?

CHILD: [Starts crying] A big one!

Bringing up monsters to a scared child is like telling them that the boogeyman lives in the closet and alligators live under the bed.

Do try, however, to let your child initiate the conversation when it comes to scary things. That way you can respond to his or her imagination, which is vivid enough without any input from mom or dad.

Don't Discipline When You're Upset

Communication can be rough on the best of days. It's nearly impossible when you're upset. You'll be much more likely to lash out and say things you don't mean if you're already in a state, especially if you're frustrated, no matter how justified.

In this example, dad walks into the house after a fractious day at work and wishes he hadn't. He starts screaming before he's even put down his briefcase.

DAD: When I came home today it was like I had walked into the wrong house. Well, I wish I had. What are you doing? Stop it. Right now! When I come home, and it's wild and crazy, then I get all worked up and that leads to impatience and screaming. Listen, if I have to tell you again, you're going to go to your room. You understand me?

My wife is a lot more patient with the kids. She can tolerate more. I tend to snap.

NANNY: I understand that this is what's worked for you in the past, but it works only for the moment. Five minutes later, the kids are doing the same thing again. They need to learn to communicate by talking and listening to one another. How can they listen when you're screaming like that?

DAD: [Screaming] Stop it! Right now!

NANNY: You need to get a hold of yourself. You're an example to your children. You know, Sam is afraid when you yell at him. Do you want your child to be afraid of you?

If you feel like you're about to blow, give yourself a parental time-out. We already discussed this in chapter 2, but let's go over the concept again.

Parents who are prone to anger can put themselves in time-out, just as they put their children in one. It is an excellent way to show your children how to use self-control in emotional situations.

Right before you explode, tell your kids what you're about to do—that you're putting yourself in time-out because you need time to calm down. Then leave the room and take a lot of deep breaths. Focus until you feel better.

Parental time-outs show your children that you need quiet, private time to calm down. You're showing them that it's okay to be angry, and this will in turn give them permission to be angry when they need to be.

If you've already lost it before the time-out, come back when you're calm, and explain yourself. Apologize for yelling or screaming, or whatever specifics you said. Say you're sorry you lost your temper, you're doing your best, and you'll try to do better in the future. Tell them that it's not right to treat anger with anger.

Because it isn't right to treat anger with anger, however justified you think it may be.

Then use AMMO: Acknowledge and move on.

Don't, however, say to your child, "I yelled. I know I was wrong, but you made me do it."

Your child may have driven you right round the bend, but you are the adult here. You are in control of your own actions. You are responsible for your behavior and your response to your children's behavior.

And you are also responsible for allowing your children's behavior to deteriorate because you didn't want to deal with it in the first place, which is the reason there's so much yelling, screaming, and naughtiness in the first place. Right?

But don't beat yourself up if and when you lose it. Admit it and move on—that's what makes us learn. Acknowledging the fact that we've make mistakes.

And hopefully we won't make them again.

WHAT TO TALK ABOUT WHEN YOU'RE TALKING

Older kids may have the vocabulary, but that doesn't mean they know how to use it. Often, they are desperate to talk to their parents but just don't know how to start.

Do Initiate a Conversation

Being able to communicate freely and openly is why we are such firm believers in family mealtime. Children who grow up in a house where they are always asked about what they did during the day as well as how they feel are children who feel confident that they are loved and who don't repress their emotions.

The easiest way to teach your children how to open up is to always ask them about their feelings—every day.

Be as specific as possible when initiating a conversation. Don't accept "Nothing" or "I'm fine" as an answer if it's obvious that it's not nothing and your child isn't fine. Instead, rephrase what you're saying so it's not so much a question, but the beginning of a conversation. Such as the following:

- You look like there's something on your mind. Let's go have a quiet talk, just the two of us.
- Did something unusual happen today?
- What do you think about kids who _____? Fill in the blank with whatever you think may be pertinent to what's upsetting your child.
- You know, when I was _____, I used to _____, and it drove my parents _____. Or something like that. Talking about something that was upsetting or frustrating to you as a child is often a good way to have your child realize you are going to be empathetic, not judgmental.

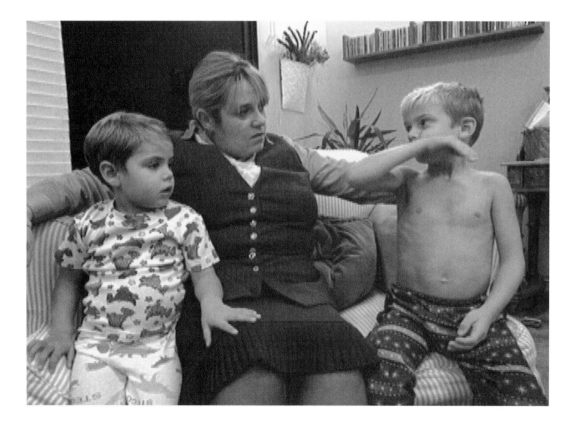

If you find it difficult to talk to your kids as they start to approach those preteen years, try finding a calm, quiet, *private* place. No child is going to want to talk about a sensitive topic in front of snooping siblings. Go back to basics. Get down to your child's level. Keep your voice calm and level. Don't interrupt. Acknowledge the problem. Reserve judgment until your child has stopped speaking. Figure out a way to tackle the problem or feeling together.

Many parents like to talk to their kids in the car. If the topic at hand is embarrassing, for example, a child may not want to make eye contact. Plus it's a confined space so no one can escape.

Another way to initiate a conversation is by leaving a note. Sometimes kids will respond in writing to sensitive topics. You can also sit down in private with your child and the notes and talk about what was written. It gives you something concrete, in hand, and can make the talk a little less threatening.

Do Be Honest and Deal with the Tough Stuff

Opening up about painful behavior is really tough stuff. It can be excruciatingly painful for grown-ups to admit to what they've done wrong—for fear of losing face, for fear of opening up their own unhealed wounds from childhood, and for fear of having their child rebuff their love.

If your child is hurting and needs to talk, find a private, quiet place. Hold the child close with a reassuring hug or touch. Go back to the basic technique for talking to a child on p. 58. Follow the steps there—get down to the child's level, make eye contact, and keep your voice low and even. Remember to breathe.

We know how hard it can be to open up. Try using any of these sentences to get the conversation flowing. Most importantly, do not interrupt your child. Do not contradict them even if you believe

they are wrong. You can follow up later. Repeat what they are saying so you can process it, as well as prove to the child that you are
really listening.

- I really love you.
- I never wanted to hurt you.
- I'm sorry if I ever hurt you.
- I want you to be able to come to me if there's something you
  need to talk about.

Here's a terrific example of parents who were honest with their
children about things they'd done wrong and wanted to change.
Mom talked to one child and dad to another:

MOM: I don't like fighting with you. And we're going to work on that because I don't want to fight with you anymore, okay? [crying] Would you like it if we didn't fight so much?

CHILD: Yes.

MOM: Okay. So we'll work together on it, okay?

DAD: That's part of the thing I'm going to work on. I don't want to scream at you anymore, okay?

CHILD: Dad, when you scream, it scared me. You scared me.

DAD: I know, I can tell it did. And I don't like to see that. When you shake a little bit, I don't like to see that.

NANNY: How do you feel when you think your kids are so afraid of you that they're actually shaking?

DAD: I feel kind of sad. It's really sad.

NANNY: You don't want children to fear you. You want them to respect you. It's a terrible feeling to be afraid or to be the person who instills fear. So by communicating, these children are going to learn to respect you and not to fear you.

DAD: Sam, I'm sorry for making you afraid.

NANNY: As an adult man, you should be proud of the fact that you were strong enough to say sorry to your child. Because by doing this, you are teaching your child that it's okay for him to say sorry. And to feel emotions and to feel sorry.

DAD: Sam, I'm so sorry. [Both are crying]

Later, they sat down with Nanny Deb and their children and had another very much needed talk.

DAD: Today was a big turning point in my life. I will never ever scream at them again. Enough. All it does is instill fear in them. When I looked at Sam, when I was hugging him, he was crying.

MOM: The same thing happened with me and Josh.

DAD: I don't want to scare them anymore.

MOM: I know. We'll get it.

DAD: I am not going to scream anymore. I'm going to really try this and talk things through with you. I'm going to work just as hard as you guys are working.

NANNY: Doug is actually thrilled to be able to come home at night, sit around a family dinner table, and eat with his boys. He realized he needed to talk to his children for them to listen to him. Diana and Doug really understand the importance of a calm tone and the keeping of a loving household.

In another family, mom is so controlling that the children obviously live in fear of her, and dad was so busy with work he was never around to listen. Instead of being able to talk, the children repressed their feelings, yelled, threw tantrums, or locked themselves in their rooms.

Nanny Deb dealt with this by insisting that the problems be confronted. They also told ten-year-old Tyler that he had to be able to open up to his dad if he wanted dad to understand how he was feeling. And dad had to be encouraging, too.

NANNY: There's no more running away and locking doors. You have a problem? You're going to talk about it. I'm asking you, Tyler, to be brave enough to say to your dad why you feel like you can't talk to him about your feelings. And I'd like dad to come and sit next to you. I want you to feel that your whole life, this is the person you can go to if you have a problem. I want you to have that relationship with your dad.

TYLER: Dad, you say, okay, that's all right. See you later. I
have to go to work. Bye. You never listen to me.

JOHN: It breaks my heart to hear this. And if there were
times that I should have been listening to you, and I
didn't, I apologize. You have to tell me when something's bothering you. Unless you say something to
someone, I don't know it. If you don't think I'm listening to you, will you please tell me, rather than just
be disappointed. I love you.

TYLER: I love you, too.

They had a long cuddle and spent some much needed time together, clearing the air so they could move forward.

IT'S NEVER TOO LATE TO START COMMUNICATING

We can't tell you enough how important it is to start communicating early with your children. The sooner you establish firm, unshakeable bond of trust, the better—and the easier it will be to build upon this foundation of love and trust when your kids get older and life gets a lot tougher.

But even if you haven't done a bang-up job at communicating so far, it's never too late to learn to start talking properly to one another.

You can always start from scratch and go back to basics, no matter how old your child is. Pretend that you've just met this child, and you're establishing a relationship, a friendship. How would you talk to new acquaintances? Well, you'd ask about their interests, where they're from, and what they like or don't like. And you move on from there.

Once they open up about their feelings, it can be a pretty amazing experience for parents to truly get to know their children for the first time.

On the show, you've seen many toddlers and preschoolers raising hell and acting out in some pretty shocking ways, until we take charge and establish order, discipline, and clear, calm, kind communication.

We tell their parents that when communication improves, they can store those lessons away and use them again when their kids approach their teenage years. After all, toddlers and preschoolers are learning how to express themselves as individuals. They're asserting themselves. They're finding their independence. They're exploring their world. They're wanting to control their appearance and may demand to wear certain clothes.

So are teenagers.

Give your children the tools of great communication that they will use for life. Give them credit for their intelligence, their spirit, and their fearlessness in facing the world.

Just remember who's in charge. You are. You're the parent. You're the teacher. You make the decisions. You set up the rules. You talk honestly about your feelings and your expectations.

Most of all, you know how to listen to your children when they need you.

CHAPTER 4
YES, PLEASE: CHILDREN LEARNING TO COMMUNICATE TO PUT AN END TO WHINING, WHEEDLING, WANTING, AND TANTRUMS

In the previous two chapters we talked about *how* to communicate. Now, we're going to talk about how *not* to communicate—if you're a child, that is. Every parent knows what we're talking about. It's that terrible sound that grates on the ear like fingernails on the chalkboard.

Yes, moms and dads, it's the dreaded sound of the whine.

Whining is usually accompanied by begging, pleading, wheedling, and wanting.

It usually precedes the total meltdown that is triggered by the I-have-to-have-it-now-or-I'll-die syndrome, which, naturally, most likely involves a toy that will end up being played with for only five minutes before being thrown off the couch and broken.

We've heard every possible sound that children can make when in the process of trying to get what they want. We've seen some pretty terrifying tantrums in our years as nannies. We've seen even the most calm and rational of parents lose it completely when their children act up and act out in public, leading these parents to fear

that their beloved children are turning into superbrats for life. What these frazzled parents do is give up and give in, handing little Jasper another candy bar on the checkout line just to shut him up, or buying little Peyton her tenth Bratz doll so she'll stop kicking and hitting mom in the mall where, naturally, everyone's looking at mom's blushes of mortification and tut-tutting her obvious lack of parenting skills.

Read on, if you want to learn how *not* to give in and how to teach your children to communicate without whining.

ALL ABOUT NO

One of the most overused words in the English language is "no." If you can learn to moderate your use of this tiny little word, you'll be in a much better position to deal with the whining and tantrums.

NANNY RULE

ONLY SAY NO WHEN YOU MUST—THE NO "NO" TECHNIQUE

Only say "no" when you really mean it and it's really necessary.

This is by far one of the hardest Nanny Rules to follow because using the word "no" is such a reflexive act that few of us even realize how many times we say it during the day. As with other negative words or phrases, such as "Don't," "Stop it," or "Cut it out," if children hear the same thing repeatedly with no consequences or inconsistent consequences, they merely tune it out and go on their merry ways, doing whatever they want to do and probably getting away with it, too.

For us, "no" is a very, very heavy word. It should be saved for the occasions when you truly need it. For these situations, "no" is inflexible and absolute. It means imminent danger, so "no!" is a true warning. When a child is about to put his finger in the electrical outlet, or tries to pull the television off the shelf, you should without question say either "No!" or "Danger!" (See The Difference Between Caution and Fear sidebar on p. 114.)

The no "no" technique should start early, when your child is a baby. When Chloe and Antonio are picking up something that doesn't belong to them, for example, you don't need the no. Instead, briefly explain why they shouldn't pick that something up. Say, "Gentle, that's Mommy's. I don't want you to touch that."

If Chloe is trying to bite Antonio, you don't need to say no, either. You can calmly pull her away and tell her, "It's not okay to hurt someone else." If she keeps trying to bite, remove her from the situation. Grabbing Chloe's hand and saying, "No, no! I said no biting!" will not be as effective.

In other words, the no "no" technique means you just announce what is to be done, without attaching a "no" to it. Simply state the facts.

One caveat: Do not give your child a dissertation on why he or she should not do something. We've seen parents go on and on about what little Chloe is supposed to do. As in, "Well, honey, you really shouldn't bite, as it hurts Antonio's feelings, and you wouldn't like it if he bit you, would you, of course you wouldn't, so you shouldn't do it either." This is just as ineffective as saying "no" all the time.

Let's say little Violet wants a glass of milk shortly before dinnertime. This is what usually happens.

CHILD: I want milk, please.
MOM: No, you can't have it now. It'll ruin your appetite.
CHILD: I want milk now! I said please!
MOM: I said no!
CHILD: Give me milk!

And the situation deteriorates from there. Instead, try this.

CHILD: I want milk.
MOM: We're not having milk right now. We'll have milk with dinner. Dinner is in ten minutes.

You can also try this.

CHILD: I want milk.
MOM: I know you want milk. You may have some with dinner.

Rephrasing your child's question into a sentence is the key to teaching yourself how to say no. By rephrasing the question, you are putting the idea into your head, and buying the time it takes to compose a calm answer without using the re-flexive "no."

Rephrasing or repeating the question and acknowledging the request also proves to your children that you really are listening, which is very important to them.

Quite often, especially with toddlers who are preverbal or just beginning to speak, when you say "no" instinctively to them, they honestly think that you haven't been listening to them. For them, saying "no" is part of their learning age-appropriate autonomy. Hearing it from you, however, is coun-terproductive.

Toddler tantrums often stem from the sheer frustration of not being understood, so if you acknowledge what you think it is they're trying to communicate, it will be easier for both of you.

Learning the no "no" technique will take quite a lot of thought and hard work to drill into your head. It isn't easy to undo years of (bad) training and stop saying "no" all the time. You have to put your brain in gear before you put your mouth in motion.

When you do get better at the no "no" technique, you'll find that your children are much more responsive to your directions, and they'll be less likely to say "no" to everything, too.

As your children grow older, however, using "no" will become less of an issue than when they're toddlers and preschoolers who need a lot of direction. Be sure that both parents have figured out when to say "no" before saying it!

. . . .

IF YOU CAN'T ACCEPT NO AS AN ANSWER, DON'T ASK THE QUESTION

NANNY RULE

One of the biggest problems we've dealt with on our show is that parents give their children far too much freedom of choice.

If you can't accept no as an answer, don't ask the question.

If you ask your misbehaving little girl, "Do you want to go to time-out?" how do you think she's going to answer?

She's certainly not going to say, "Yes, please, Mommy, I'd love a time-out!"

Rethink what you're about to say. If you have to go shopping, don't ask your child if he wants to come with you. Instead, tell him that you're going shopping. It is a fact. It's going to happen.

And then just do it.

If it's time to go outside and play, don't ask, "Do you want to go outside now?" What if your child doesn't feel like going? Then you've set up a situation where frustration or a tantrum can ensue, and there's no need to have started the mess in the first place.

When you do have to ask questions, rephrase them so the answer must be specific. Don't offer too many choices. If you do, you your child can quickly begin to manipulate what you're offering.

A lot of parents think they're getting around this by using "How about?" But we're not crazy about that, either. Asking "How about" is a choice, and choices lead to arguments.

Don't say, "We are going to get dressed now. How about your blue shirt or your yellow shirt?"

You may well hear: "No! I hate my blue shirt and my yellow shirt, and you can't make me wear them!"

Instead, say, "We are going to get dressed now, and you can wear your blue shirt or your yellow shirt."

Be firm and stick to what *you* want your child to do.

THE DIFFERENCE BETWEEN CAUTION AND FEAR

It's important for children to know the difference between caution and fear.

Caution has to do with basic rules of safety. It's a necessary part of life. When you're riding in a car, you need to be buckled in your car seat or booster. When you're riding your bike or skateboarding, you need to wear your helmet. When you're crossing the street, you stop, look both ways, and proceed carefully.

A sharp "no!" *should* be part of your cautionary vocabulary. It should be used when your child is about to do something dangerous, such as touch a hot pot on the stove or start to run across the street.

Fear, on the contrary, has to do with being scared. This is a perfectly normal feeling to have as a child (or as an adult, for that matter), as the world can be a scary place when you're small. Learning how to ride a bike *is* scary, but that doesn't mean you want to stay afraid of riding.

Overprotective parents tend to plant fears in their children, turning what should be simple caution into outright terror. Watch yourself so you don't automatically say things such as, "Don't climb on the monkey bars, or you'll get hurt," which is pretty much guaranteed to make a child more anxious and likely to fall. Or "Of course there are no monsters under the bed. Do you want me to check and see?" which not only is contradictory, but also plants the idea in a child's head that there really are monsters down there.

ALL ABOUT WHINING

Why do kids whine?

The answer is simple: Because their needs aren't being met.

Most often, they want attention. And they've learned that the only way to get it is to start with the pleading, nagging, annoying sound that drives you so crazy you give in just to make it go away.

Once you give your children the comfort, respect, and acknowledgment of what they're looking for, whining and tantrums will stop. Once you make it safe for your children to use their words and talk about their feelings, they aren't going to repress these feelings and then blow up later over something that's seemingly inconsequential.

The children we look after learn very, very quickly that whining will not work with us. Much to their parents' amazement, the little whining machines stop their annoying clinking and clanking right away. We teach them how to use their words to express themselves. And if they don't use their words, they don't get what they want.

So, what is it that children need?

THE NEED LIST

Need
Encouragement
Enthusiasm
Daily

THE ALL LIST

Attention and acknowledgment
Listened to
Love to be stated

Give your children what they need, and they'll be much less likely to whine. Let's take a look at how to do this.

Whining Starts Early : The Baby Whine

Whining can start early. Babies who are as young as seven or eight months old whine. As soon as your baby can make noises, which signifies that something is wanted—a toy, a bottle, or your attention—the whining can commence. This preverbal whining needs to be nipped in the bud—pronto!

Babies are incredibly fast learners, which, of course, means they learn to whine once they figure out that those grunts, groans, moans, and noises get mom and dad to respond. They'll usually point to something and whine. If your baby has started to whine, your response is easy.

Say, "Use your words."

It doesn't matter if the babies don't have words yet. They'll still understand the concept. It's up to you to ask them what they want. Then repeat it.

Let's say the baby wants a banana. You say, "Do you want a banana? Use your words. Yes, please. Okay, here is your *banana*." The emphasis should be on the word *banana*.

The key word here is repetition. You may have to repeat things until you're blue in the face at first, but trust us, it will be well worth it as soon as the whining stops—and it should stop quickly as long as you are consistent and don't give in to whatever it is your baby wants.

You should also reply to questions with yes, and full sentences, even to tiny babies. (Remember, you're trying to avoid using "no" as well.) This is how babies learn to speak correctly and how to ask questions. They really need to learn that the awful whining intonation is not acceptable.

The Wonder Years of Whining: Toddlers and Preschoolers

Like misbehaving brats, whiners are not born. They're made.

Whining is the stepping-stone that kids pick up during those thrilling months when they're growing by leaps and bounds, and progressing from making noises and babbling to full-blown talking.

Whining also escalates because parents are so used to attending to their babies' every need that they swoop in the minute they hear crying. This is fine for very young babies who *do* need a swift response to their distress. It is not fine for toddlers who whine and cry simply to get attention—and who've trained mom and dad will do anything to stop the crying.

At this stage, more than ever, it is absolutely essential to say: "Use your words" to stop whining from becoming an entrenched habit.

For toddlers, whining means: "You aren't listening to me. You don't know what I want. You don't understand me. You don't know what I need. So I'm going to make you pay attention in the most annoying way possible until I get what I want."

The minute you take the time to make children feel as if you understand them and that you *are* listening, whining should stop.

Your response *must* be: "I am not listening to you when you whine. When the whining stops and you use your words, I will listen to what you have to say."

Nanny Deb worked for one family where the whining from the four children was completely out of control. Mom was so entrenched in denial that she literally didn't hear it anymore. Yet the longer she ignored it, the more it escalated from annoying whining to full-blown kicking, screaming, yelling, and acting out.

At that point, she'd finally take action and put her children in time-out. They'd cry and sob and promise to be good. That lasted for a scant few minutes.

Then it was right back to whining.

After enduing *years* of this ridiculous behavior—behavior that mom and dad allowed to happen, of course—mom had not once asked any of her children what they were whining about or what they wanted.

Often, what they'd wanted was to tell mom about some crisis that was going on or which sibling was hurting them. But mom didn't listen. The whining could have been about something as inconsequential as wanting a cookie or something far more dangerous and hurtful as being punched in the face by a brother—to her, it was all the same. She tuned it all out. And her kids, devastatingly enough, knew it.

As soon as Nanny Deb stepped in with a firm voice that brooked no nonsense, telling these children to use their words, the whining stopped literally overnight.

STOP THE WHINING TECHNIQUE

1. Tell children to use their words.
2. Acknowledge the situation and shift the conversation away from the whining.
3. Ask how the child is really feeling.
4. Involve the child in coming up with a solution to the problem that caused the whining in the first place.

Here are suggestions for what to say in each step.

1. "Stop. I am ready to listen, but you've got to use your words and tell me what you mean. I need you to use your words." Do not go further with the conversation until the child has used the words properly. If he or she needs time to calm down, help them do so.
2. "I understand. Your brother grabbed your toy and won't give it back." Repeat what you've heard to acknowledge that you are listening.
3. "I see that you are upset. That isn't fair, is it." Sometimes it helps to be extremely specific when asking about what's gotten the child upset. Ask how he or she is feeling. Ask, "Are you feeling mad," or "Are you feeling bad?" You're

giving the child the words to articulate the particulars and often this is all it takes to instantly shift the mood away from whining. When children are upset, it can be difficult for them to get started talking about how bad they feel. The same goes for adults.

4. "Let's see what we can do. What do you think you can do?" Involving children in coming up with solutions to the dilemma at hand shows them respect for their judgment and ideas, even if they are toddlers or preschoolers. It puts the ball back in their court. The situation will no longer be out of their control. If a child has trouble coming up with a solution or remains upset, try suggesting an idea yourself. Say, "Hey, I have an idea. Why don't we do it that way, and then we'll see what happens."

Even well-behaved and normally whine-free children do succumb to the big whine from time to time. It's perfectly normal and no big deal. Simply ask the child to tell you what the problem is. Take the time to acknowledge the situation. It may not seem like a big deal to you, whereas it may be a huge deal to your child. You won't know until you ask.

Teaching your child how to communicate without whining is essential training for so much in life—for school, for friendships, and for growing up. The way that grown-ups make their way in the world and the way they keep learning is by asking questions and making compromises. Children really do need to learn that both stating their needs and engaging in effective negotiations never result from whining.

THE BABY FOREVER SYNDROME

Usually, the very worst of the whiners have been created by parents who want to keep their children forever. These parents end up doing everything for their preschoolers—feeding them, dressing them, crawling into bed with them, and carrying them. Trust us, if you treat your children like babies, they will continue to act like babies and become very, very spoiled, through no fault of their own.

It must be said that we've seen moms do this far more often than dads. Mom wants to be seen as the nurturing, coddling parent, to the point of where she ignores the indisputable fact that she's in the process of creating monstrous little brats.

Take this Mom. It's an hour past her four-year-old son's bedtime, yet she's still sitting on the floor near his bed, trying to put him down.

MOM: If you keep bouncing around I'm going to leave.

CHILD: [whining] Why? Why? Why?

MOM: Because this is reading book time and then I need to go to bed, I'm very tired.

CHILD: [whining] But I need to do this.

MOM: Then I'm going to leave.

CHILD: [screaming] No, you can't!

MOM: Okay, five more minutes.

Mom stays for another hour.

In this case, a four-year-old girl can't put her socks on because she's never had to do it before. Mommy always does it for her. Nanny Deb explained that a four-year-old is perfectly capable of getting herself dressed. Mom is having a very hard time trying not to give in.

CHILD: I don't know how to put on my socks. [Whining] No, no, no, Mommy, no.

NANNY: You do know. You are choosing right now not to do it.

MOM: I'm not sure I'm going to adjust to this so well. I think I'm probably going to still jump in and help her with this.

CHILD: Can you do it? Please? *Please*!

MOM: No. You can do it.

CHILD: [whining] *Please*!

MOM: Okay, come here.

NANNY: For four and a half years, she's gotten upset and you've let her get away with it. She's really testing your boundaries right now. But what's going to happen to her in second grade when she's not doing her math because she doesn't want to? She needs to know you're not going to give in to her.

This mom finally admitted she was having trouble adjusting to her child becoming self-sufficient and that her giving in to the whining met *her* needs, not her child's.

I WANT DOES NOT MEAN *I NEED*

NANNY RULE

You've probably heard us say this quite often to the families on our show: "*I want* does not mean *I need*." When we say that, we're teaching children the difference between whining and manners. They need to learn, early on, that wanting something and needing something are very different indeed.

First off, if and when they do want something, it must be asked for with manners and no whining.

Not: "Buy me that Barbie, Mommy, right now!"

Instead: "Please may I have a new Barbie?"

Second, it's essential for children to understand that even if you ask for something politely, this doesn't mean you're going to get it.

It's as crucial to nip the "I want" mantra in the bud as it is to nip the whining. Kids are always going to want things, and they're going to use all the weapons in their whining arsenal to bombard you until you give in. It's up to parents and caregivers to stand firm.

With situations that involve temptation, such as a trip to the mall, warn the children ahead of time about what's going to happen to stave off tantrums. Tell them, for example, that they can look at the toys, but they aren't going to get any today. And that this fact is not open for discussion. This will make it easier for you to say "We're not buying any toys today" when the inevitable pleading starts. You can simply state, "I told you before we left that we're only looking today. So we're just looking. Now let's go to the supermarket."

If you do give in, brace yourself for even more whining next time.

· ·

ALL ABOUT TANTRUMS

Whining is often the wind-up to the full-blown tantrum. Children start nagging and pleading, and then wind themselves up so badly they blow up.

Rare indeed is the child who doesn't have a tantrum at some point or another. They often start between the ages of one and three, when they are learning to communicate. They know what they want, but if they aren't yet completely verbal, they can have a tantrum because they can't make themselves understood. Avoid trigger words like "no," as they will make matters worse.

Redirection usually works well here, as toddler moods come and go in a flash. A child who's losing it because he can't get his tow truck hook to work can be surprised out of throwing a tantrum when you hand him a pirate ship instead. You may also want to pull out a book and ask him to join you for a story or start doing a game with a stuffed animal. Redirection works best when what you choose to do is something completely different from what's triggering the tantrum.

The "I can't communicate" toddler tantrum will be outgrown as soon as a child starts speaking clearly enough to make his or her needs clear, and has a longer attention span and better motor control. In the meantime, tell children to use their words, and repeat your own words to help figure out what it is they need.

If your child becomes violent during a tantrum and starts hitting or throwing things, for example, then it's straight into time-out without a warning.

Some parents have used sign language to help their children communicate at this stage and found it very helpful. If you decide to teach and use simple signs, remember that this should not be used in place of talking and teaching your child how to communicate clearly with language.

Once your kids are old enough to make their needs clearly known, however, the "I'm having a meltdown" behavioral tantrum can start. And it can continue until it becomes so bad that you'll be afraid to go anywhere in public for fear of having screaming, shouting, enraged children, who fling themselves on the floor, kicking their heels and having an absolute, mortifying fit.

There is never any reason to allow a tantrum to happen, at home or in public. The way to stop tantrums is to make it absolutely crystal clear to your children that you are there to listen to them when they are calm enough to talk, and that the tantrum will not work. Not now, and not ever. There can be no negotiation about this point.

With tantrums, it is also absolutely critical for mom and dad to be on the same page. Both must be consistent, and one parent must not undermine the other, giving in because it's easier to stop the whining and pleading that way. It's not okay for mom to say "We're not buying any toys at the store today," and then for dad to give in. This makes it likely that the next time mom says, "No toys," a tantrum can ensue. In this case, dad ought to get a time-out, too.

What should have been said before leaving the house was, "We're going to Target today and this is what we are buying."

State the rules and make all plans known to your children before you go out. Let them know what to expect and what the consequences will be for transgressions, and they'll be much less likely to lose it. Sure, your children will still test the limits—that is their nature! But it's your job not to give in.

Stopping Tantrums at Home

Although conventional parenting wisdom follows the "just ignore it" concept when it comes to tantrums, we know it's more complicated than that. Without getting to the root of what's causing tantrums, they're much less likely to stop. Furthermore, we don't believe that ignoring a child in distress is the best way to manage this distress.

Follow our system of communication, even with a child who throws a tantrum. Say, "Use your words. I will listen to you when you are ready to talk."

One mom we know would lose her temper as soon as her son Walt started a tantrum, and she was very upset about this. She'd pull out the vacuum and literally vacuum around the kicking and flailing Walt, as she needed the physical distraction to keep herself from losing it.

We told her to do this instead. Say, "Walt, use your words. I will listen to you when you are ready to talk to me, but you need to calm down. Right now I need to vacuum, but as soon as you are ready to talk to me, I will be happy to put the vacuum away and sit and listen to you."

You can also try whispering as a way to diffuse the anger. A child who's screaming can't hear a whisper. Coming close to you to hear what you're saying will often switch off their tantrum. It also gives you an opportunity to control yourself because you can't lose your temper when you're whispering.

Actions have consequences, and a tantrum is going to have strict consequences. These consequences have to follow whatever decision your child made in the first place. If your daughter has pulled the legs out of her favorite doll in a rage, then explain that you are taking that doll away. Don't confuse your daughter by telling her that she won't have her favorite dessert tonight. She broke her doll, so the consequences are about her having broken the doll. Then do it. Brace yourself for more (temporary) screaming. Explain that she will get the doll back when she has proven that she can reliably take care of her toys.

Don't give in, or there will be another tantrum.

If your child has crossed the line and either hurt a person, or destroyed property, such as a toy, there must be appropriate discipline. Start with a time-out. Then use whatever House Rule is in play for the replacement of anything that is broken. Some families have the House Rule that parents will replace an essential item such as a bike helmet once, and if it's broken by the child another time, payment comes out of the child's allowance. Other families enforce a loss of privileges.

Be sure that your response to tantrums is consistent. The sooner you act—and stick to your guns—when a tantrum starts, the sooner you will see tantrums disappear.

Stopping Tantrums in Public

Children who have stopped throwing tantrums at home also need to be told that tantrums in public are equally subject to consequences. This can be very tough for parents. When your precious little angel kicks up such a fuss in public that the stares, critical comments, and tut-tutting of busybodies become overwhelming, you can feel like a complete failure as a parent.

If your precious little angel starts having a tantrum in public, your response must be immediate. Tell the child that you are not going to tolerate this behavior, but always start with a time-out first, in a place where the child can try to calm down. Follow the following steps:

1. Tell the child that if he or she doesn't calm down, he or she is going to have a time-out. Then count to five as your warning.
2. Take the child to a quiet spot for one minute per year of age.
3. Ask if the child is ready to discuss the matter calmly.
4. Listen to the child, and thank him or her for talking. Take him or her back to shopping, eating, or whatever activity you were doing.
5. Go back to what you were doing.

Only if the child is unable to calm down do you tell him or her that you are leaving, and then follow through, with your wild-eyed, frothing-at-the-mouth child in tow.

We've left stores. We've left items on shelves. We've told children that if they don't calm down, they will be sitting with the security guard until lunch is over. We've walked out of restaurants before the meal has been served, with six siblings in tow, when one child is acting impossible (and then gone back in to eat when the child has calmed down).

The only exception is that if you're in the middle of an important transaction, such as standing in a long line to buy essentials, such as medicine at the pharmacy or you're just about to pay and you really can't leave. If you have to temporarily ignore the tantrum, make it clear that consequences are going to be swift once your transaction is over.

Remember that the more you prepare your children in advance for what's going to happen when you go out, the less likely they will be to act out. And when you follow our system of communication, children will be far less likely to have tantrums at all.

Tantrum Trigger Points

To be fair, many times tantrums are triggered by situations out of your child's control. There can be certain things that push their particular buttons, and if you know about these yet choose to ignore them (or, being human, you temporarily forget), you'll have to brace yourself for the storm that ensues.

The most common situational tantrum triggers are the following:

- **Hunger.** Many children go bonkers from plummeting blood sugar levels. Nannies always go outside with their bags stocked with nutritious snacks—a piece of fruit, a box of raisins, some whole-wheat crackers, or string cheese—to nip a hunger-based tantrum in the bud. One Mom, who has a child with bipolar disorder, must follow a strict diet, as certain foods, particularly those with high sodium contents, are known tantrum triggers. At dinner one night, this child asked if he could have more of the really salty food. His mom knew the answer would be no, but instead of saying it, she calmly said, "We can discuss that after you've eaten what's on your plate." When he had eaten all of his meal, she diverted him by saying, "I have a little treat for you now," and gave him something he was allowed to eat. A potential nightmare was prevented very smoothly.

- **Fatigue.** When they're really pooped, kids can go from zero to sixty in about three seconds flat.
- **Frustration.** Children have a low threshold for patience, especially when learning something new and more difficult than usual. Frustration at not being good at something or at losing a game can end up as a tantrum.
- **Not giving a warning.** Children like to be prepared for changes. Toddlers, especially, need to be prepared. If you have to get to the store before it closes, and you swoop in to pick up your happily playing toddler with no warning, chances are high a tantrum will result.

    Try to give warnings whenever possible. Start at the ten-minute warning. Then five. Then three. Then announce it's time to go. Be sure your child has really heard you, as little ones can often be so engrossed in play that they nod yes but really aren't paying attention. Come over to them, get down to their level, and tell them what is happening.
- **Rushing.** Some children are very particular about their routines, and need to do things in their own time and in a slow-as-molasses (for you, at least!) way. If you know that your child can't stand being rushed and will go bonkers if that happens, give warnings way in advance. First say, "We're leaving in twenty minutes." Then: "This is the ten-minute warning. Your coat is ready." Then: "This is the five-minute warning. Please put your shoes on now."
- **Overstimulation.** Children can get wound up in their play or other activities and get so cuckoo they literally don't know how to get out of having a meltdown.

- **Feeling disrespected or unacknowledged.** While we've said that it's not a great idea to offer too many choices to young children, as they get older, they're more competent at handling them. Once a child reaches three or four and up, their opinions are very important to them. While we don't recommend you give them too many choices, when it comes to issues more important than going to the grocery store, we don't suggest that your discount their feelings entirely. Not including them in a crucial decision-making process, for instance, can make a child feel terribly disrespected, and they can blow big time. What you'll usually hear is something along the lines of "You never listen to me. You don't care about me." Tantrums stemming from disrespect often are a long time in the making, rather like a volcano that erupts without warning. Often, the tantrum tripwire can be something unrelated to the feelings of hurt, disillusion, or worry. When this happens, it's essential to calm your child down using the techniques outlined in chapter 2, then ask what's going on, and listen without being judgmental.

- **Needing a parent.** Sometimes, a child loses it for the simple reason that he or she needs mom or dad. Perhaps there's a new baby or a stressful situation at school. Perhaps Belinda or Bryant is just feeling lonely or blue and needs a hug and some extra attention.

  Pay attention when your child is showing signs of needing you. Ask what's wrong, and listen carefully. Acknowledge the distress. If it's impossible to spend the extra time with that child at that very moment—perhaps you're about to serve the family dinner, and have bubbling pots on the stove—set a time for when you can continue the conversation in private. Perhaps you could use the kitchen timer or an alarm clock to go off at this specific time, to reassure the child that you will indeed be there and ready to help later. Often, acknowledgment

TOO MUCH PRAISE

We've seen countless parents praising their children so much for their genius, cleverness, intelligence, and cuteness, that you'd think all world problems would have been solved by now.

Too much praise is just as bad as not enough. If you make your child the center of the universe, you're not preparing them for the rest of the world. There is always going to be someone who prettier, smarter, more artistic, or more athletic. But a child who thinks he or she is the center of the universe is very likely to be a whiner and complainer. Worse, when they go off to school and they find out they're not perfect, they'll be devastated.

Instead of saying, "You are the most special child in the world," say, "You are very special."

Instead of saying "You are the smartest six-year-old ever!" say, "You are the smartest six-year-old I know." Or, "I think you are one of the best football players I know."

When a child does something wonderful, say, "Great job!"

Don't get into the habit of complimenting children for doing things they're supposed to do, like eating their vegetables or cleaning up their mess. We don't tell children who are already potty trained that they're brave for peeing in the toilet. Soldiers are brave. Kids going to the bathroom are not.

of the distress is enough to help prevent the tantrum in the first place.

HOUSE RULES

5

THE BASICS OF HOUSE RULES: ESTABLISHING ORDER

Here's a helpful list of House Rules to keep you from scrambling for answers!

THE SCRABBLE LIST

Say only what you mean and mean it

Consistency

Routine

Attention

Boundaries

Believe you can do it

Lots of love

Enjoy

Rules. Boundaries. Structure. Order.

You've undoubtedly heard these words a lot on *Nanny 911.*

They're just about the most important words you can hear. In fact, along with good communication skills, these words zing right to the heart of our message.

Children need rules and consistency in their lives. In fact, they *crave* them. They'll do all sorts of crazy, naughty, out-of-control things just to get their parents to enforce some rules to curb their behavior. That's one of the wonderful paradoxes of a child's development. More rules that define their behavior and boundaries will actually produce more freedom to grow and blossom. Rules make children feel safe. They give children a defined world. They spare children from having to make adult decisions because the adults have made the proper decisions for them.

It's part of human nature to crave limits—and to test them.

Suffice to say that a child without limits can't learn how to self-regulate. Without rules, there is no order. Without order, there are screaming, crying, miserable children who act the way they do because they don't know any better.

Okay, now that we've gotten that out of the way, let's move on . . .

The reason our system works as well—and as quickly—as it does is that it has a very defined structure. We come into a family's home, we observe, we take notes, we discover the family dynamic, and we figure out a plan.

Then we sit down with everyone and unveil our new House Rules. And watch the reaction. It's usually the same: Skepticism from the parents, and shock, if not downright rebellion, from the children.

With every family, we make it very clear that parents are ultimately responsible for deciding what goes and what doesn't. We do say that all children need to live in a home that is organized and can meet their basic needs of comfortable shelter. (On one of our shows, the family's house was practically a construction site, with exposed wiring and nails. None of the kids had their own room. They slept with mom; dad slept on the couch. Everyone was grouchy and miserable, until a kid's room was set up in the attic.

Here's how to start making your own House Rules.

FIGURING OUT YOUR OWN HOUSE RULES

It's relatively easy for us to visit a family and figure out what works and what doesn't, as we've got trained eyes and ears. For instance, whenever mom is frazzled to a crisp along with her bacon before breakfast is even over, and the kids have missed the school bus again, we've got a really good hunch that there is no timetable or routine in this family.

With a little bit of work, you can confront your own family dynamic, assess what's good and what's not, and sort out your own plan. It does take a little bit of brutal honesty, but if you're reading this book we know you're up for it.

There are several ways to do this.

1. Get a notebook or a few sheets of paper and a pen, and take notes for a day. Write down everything that happens, along with the precise time. See who acts out first. Identify the ringleader of sibling misbehavior. Make a note every time you see your kids jumping on the bed, throwing food at dinner, fighting with one another, squeezing all the toothpaste out of the tube and into the toilet, running into the basement instead of going to bed, refusing to clean up toys, shredding the upholstery on the new armchair, or slipping their vegetables to the dog—you get the drill.

   If it's too hard for one parent to do this, alternate so that dad takes the notes during breakfast and mom does them later. You can also take notes over several days. Then compile them into a coherent list that starts from the minute you wake up until the minute you collapse into bed.

   You may also want to set up a tape recorder if it's hard for you to take notes and transcribe the significant scenes later.

2. Do the same, but this time videotape everyone. Watching your family in action can often provide the shock necessary to galvanize parents into action.

3. Invite a trusted friend or relative into your home to videotape your day. Tell them they can do it only if they refrain from interfering or making any judgments. They're there to help you.

   Single parents may find this the best option.

Once you've got the blow-by-blow of your day outlined, make several copies so you can write all over them. Sit down when both parents have the time to do this properly—not when you're exhausted and in a bad mood after a rotten day at work. (If you're a single parent, find a quiet, calm time to devise your list.) Then do the following:

1. Prioritize the issues.

    Be honest! Which is the most important? You may decide that all have equal weight.

2. Make a new list of the good and bad behavior.

    It may help to make a scale from one to ten and rank what happened and who did what.

3. Devise a strategy and pick the House Rules you think will be best for your family. We'll show you how to choose different rules in the next four chapters.

4. Mom and dad must work as a team when both are devising the House Rules—and enforcing them.

    If you can't work together now, the House Rules will not please anyone. And they won't work, either.

5. Pick your battles.

    Agree on divvying up the tasks. As always, have realistic expectations. Set up only the House Rules that you know deep down are something you can stick to. Be blunt about what you know you can follow through on. (For example, will you really take the kids back to bed every night, or should you admit to yourself that you still want them to be sleeping with you?)

6. Agree to be consistent.

    Good parenting equals consistency and teamwork. Any inconsistencies will immediately be pounced upon and exploited to the max by your children.

If one parent is vehemently opposed to an idea by the other, take the time now to figure out why, and decide who's going to win on this issue, or what the compromise will be.

As you know by now, the ability to compromise is a crucial element if families are to live together in harmony.

7. Pledge to each other that you are in this together.

If there is *any* undermining of the rules by either mom or dad, you may as well throw them out and go back to living in chaos.

Now is the time to air any grievances, before setting up the rules, and then punishing your spouse by not enforcing them.

With one family, mom told Nanny Stella that dad had agreed to do it her way. "My husband doesn't object to any of these rules," this mom declared, "because he doesn't know any better."

Nanny Stella's response was, "Well, what about 'our' way? You're a team, and you need to do this together."

The fact that mom may stay at home with the children doesn't mean she has the right to make all the rules. Dads need to be involved with their children, too.

8. Admit that if you want your children's behavior to improve, yours may need a little bit of improvement as well.

Set up some private House Rules for yourselves as parents. Then stick to them!

Once you follow these steps, we hope you'll give each other a pat on the back, as you're on your way to doing the work you'll need to do to communicate honestly and effectively with each other about your family.

RULES ARE NONNEGOTIABLE

Don't present the rules as something the children can decide. It's not their responsibility to be the parent.

We suggest you say something along the lines of, "When you are an adult and you have your own house, you can set the rules. These are the rules for this house at the moment.

"And they're nonnegotiable."

Don't say this in a forceful, angry way, of course. It's best to set up a family meeting when everyone is home, no one is tired or hungry, and the expectations have been set that something important is going to be discussed.

Trust us on this one—establishing a good habit of enforced and consistent House Rules will help your entire family once the teen years approach. You know, those wondrous years when everything you say or do will be challenged by your beloved child who seems to be morphing in front of your very eyes into somebody new. You'll undoubtedly be hearing yourself say the same things to your teen that you did to your toddler. You should be telling a toddler: "These are our rules. There is no hitting in this house." A teen will hear you say, "These are the rules. If your curfew is ten, then it's ten."

You have been warned.

HOUSE RULES ARE NOT NECESSARILY SET IN STONE

Don't worry—we're not contradicting ourselves!

Even though the rules you've decided upon are nonnegotiable, they can and should evolve over time. Just as children grow and change, and their needs change with them, so should the House Rules. While some basic rules will always remain the same, especially those pertaining to routine and structure, a six-year-old certainly doesn't need the same rules as a two-year-old. A six-year-old doesn't need to be treated like a two-year-old, either.

Always feel free to edit and change your House Rules as your children grow. With age and experience come different kinds of behavior, and different parenting styles.

You may want to call a family meeting every few months to review the rules. Tell the kids that you will consider their suggestions at that time. (The key word here being *consider*.) This can make the kids feel that they have more a say in the House Rules, even if they really don't. (But they don't have to know that.)

Evolve along with your children, and you'll be much more likely to have a happy household.

HOUSE RULES DON'T CHANGE FOR GUESTS

Once you've established the House Rules, they're going to stay in place for a reason. No matter who is looking after your children—a babysitter, an aunt, an uncle, a neighbor, or a friend—your House Rules are unchangeable.

Obviously, children quickly learn that different places have different rules. Grandma Joan may be more lenient about TV watching than Grandma Jennie. Dad may have a strict policy about touching anything on his desk during visits to his office, whereas Uncle Benny invites his nieces to play on his computer and doodle on his notepads.

It's up to parents to tell visitors, especially babysitters, what these rules are. Post a list with the kids' routine in a visible place, such as on the refrigerator. Make it clear that the rules are enforced, no matter how much the kids may say they aren't the minute you're out the door!

We've found parents often have trouble enforcing the House Rules when other children come over for playdates or visits. If little

Sebastian is used to jumping on the couch at his house, and your rule is no jumping on the couch, don't bend the rule to make little Sebastian happy. Sending a message like this makes your kids feel as if placating guests are more important than they are, and it can be very confusing. Simply tell your kids that "If they're allowed to jump on the couch at Sebastian's house, go right ahead. That doesn't mean you can do it here."

Enlist your children in helping visitors understand the House Rules. With one family, Nanny Stella sat down with a cup of tea in the living room, not knowing that the House Rule was no drinking in the living room. The kids were only too happy to point this out to her, and she quickly apologized and took her tea into the kitchen. With another family, Nanny Deb watched happily as their three-year-old daughter told a friend, who was over for a playdate, "When Nanny is here, we could do this and that and I just have to tell you the new rule." This little girl was very proud of her ability to both remember the House Rules and share them with her friends.

It is okay, of course, to make special exceptions to House Rules. Let's say Auntie Sue is the regular Friday night babysitter, and she likes to spend some extra time with her favorite nieces and nephews. So on the Friday nights when she comes over, the House Rule for Auntie Sue is that the kids can stay up late, or watch a DVD, or whatever you decide, as long as it's consistent.

Having occasional exceptions to House Rules can be really fun for children, as long as they're agreed to in advance. And not exploited by the children who will most likely do everything in their power to wheedle more exceptions out of you.

DON'T BREAK THE RULES YOURSELF

Many of the children on *Nanny 911* have confided to us that their parents tried having some House Rules before we arrived but couldn't stick to them. They've merrily announced that, "Well, my Mom said she was going to do this before and she didn't . . . so this time it's not going to work, either!"

Nanny Stella worked for a family where the agreed-upon rule was that Alex, who was thirteen months old, would be put down for his nap, and left to fall asleep on his own, which he did with a minimum of fuss. Nanny Stella would walk out of the room, saying, "Have a nice nap," then turn on the baby monitor in the kitchen and make lunch.

One weekend, she was asked to babysit in the afternoon, and she arrived at Alex's naptime. She went into his room to check on him, and there sat dad by the side of the crib, reading a newspaper. It turned out that Alex could only fall asleep on weekends if dad sat with him. Of course, Alex never needed Nanny Stella to sit with him. He already had figured out that dad was a pushover. Because Nanny Stella had made the rules clear, Alex knew they were not there to be broken. But dad? Well, after indulging his sweet little boy just once, this behavior went from being a treat to a habit.

We know how tough it can be to get used to having House Rules and enforcing them, but remember that you're the parents, and you're the grown-ups, so self-control is a habit that should be a little bit more ingrained in you by now. We're sure you catch our drift! We've seen far too many families where the kids come on board with the House Rules seemingly overnight. This doesn't surprise us—we know that children are desperate for rules. But it does often surprise their parents, who aren't quite with the program yet!

House Rules are family rules. They're not just for your children. Don't let these children down by breaking the House Rules yourself.

If you have trouble following the rules, expect to be disciplined the same way as your child.

DON'T PENALIZE EVERYONE WHEN ONE PERSON BREAKS THE RULES

This is an issue that is all too common, and when you think about it, it's really quite unfair.

Parents often discipline or punish everyone when only one child has misbehaved. We suppose their logic is that this will serve as a deterrent for the next time. Usually, this concept backfires and leaves a lot of angst behind. The naughty child gets all the attention for being naughty.

But will the siblings be rewarded for their good behavior?

Let's say it's time for a family picnic. Nine-year-old Samantha decides it's time to be naughty. She has a tantrum—for whatever reason. Mom and dad get so mad that they yell, "Right, that's it, forget about the picnic. We're not going."

Everyone is disappointed and angry. Samantha's siblings turn on her, with some justification in their minds. She becomes even more enraged . . . and you can imagine the rest of the cheery afternoon spent in this house.

Whoever is breaking the House Rule or acting out should be dealt with in the appropriate manner. Children who are following the House Rules shouldn't be on the receiving end. If only one child is acting up, do you put all the siblings in time-out? Of course not.

With one family, one of the punishments when a serious House Rule was broken was that the older girls weren't allowed to go to track team practice and cheerlead. But when the girls deliberately flouted the rules, mom let them get away with it. Nanny Stella stepped in and reminded her that the House Rules needed to be enforced.

Mom replied, "But they have to go. They're letting the team down."

Nanny Stella calmly said, "The first team they have an obligation to is this family. So they're not going."

They didn't go to practice. Their cheerleading teammates were furious. But guess what—neither of the girls ever flouted the rules like that again. They learned that serious actions have serious consequences—not just for them, but for other people they care about, too.

FAMILY CONTRACTS

A wonderful way to manage specific House Rules, or a rule that may only be applicable to a certain child, is to make a family contract. This works best with older children, who can write up a contract, and make a pact with mom and dad about either something to be done, something that's wanted, or someone's behavior.

Let's say Nathaniel, who's ten, wants a custom skateboard. A family contract can be drawn up, stating that if he maintained a B+ average at school, had a good attitude to his younger siblings, did extra chores for an additional allowance, and paid 50 percent of the price with the money he'd saved, he would get the skateboard of his dreams. Some of the items on he list may be negotiable, depending on circumstances (say, perhaps, he comes down with the flu over a weekend and can't earn the money he would have made washing the neighbor's cars as he usually did). Others, such as grades, may not. The family contract can specify all of this in detail.

Your children can also draw up a family contract, where dad promises to stop swearing at bad drivers when he's driving with the kids, or mom promises to stop nagging about how the beds are made.

What works so well with family contracts is that they give your children an opportunity to be proactive, both about their expectations for something of their choosing, as well as their expectations of *you*. Have some fun with this. It can be a terrific way to enhance family teamwork.

6 HOUSE RULES OF DISCIPLINE: ACTIONS HAVE CONSEQUENCES

We've never met a parent yet who didn't know how to love their children. But we have met hundreds of parents who didn't know how to discipline their children.

Sometimes parents don't discipline their children because they think this means their children will turn on them. Take this mom. Her three-year-old was sobbing for her sippy cup. Nanny Stella explained that three-year-olds don't need to drink out of sippy cups and certainly not in bed. Mom wasn't so sure.

CHILD: [crying] I want my sippy cup. Now!

MOM: I feel if I'm being really strict with them, then they feel that I'm not loving them.

Mom has confused limits with love. Never mind the fact that denying a preschooler a sippy cup is not what we would call "strict!"

Children love their parents. But parents mistakenly believe that their six-year-old son, who yells, "I hate you!" when dad tells him he can't have another new Star Wars toy, really means it. Of course this six-year-old doesn't hate his dad. He just hates not getting his way.

Children love their parents dearly even while testing every limit, punching every sibling, spreading dog food all over the bathroom walls, pinching, biting, screaming, kicking, and swearing at the their beloved mom and dad. They're figured out that love does not equal respect, long before mom and dad do.

Which is why, when we arrive at a family's home, somehow the kids know that things are going to be different from the instant the door opens. It isn't our uniforms. It isn't our charming English accents.

It's that we mean business!

We grow to love the children we care for, and they grow to love us, but we aren't taking the job to make friends, or for gushing devotion. As these kids get to know us better, and see what we're like, they also quickly realize that we aren't going to *demand* that they behave. We don't scream or shout or cry or plead or beg as their parents do. We don't lose our tempers. We are consistent in what we say and what we do.

They soon learn who's in charge because of this absolutely crucial Nanny Rule.

NANNY RULE

ACTIONS HAVE CONSEQUENCES

Actions have consequences. Without consequences, there is no incentive to stop doing anything naughty, cruel, violent, silly, dangerous, or hurtful. And believe us—kids won't stop acting out unless they have to. Children whine, scream, cry, and throw tantrums because those things work. Children know that if they keep at it long enough, someone is going to give in—and it's going to be mom and dad. They've trained their parents well.

As we've already discussed in Part I, many children don't know how to communicate. They can repress their feelings for so long that they eventually blow, with frightening results. Siblings can really hurt each other. Nanny Deb worked for one family where a nine-year-old girl held a pillow over her young brother, smothering him so badly he was literally left gasping for breath.

In other families, the children can *only* express themselves through anger, either with words or by lashing out physically. Often, the children don't exactly have the world's greatest role models—this means you, mom and dad. Screaming at your kids to stop screaming is not going to do anything except give you a sore throat.

When it comes to discipline, the House Rule is clear.

. . . .

HOUSE RULE: BAD BEHAVIOR COMES WITH PENALTIES

NANNY RULE

Bad behavior will not be tolerated. Bad behavior has consequences. End of discussion.

It's up to you to decide what kind of bad behavior needs to be spelled out in a House Rule. Some that you've seen often on *Nanny 911* are as follows:

No biting
No grabbing
No hitting
No lying
No throwing
No yelling
No jumping on furniture

Whatever you decide upon, mom and dad must work as a team. There's no point in having a House Rule about jumping on the couch when it bugs mom and it makes dad laugh.

Pick your battles here, and compromise if need be so that

there won't be any undermining of one parent's decision by the other. Be consistent about which rules are the most likely to be enforced.

Let's take a look at what some of these consequences should be.

. . . .

HOUSE RULE: THE TIME-OUT

Time-outs are a nanny favorite because *they work*. Time-outs are not punishment. Time-outs are a useful tool to teach children that when they are out of control, they need to take the time to themselves to figure out their thoughts and feelings. Then, after they are calm, they can talk about them. So think of time-outs as time for children to think and to breathe. By doing this, they help teach patience and responsibility.

There are several steps to an effective time-out.

1. **Give warnings.**

   Warnings should be the precursor to the time-out.

   Don't just swoop in and grab the child and dump him or her in time-out. This is just going to make your child even more angry and with good reason.

   Decide whichever warning system works for you, and have that be part of the time-out rule. Some families give only one warning. As in: "We don't hit in this house. If you don't stop hitting your brother, you are going into time-out." Others like the three-strike concept, and the time-out starts with the third strike.

2. **Countdown to the time-out.**

   Part of your warning should be a precise statement of when the time-out will begin. This will help you be consistent, and it will help your child realize you aren't kidding.

   This is also very necessary for young children, who don't yet have a grasp of what "time" is. Telling two-year-old Allegra that "We're leaving in five minutes" doesn't really mean very much to her; nor should it. If Allegra throws a fit when, five minutes later, you say, "We're leaving now," it's perfectly understandable to her because five minutes is the same as five seconds to a two-year-old's brain.

Try using visual clues to make your point clear. Instead of saying, "We're leaving in five minutes," say, "When Mommy puts on her coat that means we are going to start to get ready to go."

Make sure your child has heard you, and has acknowledged that he or she has. Often tantrums erupt because a child simply has been too engrossed in play to listen to what mom was shouting from the other side of the room. We're sure you know by now how easy it is for children to tune out what they don't want to hear!

Use the communication skills we've already taught you: Get down to the child's level. Speak calmly. Sometimes a physical touch on the arm or shoulder as well helps get their attention. Be sure they acknowledge that they've both heard and understood what you've said.

Or, you can simply set the timer, and tell Allegra that you are leaving when the timer dings. Be sure she's heard you.

Then leave, whether she's happy about it or not.

3. **One minute of time-out for each year of age.**
Trust us, three minutes is a very long time for a three-year-old!

Time-outs work best starting at around age two, as a child younger than two can't really understand the concept. A kitchen timer or alarm clock is set.

The time-out should always take place in the same spot. For children age two to about four, we like to keep the children in a time-out spot where we can see or at least hear them. We prefer a hall or a spot where they can't get into mischief! (We do not recommend that you use the crib or toddler bed, as they're only for sleeping.) We do not make any contact with a child in time-out, but he or she certainly knows that we are there.

Older children can be put in time-out in a room by themselves, as long as it's a calm, quiet place, and there are no distractions, such as a TV or a computer.

Do not ever lock a child in a room during time-out. That is unsafe, scary, and cruel from a child's perspective.

4. **Use a timer in plain view of the child.**

We love our trusty timers. They have large numerals, make noise, and come complete with a loud ding at the end.

Make sure your child can see the timer or clock. Older kids who can tell time fully grasp the concept of time passing slowly when they sit in a time-out with nothing to do but look at a clock!

5. **Leaving the time-out spot or area starts the clock all over again.**

It doesn't matter what the infraction is, or that your seven-year-old has been in time-out for six minutes and forty-nine seconds. If he or she gets up, the clock is started all over again.

This means no negotiation, either. Kids love to try and wheedle their way out of the time-out. If children want to sing, dance, wiggle, or hum during a time-out, however, that is their priority. Some children find it absolutely impossible to sit still while they are thinking, so forcing them to will only make the situation worse. The timer is reset only if the child physically *leaves* the time-out spot or area.

6. **Parents do not interrupt the time-out.**

No matter how much begging or pleading ensues, stand firm and do not give in. Otherwise you may as well just kiss the time-out goodbye.

Parents must work as a team with time-out. Often one parent can't bear the crying, and wants to go in and soothe or talk to the child.

Sit tight. The time to talk will come soon enough.

7. **A talk afterward is an essential part of the time-out.**

Actually, we ought to call the time-out the time-out-and-talk.

Time-outs need talk afterward. This is really important, and parents often neglect to do it. They let their child strew and brood instead.

A talk after the time-out will clear the air. Sit down and ask children what was going on, what they were feeling, why the naughtiness happened. Ask them these questions calmly and listen without judging. (See our guidelines in chapter 3 if you need a refresher about how to talk to your child.) You may be surprised at what you hear.

. . . .

WHY DOESN'T TIME-OUT WORK FOR ME?

Parents often complain that time-outs don't work. They will work, if you follow the steps outlined above. You must be consistent both with the warnings, and with strict adherence to the time limit. In most cases, a large timer in clear view of the child in time-out is a must.

Parents also need to be realistic about enforcing the time-out. It's not just something you can try for a few days or a week and give up later on. It is a House Rule, for now and the foreseeable future. The message must be clear and nonnegotiable.

This mom blew the time-out because she couldn't bear to hear any misery from her three-year-old boy, Theron. She'd allowed him to persist with an absolutely terrible habit of hitting her and had the bruises to show for it. Nanny Stella showed Theron what she was going to do. He'd already been warned and told he was going into time-out in the den for punching his mom.

NANNY: To help mom enforce time-out, I'm bringing along my trusty old timer. When this ding, ding, dings, you can come out, okay? There you go.

MOM: That's the nanny's timer. Whenever you hit mommy or if you hit anybody, you're going to be put in time-out. Now Mommy's going to put three minutes on the timer.

CHILD: [crying] Noooooo!

MOM: The reason you're here is because you hit me. You cannot hit Mommy.

Theron runs out of the room. Mom starts negotiating. Dad walks into the room, and he starts negotiating, too.

MOM: No, you need to go back into time-out.

CHILD: NO!

MOM: You need to go back to time-out.

DAD: Just sit down.

NANNY: When the timer goes beep, beep, beep you can come out.

CHILD: No.

NANNY: Go back in time-out, Theron.

At this point, Theron had done only one minute, and his time-out had become an effective exercise in getting more attention from mom and dad. A scant minute later, out bounded Theron. Mission accomplished—for him.

CHILD: I hate time-out.

DAD: You'll be okay.

MOM: You may come out now. Thank you for being a good boy.

Nanny Stella was understandably disappointed with these parents, who didn't listen to her. Mom stepped in with one minute left on the clock, and abruptly pulled Theron from time-out. He was confused because she'd sent him a mixed message. Plus, she undermined her husband, who may have been negotiating but was clearly not about to lessen the time Theron needed to spend in time-out.

Time-outs *will* work if you do them properly.

Don't go overboard with time-outs for very minor infractions, however. Often what a child needs is a good long talk instead.

Once you install a reward system, as outlined in the next section, you may be able to cut down on the time-outs and other House Rules of discipline as well. Taking away a reward in addition to a time-out is often going too far. Once you get used to having a reward system as well as time-outs as part of your House Rules, you'll be able to decide which form of discipline to best use.

Whatever you decide, as with everything, just be consistent.

And remember: Do not punish all the children when only one is acting up.

THE TIME HAS TO FIT THE CRIME

NANNY RULE

If Celeste takes Marcus's toy and breaks it, Celeste has to replace it. If Celeste breaks one of her own toys while she's having a tantrum, she is also required to replace it.

Children need to learn that actions have consequences, and they are responsible for the consequences of their anger or inability to share. These consequences need to pertain to the exact crime. Don't discipline a child who's made a mess by taking away dessert later. Simply deal with the mess.

· ·

NANNY RULE

HOUSE RULE: GOOD BEHAVIOR COMES WITH REWARDS

What every family needs is a reward system. Or, if you don't like the word "reward," try "incentive."

The premise is simple—it's the actions have consequences rule played out with objects. Good behavior or doing a specified task earns a reward. Bad behavior or noncompliance means a reward is not granted or taken away.

A reward system shows children right away that what they do is going to affect their ability to earn a reward. The operative word here is "earn."

THE FAMILY TIME-OUT

In large families, it's often difficult to stop the squabbling and the finger-pointing. One mom we know came up with a great solution to problem settling, especially in situations where more than one child was acting up.

If the kids came to mom or dad (or both) to settle the problem, then *everyone* involved would start a family time-out. Everyone had to sit down in a comfortable place and be quiet. The parent would get out the timer, or a stopwatch, and set it for an allotted time, such as a minute or two for each speaker. Then each child would have a chance to state their specific complaint until the timer went off. No one could interrupt while a sibling was speaking. (Be sure that a different child gets to start each time, otherwise you'll be accused of playing favorites.) Then mom or dad would discuss alternate ways to solve the problem.

A family time-out works incredibly well with older children. It teaches them that they can be part of the solution, which makes them proud of their own decision-making and creativity in finding answers. It also teaches them patience, as they must listen to differing viewpoints. This is much easier to do when they know they will have their turn. It also demonstrates that you respect their voice, even if you don't agree with it.

Most of all, it teaches children that problems can be settled with calm conversation, not hitting, screaming, yelling, whining, and crying.

Children love the concept because they can see results right away. It gives them a sense of values, and pride in a job well done. Plus they love to collect things.

We use different objects in our systems, such as a marble jar, a magnet board, or a sticker board.

With a marble jar, set up a large jar for each child that is labeled with the child's name. Use a clear jar and different colors for each child. Keep the jars out of reach.

With a magnet board, use a large magnetic bulletin board, dividing it up into sections. Use small magnets. With one family where dad owned a pizza restaurant, we painted the magnets to look like slices of pizza. Be creative, if you like, and come up with objects related to something your family really likes, such as pets or sports. With another, each child was given a toy pirate chest, and the rewards were small jewels.

With yet another, they used tickets. Whatever you choose, just make it fun.

To set up a sticker board take a bulletin board with a section for each child. Buy economical rolls of stickers. You can use cardboard for your board, so this will cost next to nothing, and once one board is used up, you can set up a new one.

Be sure the jars or boards are in a very visible place.

It's up to you to choose whichever system you like best, and to decide what your House Rules are going to be for earning or losing a reward.

With younger children or in families where this is a very new concept, spell everything out. Cut out pictures of the chores or tasks that must be done everyday—brushing teeth, making beds, not dumping jackets on the floor, taking out the garbage, and so on—and put these pictures on the board. Or make a separate checklist.

You can get very, very specific with the rewards. A child who is learning to sleep in his own bed, for instance, can earn a marble for getting into bed by himself, for staying in bed, and for staying in bed all night. So if he goes to bed and stays there, he's earned three marbles for one night's work. Likewise for toilet training: you can use a marble for announcing that you have to go, one for sitting on the potty whether something comes out or not, one for pulling up your pants, one for flushing, one for washing hands. Each trip to the potty can earn up to five marbles. And can make training much easier.

You may also want to make a reward jar, with different rewards written on slips of paper. When a child has earned a reward, he or she pulls out the slip, and the reward is a nice surprise.

Perhaps you decide that a reward will be earned after there are fifty marbles in the jar. Decide in advance what the reward is going to be. You don't need to spend a penny on the rewards—and frankly, we hope you don't, although for older kids you may decide that it's okay to trade in marbles for an allowance. Rewards should be tailored to the unique needs and wants of each child. One of the best rewards is for a child to spend extra one-on-one time with a parent. Or it could be an hour of television on a school night, or extra computer time online, or an outing to the aquarium, or a skating lesson. Or a contribution to the piggy bank for a child who is saving up for a special toy.

It also helps that mom and dad are up on the board. Parents—you can have their own marble jar, too. This is a House Rule, after all. Kids love it when dad is naughty and has a magnet taken off the board. (This works especially well with parents who yell. They lose a marble or magnet each time they start shouting.) It helps establishing the fact that rules are for everyone. Not even mom and dad are exempt from bad behavior.

As with everything, you absolutely must be consistent with a reward system. Don't forget about it or it won't work. And as House Rules can evolve as children get used to them and grow older, so can the rewards. Call a family meeting and decide what the reward system should be—how many marbles, for instance, to earn a reward. Or you can up the ante.

And don't forget that the reward system is not just about behaving, or not doing something naughty. Give your child a reward for just being good for good's sake. Drop a marble into their jar out of the blue, just because you love them. This teaches a valuable lesson that life is about doing good because it's the right and wonderful thing to do.

· ·

7 HOUSE RULES OF ROUTINE: MANAGING YOUR DAY

We love routine. We can't work without it. And we watch families positively blossom once they learn how to shape their days around a regular routine. Suddenly, there are more hours in the day to do normal things like have a meal without tantrums, do chores, or—especially crucial—to have fun. More important, kids can relax and be kids when they don't have to spend any time worrying about what's going to happen to them (or not happen). Believe us when we tell you how much anxiety we've seen in because their parents were so frazzled and disorganized that mealtimes never followed a fixed schedule.

When you ask most adults about their fondest childhood memories, you'll often hear about Sundays in church, a book being read by mom at bedtime, or grandpa tucking you in at night, playing board games, after-dinner strolls for ice cream on hot summer nights, or the Saturday night potlucks with the neighbors who lived around the corner. These memories are almost always centered on a routine—well, okay, some of them are centered on food, too. Routines stick in your head precisely because they make you feel safe.

Both of us have spent many years as baby nurses, and one of the primary reasons we were so good at our jobs is that we established a routine with the babies we cared for, the minute they came home from the hospital.

Children should not be expected to fly by the seat of their pants. They need the stability of a regular routine to make them feel safe. As with all good boundaries, the more they're in place and consistently used, the less they're needed. They become good, intrinsic habits. If you can establish a secure routine for your children, it will help them be able to fly when they're older. They'll be able to improvise and soar because they can always fall back on that solid foundation of safe routine.

Here's how you can set up a routine, too.

HOUSE RULE: REGULAR ROUTINES ARE A MUST

NANNY RULE

What happens during your day? Food, activity, and sleep. Those are essentials. You get up, get the kids up, try to pull yourself together, get the kids off to school, go off to work or figure out what you're going to do if you're a stay-at-home parent, then the kids come home, it's time for dinner, some evening activity, then collapse into bed. On all of the *Nanny 911* shows, you'll recall that this daily activity was punctuated by screaming children and frustrated, frazzled parents. Tempers flared over something as simple as finding a shoe. We've seen parents unable to get their kids on the school bus on time . . . even when the bus literally stopped in front of their door at the exact same moment every morning.

What we do with all these disorganized families is impose order in the form of a timetable. Most parents freak when they first see it, and say it can't be followed, but in a remarkably short time, they have all come to realize that the timetable is actually the life preserver they needed to save them from drowning in a sea of chaos.

· ·

SET UP A TIMETABLE BOARD

Some parents are by nature super planners. They like to know everything well in advance, and they write it all down.

Most of the parents we meet, however, are not.

While we encourage everyone to plan, don't go overboard, especially if your spouse is a non-planner and prefers spontaneity to everything being decided months in advance. Find a good way to compromise.

We suggest you buy or make a large calendar (using poster board, oak tag, or with an erasable surface—be creative), and use a color-coded system where every child has his plans laid out in his or her own color. This makes it much easier for them to see what's going on. Check the calendar before you leave the house for the day, just in case.

Post-it notes are also very useful. Simply write down what needs to be done and put it on the door so you can't miss it in the morning.

GETTING ORGANIZED FOR THE WEEK

On a quiet calm night when the kids are asleep, or on a weekend afternoon when they're out at a playdate, mom and dad should sit down with either a pad of paper or their computer, and figure out a family timetable.

First, do a timetable of your life as it is now. Write the hours of the day on the left. Then write the activity on the right. Have each parent do a separate schedule, and one for each child. Put in all the unchangeable basics, such as school and work, with hours that are by nature inflexible.

Then, highlight the hours that don't work. Break each hour down into minutes if you have to. Here's one mom's schedule.

6:45 A.M. Wake up.
7:00 A.M. Get out of bed. Make coffee.

7:07 A.M. Finish shower.

7:21 A.M. Finish getting dressed and applying makeup.

7:22 A.M. Wake up kids. Kids get dressed.

7:35 A.M. Finish cooking breakfast. Call kids to table.

7:50 A.M. Kids finish eating breakfast.

8:02 A.M. Kids at the door.

8:10 A.M. School bus pick up.

When you look at this timetable, you will immediately see that there just isn't enough time for the kids to get ready. Their wakeup time needs to be earlier. Mom also needs to set her alarm for 6:30 if she wants to spend a few minutes in bed, waking up at her own speed.

In another family, dad was always late for work. He needed to be out the door at 8:00 A.M., yet he never quite makes it. His wakeup time needed to be pushed back an hour earlier.

Get out a new piece of paper or computer file, and write down the hours again. Now make a new timetable. Be realistic—and be ruthless. Give yourself more time than you think you may need. Once you get used to the timetable and organize yourselves properly, we guarantee it will take you much less time to get ready, and you will be able to redo the timetable for the last time.

It may help to go backward when you set up the timetable. If you have to leave the house at 8:15 A.M.on the dot, ask yourself how long it takes to do each step before that. If your children are school age, what do they have to do? Wake up, get up, brush their teeth, get dressed, make their beds, go to the bathroom, eat breakfast, get their backpacks, then leave for school. When you're done, you'll be at the time you need to wake up. And if you have trouble figuring out the precise times, clock yourself one morning. Give the kids a stopwatch and turn this into a game.

Starting the day without a huge rush makes the rest of the day that much nicer.

Whatever you decide, *do not* allow the children to participate in the making of the schedule. It is not their responsibility. If they want new activities, naturally they need to be discussed with you— but it's up to parents to decide who does what, and when.

We are big believers in spots for your belongings. The book backpack has a spot (not on the floor—floors are for shoes). Your coat and hat have a spot. The spots can be on a hook or low shelf, or in a closet—as long as the spots can remain tidy. Some parents use labels, as kids are used to this at school. It's up to you. Just be sure that each child has a well-defined spot, and they understand that they are responsible for their own property being placed in its own spot. The consequences for not using the spot should become a House Rule.

As soon as your child has a precise spot, this should put an end to the "Where is my _____" whine. It will also put an end to the earning morning scramble for belongings.

One thing all parents can agree on is that the biggest problem after school vacation is getting the kids back in a routine. The solution is to start easing into the school year routine a few days before school starts.

ORGANIZING AFTER-SCHOOL

When Nanny Deb started working for a family with four boys, they had to do a little bit of work on their after-school routine. As soon as they bounded in the door, dumping down their backpacks and leaving their coats on the floor, they'd dash into the kitchen, where a nutritious snack of cut-up veggies, whole-wheat crackers, and string cheese would be waiting for them on the table. As soon as the snack was finished, Nanny Deb said, "All right, go get your homework." At first, they would meander about and wonder where their backpacks were and whine that they couldn't find their backpacks. That lasted for exactly two minutes. "Do I look like I will go find your backpack for you?" Nanny Deb asked calmly.

The answer, obviously, was no.

Set up an after-school routine using the same timetable technique you used for the morning. Backpacks are put in their spot as soon as the kids walk in. Coats are put away. A wholesome snack is provided—not sugary junk.

Then it's time for homework.

If your children are in extended after-school care, they should be doing their homework there. If they're in sports programs, figure out when the best time to do homework will be. A child can't concentrate if he or she is ravenous, so you may have to have a timetable that's more along the lines of get home, have a shower, eat dinner, do homework, then have a specified amount of computer time if and only if the homework is done within the specified timetable. Figure out what works best for your entire family.

And remember that homework always takes precedence over sports or other activities.

ORGANIZING CLOTHES

Many parents said a fervent prayer of thanksgiving when schools made uniforms mandatory, as this made the daily battle over what to wear nothing more than a bad memory!

If your kids don't wear school uniforms, we suggest you either have them pick out or you help them pick out the outfits for a week. Do this on either Saturday or Sunday. If your child is notoriously picky about clothes, as many are, this will give them the time to do this task properly, with no grumbling and no parents screaming that they're going to miss the bus if they don't hurry up. There are inexpensive closet organizers that have seven cubbies, so you can sort out the clothes this way, or put the outfits on hangers, then lay them out on a chair or table the night before. Your kids should already know where their underwear and sock drawers are.

This will save you tons of time in the mornings, and will spare all the arguments about "I don't wanna wear this today" in the morning when your child may be cranky.

ORGANIZING MEALS

So much of a child's routine is centered on eating. Children mark time by increments—and these increments are marked by food. When we first start working for our families, the children always say things such as, "I go to gymnastics after dinner," or "I come home for lunch," or "Where's my snack?"

We'll discuss meals in much greater detail on page 166, but we suggest you plan your meals for the week as you would plan what you'll be wearing. This will not only make your grocery shopping much more efficient and much less expensive, but will also free you up for spending the time with your children instead of squawking about what you're going to make for dinner. Set aside cooking time for one night or a weekend afternoon whenever possible, and cook large amounts to freeze. Label them clearly. You can involve everyone and turn cooking time into family fun time, if you get creative in the kitchen. Put down a large plastic mat and give the kids something to make. Let them get messy. Flour and water, for example, make a lovely, gooey paste that will occupy both toddlers and bigger kids while you cook.

The point is, you don't need to survive on fattening, unhealthy, and expensive fast food when you can so easily learn how to be efficient in the kitchen.

ENFORCING THE ROUTINE

As with every other House Rule, following the timetable and establishing a routine can not be negotiable. There will be the usual consequences for not sticking to it. It's really easy to let the routine slide or get sloppy once you're used to it, so be consistent, and enforce the rule. And don't let one child get away with something if another has been disciplined for the same infraction, no matter what the excuse is.

SETTING UP A ROUTINE FOR YOUR BABY

We've spent so many years as baby nurses that we know how crucial it is to set up a routine for the baby, as well as the parents. For one thing, having this routine helped nervous new parents learn how to cope with the demands of a very small infant. It also helps with sleep-deprived parents who can't remember what they did five minutes before much less worry about how much formula the baby just drank.

A routine makes it much easier for working parents to separate when they have to go back to work. Routines also help new caregivers or babysitters, as they'll be told precisely what to do, and when. This eases the transition for both parents and baby. If a baby goes to daycare, there would be a well-established routine to quickly learn there, too.

Babies thrive when they have a routine. Once you know your baby's pattern and naptimes are consistent, then write down the routine and stick to it. If it's baby's time for playing on the floor with you, forget about folding the laundry.

Establish a morning routine even if you are a stay-at-home parent. Get up and get dressed. Sort out the tasks you have to do. Get your baby up and dressed. Even if you don't go to work, parenting is your work, and should be taken seriously.

A nighttime routine for babies should always be the five B's: bath, book, bottle/breast, brush gums/teeth, and bed. There is no playtime for babies after bath time. We also believe that you should talk to your baby about every single thing you're doing with him or her. They'll soon grow to recognize your facial expressions and body language, long before they can speak. It will also give them a huge jump on language acquisition and vocabulary when they hear normal adult speech. Not that we're against baby talk—just baby talk all the time. So, we'll speak to the baby about such mundane things as, "George, I am going to pick you up now. We need to change your diaper. I'm going to put you on the changing table. Now I'm going to open your diaper. Ooh, feel the air. Here comes the wipey, it's cold! Let's put your diaper on. It's nice and dry. Okay, we're all done. I'm going to pick you up again."

Warning a baby before you do anything makes them less likely to get startled or to cry.

MEALTIMES

Family time at the table is absolutely essential. It's not just about bonding as a family—it's about socialization, about manners, and about good conversation. It's about everything that children need to know. It's like a recipe. Good ingredients make for good meals. And good children are made from the love and discipline you put into them.

NANNY RULE

HOUSE RULE: FAMILIES HAVE DINNER TOGETHER

You've undoubtedly seen some pretty horrific meals on *Nanny 911*. Families with no boundaries or House Rules don't usually like eating together because there's so much fighting and whining. Parents are exhausted after long days at work or chasing after their fractious brood. If there's no timetable or routine, most people are frantic by dinnertime. They're also starving. So it's

easier to shoo the kids away or plunk them in front of the TV, just so you can have a moment's peace.

Once you follow our House Rules of routine, however, you won't be so tired. Dinnertime will become one of the most enjoyable hours of your day. Instead of saying, "Oh God, I can't wait for this meal to be over," or, "Shut up and go eat in the living room," or "Get out from under the table," you'll be happy to be together.

EATING TOGETHER

We absolutely insist that families eat together. We know how busy everyone is, and how easy it is to let this slip if only due to logistics, when different siblings have widely differing schedules, and it just seems so impossible. But we simply can't underestimate the importance of this family time together. Mealtimes are when families learn how to connect.

If only one parent can make it home in time for dinner, then so be it. One parent is better than none. Try to come with a flexible alternative. If Dad works late, perhaps the kids can have a substantial snack when they get home with Mom, at the table. Then they can do their homework, get ready for bed, watch TV for half an hour, and then sit down at the table again with Dad, of only for some fruit. They can eat dessert while he eats his meal.

Nanny Stella worked for a family where the dad had a strenuous work schedule, and was often out of the country on business. No matter where he was traveling, or how tired he was, he did his utmost to be home on Sundays for family dinners together. He

would take his children out to a restaurant. It became a special treat for everyone, something they looked forward to all week. It was a workable compromise with his tough schedule and his children's need to eat with him.

On nights when there is a babysitter, the House Rule is still the same. Everyone eats together. Unless, of course, you have made and announced the exception, such as the kids being allowed to play Campfire Picnic with Uncle Stan, and everyone eats on the big blanket in the living room on nights when he comes for dinner.

MANNERS AT THE TABLE

Once you sit down, it's time for manners. You use a napkin. You eat with a fork or spoon or, for toddlers, fingers. You keep your

mouth closed when you chew. You never have the TV on. You never eat standing up. You never wolf down your food. You ask politely for someone to pass the salt.

If someone wishes to leave the table, he asks, "May I please be excused?" And he shouldn't expect that the answer is always going to be yes, either, even if he's finished his food first.

Family mealtime is also family cleanup time. Everyone should have a specific task to do—setting the table, clearing, loading the dishwasher, putting dishes in the sink. You can rotate these chores each week. (For more information about chores, see page 172 in chapter 8.) Part of good manners involve being helpful and courteous, too. As in, "Are you finished? May I clear your plate?" Not: "Gimme your plate!"

Good manners at home will translate to good manners out in public. (For more about Manners, see page 236 in chapter 10.) This way, you'll be confident that your kids will know how to behave in a restaurant or at someone else's house—and so will they.

MEALTIME IS TALK TIME

One of the most important reasons to have family meals is the need for family communication and conversation. Families need to talk, about anything and everything.

A good way to improve your conversation skills is by asking specific questions. Instead of saying, "How was your day?" and getting a mumbled "Fine" in response, try asking, "What was the best thing that happened today? And what was the worst?" Or, "Did your teacher say anything goofy?" Or, "What made you laugh?" If nothing had made anyone laugh, try to come up with a joke.

Be sure that every child has equal conversation time. This teaches kids how to talk—and, just as important, how to listen. Since you should be asking specific questions of each child, don't

Parents, are your kids literally climbing the walls? Are they out of control?

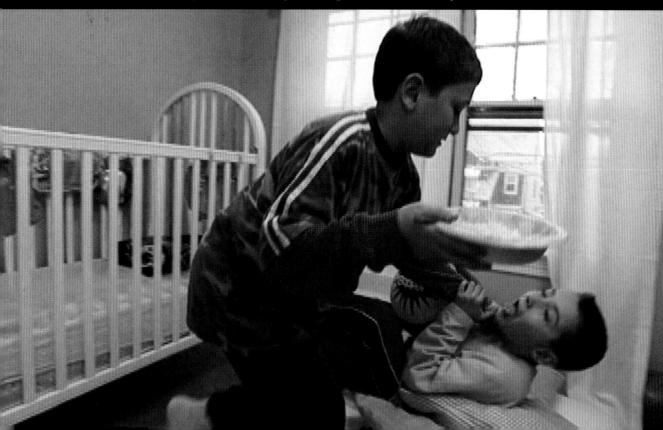

Nanny Deb (*top*) and Nanny Stella (*bottom*) are on the job
to help you solve all your parenting troubles.

This is what happens when parents set no limits and
abdicate their parenting responsibilities: total chaos.

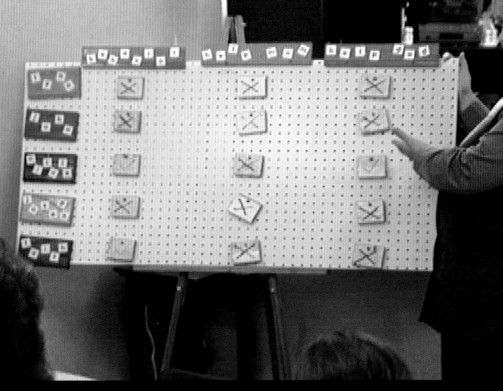

With years of experience, Nanny Stella's tough love will help you create a structure that will allow your children to flourish, no matter how rough the initial going.

Parents, it's never too late to get rid of bad parenting habits! Stop your yelling and spanking, and get your kids to sleep through the night in their own beds.

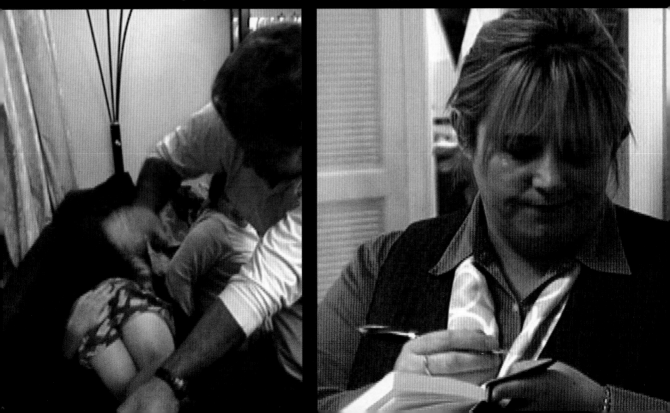

Nanny Deb's Nanny Rules and chore charts can help even the most frazzled parents create order out of chaos—always with fun and love.

The nannies have helped these children to redirect their excess anger and energy—punching pillows instead of siblings and sitting quietly in a time-out to calm down and think things over instead of running wild.

It's always a teary but joyous good-bye when the nannies transform a family on the brink of falling apart into a loving and flourishing family unit.

always start with the oldest. Start in the middle for a change. Let everyone have an interrupted amount of (fixed) time in which to speak. Feel free to devise whatever House Rules for table conversation you like. Some topics may not be suitable mealtime topics, such as bathroom talk.

When children know they have a safe time and place to talk, they're going to grow up feeling confident with both their ability to hold a conversation, and to participate in talk about a wide range of topics, with good manners and good listening. This is a priceless gift that will serve your children over a lifetime.

KEEPING A ROUTINE WHEN YOU TRAVEL

When Nanny Deb was a child, her family had moved sixteen times before she turned twelve. It was an awful lot of upheaval for a little girl to handle. Her mother helped her tremendously by creating a routine. Whenever they moved, the first room that was unpacked was Deb's. Her furniture was always put in the same places: the bed against the wall, and the dresser against the opposite wall.

Now, no matter who she's working for, Nanny Deb organizes the kid's clothing. all pajamas go in one drawer, socks and underwear in another, etc. This helps the kids find their clothes when they're getting dressed.

And it helps them know where everything is when the family travels. Any kind of travel, even on a much-anticipated vacation, causes upheaval for kids. Try to stick to a routine during any trip. Meals should be at the same time of day, if possible. Bedtime routine should be the same. Clothing should be put in the same place in the hotel room dresser as it is at home. Even something as small as knowing where the shirts are can help a child whose routine is thrown out of kilter on a trip.

8 HOUSE RULES OF ORGANIZATION: CHORES AND CLUTTER

Every house needs order.

We can tell this the minute we walk in the door. After all, we've seen every extreme in hundreds of different homes: Some are so sterile and have so few toys that we wonder if children really live there; others with few toys seem homey and cozy and full of love. Some are so clean you could practically eat off the floor. Some are such a mess that we nearly called the fire department in to tell the family that their property is condemned.

As with everything else, children learn where they live. Every home is a house, but not every house is a home. This is especially true with parents who are super-clean neat freaks, dogmatic about tidiness and obsessed with keeping everything in its place. If you spend more time cleaning than playing with your children, what kind of message does that send? If your home is in physical chaos, chances are extremely high your home is in emotional chaos, too. We believe that when a house is a disorderly disaster area, the children always follow suit.

Children can't live in an environment where they're afraid to touch anything for fear of sending mom off in a tirade. Nor can they live in mess. Clearing clutter can be amazingly freeing. Unwanted clothes, toys, and closet-clogging stuff need to go—and they need to go, now!

The first step to getting the mess in order is to delegate chores. To *everyone* in the family.

HOUSE RULE: EVERYONE DOES CHORES

NANNY RULE

Children develop self-esteem from being competent.

One of the easiest ways to teach competence is with chores. They need to be a mandatory House Rule. Everyone does chores. Everyone pitches in. This is a family rule. You're in chore land together.

Frankly, we find it astonishing when parents do everything for their children. There's no reason in the world to feel like a bad parent for asking your children to simply pick up the clothes they just peeled off and flung in the corner. Children at preschool are given tasks to do, and they do them without complaining because the teacher expects them to. Well, school tasks are chores. The difference is expectation. A teacher announces the rules. Students don't question them. They just do them.

Chores are an equal opportunity for teaching competence and responsibility, no matter how much money a family has. Nanny Stella worked for a family as a baby nurse. The family also had an older child who didn't need a nanny, but the older child and Stella shared a room when they traveled. This girl's side of the room was tidier than Nanny Stella's—but at home, the girl would drop a towel on the floor after her morning shower and it was laundered and hung up by the live-in housekeeper by the time she came home from school. She was bragging about this one day, and Nanny Stella asked her what would happen if her family suddenly lost all their money. Who would pick up and wash her towels then?

No more towels on *that* bathroom floor!

It's really a tragedy when some of our wealthy employers allow their children to grow up without instilling the necessary sense of task-mastering, of regular responsibilities, of being able to do for themselves. It ruins children by making them feel as if they are masters of the universe, and *entitled* to have someone else do their "dirty work."

Visitors are often amazed when they see the two-year-olds in our families sorting the colors and the whites in the laundry, or loading their plastic cutlery in the dishwasher. Small children are perfectly capable of doing far more than they're given credit for. Trust us—if they can pull a toy off a shelf, they can put it back.

Families need to make a House Rule about which chores are done simply because they're a part of family living, and which

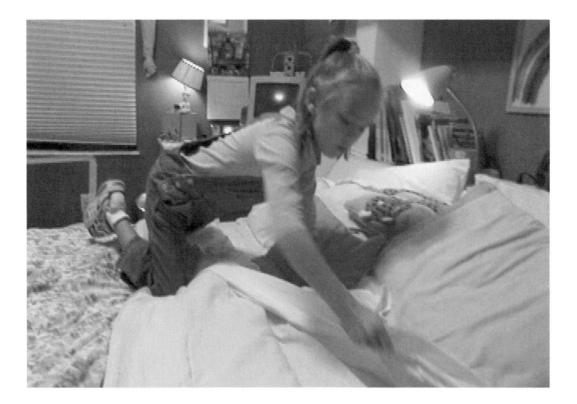

are special chores that are worthy of an allowance. Everyone will have different ideas about this, but mom and dad need to agree and be consistent, and always pay up if the rule is that this specific chore earns money.

As ever, if chores are not done, then regular discipline, such as losing marbles from the marble jar, is the consequence. For older kids, not doing chores should result in a more serious consequence, such as having a cell phone taken away for a set period of time. Make sure that the House Rules about these consequences are crystal clear to everyone beforehand.

Here's an alphabetical list of daily chores that should be delegated to different family members, depending on their age and skill level. Chore delegation will change, obviously, as kids grow up and become more physically dexterous as well as taller. Children who can't reach high shelves shouldn't be expected to put dishes away, for example, or handle fragile glassware.

. . . .

DAILY CHORE LIST

Everyone is responsible for keeping his or her own room tidy.

Bed: making, changing sheets and pillowcases
Clothes: picking up, putting away, putting in hamper
Dishes: putting in the sink, rinsing, washing, drying
Dishwasher: loading, turning on, unloading
Garbage: bagging and taking outside
Laundry: sorting, putting away, turning on washer/dryer
Table: setting, clearing
Toys: putting away, tidying
Wiping: kitchen/dining room table, floor, and wherever there are spills

CLEANING AND OUTDOOR CHORES

It's great if you have time to do these every day, but we are realistic about what can be accomplished, and certainly don't expect over-burdened families to be dusting the entire house on a daily basis. Decide whether seasonal chores such as gardening and shoveling are worth an extra boost to an allowance.

Car washing and cleaning
Dusting
Garden work: weeding, planting, trimming, and raking
Mowing the lawn
Sweeping

Vacuuming

Washing floors, windows

However you delegate the chores, remember that positive reinforcement will go a very long way to making chore time less of a, well, chore. This mom was a neat freak, who couldn't stand it when her children tried their best to make the beds.

> **MOM:** They put the blanket on horizontally instead of vertically. And it's driving me a little crazy. I would probably already be finished making these beds and onto another room already.
>
> **NANNY:** Then go vacuum another room and leave them to it.

Instead of praising them, she was ready to criticize their hard work because it didn't meet *her* exacting standards. She had to come to grips with the realization that this was *her* problem, not theirs. If you're an excessive tidier, don't expect the same perfection from your child. Nagging will never work. And we're always a bit disheartened when we work in a home where parents (usually mom) are so obsessed with cleaning and tidying that they spend more time with a hot iron than they do with their children. If your child needs you, a wrinkled shirt can wait. A child cannot.

Now, let's tackle the specifics of getting rid of a mess.

HOUSE RULE: EVERYONE DOES CLEANUP

NANNY RULE

Once you've delegated the chores, then you can begin to tackle the mess. There must be order in the house.

The obvious place to start is in the children's rooms. Nanny Stella went to a house where there was so much mess on the floors, she literally had no place to stand. That was not surprising, because as soon as the kids returned home from school they went into their rooms and dropped everything: their backpacks, their coats, their sweaters, their toys that had been looked at for a minute then tossed down again. Mom was too frazzled to figure out what was clean or dirty, so it was easier for her to pick everything up, dump it in the washers, and do the clean clothes all over again.

So Nanny Stella took swift action. She informed everyone that there was a new House Rule: Anything left on the floor was going to be put it in a large black trash bag and thrown away. You can also tell them that it will belong to you for a week, but these children needed the sharp shock of thinking their things were going to be gone forever. The kids had to get everything up before the timer she set dinged. Any time after that, anything left on the floor was fair game for her large trash bags, too.

NANNY: You know how we talked about this mess on the floor? Okay, boys, remember I said anything I find on the floor gets thrown away.

CHILD: Hey, you can't—

NANNY: No, sorry you didn't do it in time.

CHILD: It sure was mean of nanny to put this stuff in the bag and she shouldn't be bossing us around.

DAD: You were warned.

NANNY: The whole family was horrified because that had never happened to them before. They were learning that the difference between me and their parents was that what I say, I mean.

Of course Nanny Stella didn't throw anything away. At the end of a week, she returned all the possessions from the trash bags she'd stashed away. By then, all the kids were cooperating, and the floors were clean and tidy. She'd taught them to take responsibility for their things, and to understand that actions have consequences. They'd also learned that their house needed to be respected as much as the people in it.

This timer technique, with drastic consequences, is best used for emergency messes. Parents and children finally coming to grips with the mess that's been brewing for months on the floor certainly qualifies. For regular messes, simply set the timer and tell the kids that have a set amount of time to pick up what's there, and anything left over after that time on the floor will belong to mom or dad for one whole week. As soon as the timer starts, you'll see that the kids will pick up the stuff that is most important to them first, and then if there are crayons left by the time the timer goes off, they won't be as upset about losing those as they would a Gameboy.

Timers work because kids have been known to dilly-dally at cleanup without them. We do help children under age three with the picking up, but after age three they can certainly do it by themselves.

As with everything, parents need to be consistent about cleanup, and not give in to the inevitable tears or whining. Parents will give in because they can't bear to hear any crying, and say, "I'll help you just this once." One time is one too many.

Or parents come up with excuses and say, "Well, he's only two, and it's easier for me to do it." A two-year-old who is capable of getting his favorite car is just as capable at putting it back where he found it. And two-year-olds can do chores just as easily as their five-year-old and eight-year-old siblings. Cleanup is one of the easiest chores for toddlers to learn.

Whatever you do, don't criticize your kids when they are cleaning up. Of course you can do a better, quicker job. You're twice their size and have years of experience! Allow them the opportunity to try their best, and praise them for a job well done. If a spot has been missed when they're wiping down the table after dinner, simply point it out as a matter of fact, not as a criticism.

If you are consistent about the House Rule of daily cleanup, you'll soon find that you won't need a timer, and you won't need to nag. Cleanup will be done because it's expected to be done.

And then you can use the large black trash bags for real trash!

You can also make House Rules about where toys are to be played with, or put away. If the playroom is downstairs and the kids want to play with the toys upstairs, simply make the rule that whatever toys are taken upstairs must be put back in the playroom as part of cleanup. Children are perfectly capable of putting toys in a small laundry basket to make this task easier.

Be fair to your children and make it easy for them to do cleanup. Buy lightweight, different sized and colored boxes to store the toys in. Try to get some with handles for easy carrying. Organize their rooms with open shelving so it's not a struggle to figure out where to put the toys. If you live in a small apartment or house and don't have a playroom, or room for toys in the children's bedroom, then find some nice shelving or large toy bins to fit in the living room that are unobtrusive yet still fit in with the décor. There's no excuse for parents not to help their kids out with an organization system for their possessions.

Nor should parents get stressed about normal mess. Nanny Stella took care of a toddler who loved watermelon with a passion. Every summer, as much watermelon wound up in a sticky mess all over the place as in his mouth. Nanny Stella decided that she would rather have fun with her young charge than spend time cleaning up watermelon pits and sticky mess, so she made a

House Rule that watermelon could only be eaten in the sink. The toddler just loved stripping off his clothes in warm weather and doing this, and Nanny Stella hosed him down afterward with the sink spritzer, and everyone was happy.

Sinks, by the way, are a great place for kids to play when you're working in the kitchen. Put them on a small, safe stool, place large towels or a plastic mat on the floor around the sink area so you won't have to clean up the floor afterward, and give them some measuring cups, plastic spoons, and small bottle of liquid soap or bubble bath. Contained mess is great fun for kids and doesn't create a real mess for you to have to deal with.

MAKE CLEANUP FUN

When teaching children about responsibility, it's always best to keep the lessons fun.

Turn cleanup into a game. Set the timer and see who can get the most toys put away by the time it dings, and give the winner a reward, such as a marble in the marble jar. Or, make up a story about the toys that are being put away—a quick story that's finished by the time cleanup is done.

If there is already a toy out and your child get another one and then another one, we like to say, "Wait, we have puzzles out. We have blocks out. We won't have room to play and I'm going to start tripping over things, so which one would you like to put away?" Let the child decide, and do it.

When you get boxes for storage, let the kids decorate them, with paints or crayons or stickers, coded to the objects inside. Older kids can cut pictures of trains out of an old magazine and clue them on their train storage box, for instance.

Kids love spray bottles, so fill theirs with Nanny's secret cleanser—a teaspoon of baking soda dissolved in warm water. It will clean just about anything without ruining it—including crayons off walls—has no toxic smell or chemicals, and costs next to nothing—and you can let them spray where you point them.

As kids approach the teen years, however, room cleaning may become a bit more of a struggle as they become more private about their things. Jake was a ten-year-old who'd clean up his desk by putting all his papers in one spot on his desk. That wasn't good enough for his mother. A battle ensued. Mom should have respected Jake's space and left his desk alone. He has his own organization system, and it worked for him.

As hard as it may be with older kids, bite your tongue and respect the fact that a child's room is his or her domain. You may not like how they clean it, but as long as they're trying and it's not a total disaster, use the AMMO technique. Acknowledge and move on!

NANNY RULE

HOUSE RULE: CLEAR YOUR CLUTTER

Pack rats drive us crazy. This is an adult problem that can lead to serious consequences for children who learn from their parent's example of being unable to throw out a phone book from 1997. You can't expect your children to do something if you're incapable of doing it yourself. Worse, if your children are living in an environment that isn't organized, their minds are going to wander. They're not going to be able to sit in school and focus. And frankly, saving *everything* means that *nothing* is important.

This mom was one of the worst pack rats we've ever seen. She could barely bring herself to throw anything away, and that included old, broken toys, and dangerous bits and pieces of junk. It was hard to walk through the living room without stepping on something and twisting an ankle, and it was impossible to play in the toy room as it was such an appalling mess.

Nanny Deb had to convince mom and dad that their inability to deal with their things was ruining their lives. Dad dealt with the cleaning by getting the broom, making a big pile, and literally sweeping everything into the closets—and the kids would help by literally throwing their things into the closets, too. Mom and dad were both knee-deep in denial—and clutter.

DAD: Out of sight, out of mind, and that's the best way to get it done.

MOM: That doesn't work for me. It just seems like it's faster and easier if I just do it myself.

NANNY: You can't do it all yourself.

MOM: I guess I don't even think that they can do it and that's probably part of the problem.

NANNY: You enable these children too much. You do everything for them. So the house ends up in a mess. What we really need to work towards here is finding that middle ground.

Nanny Deb came up with a fun way to throw out all of their broken toys. But mom stood there wringing her hands and fussing, and her anxiety about holding on to her useless junk had been transferred to her children. Her son began hyperventilating at the mere thought of giving away a broken toy he hadn't seen or played with for two years, and mom fed right into the fears she'd created in him in the first place.

NANNY: You can see the problem here. We have too many toys, But guess what—I have a solution. So let's go. Follow me outside. Let's climb over the mess. Now we're going to do something really fun with these two big trashcans. All of the toys that you don't play with anymore, we're going to put in the happy face trashcan because we're going to make somebody

happy by giving them some toys. All the toys that are broken, we're just going to put in the sad face bin, okay?

CHILD: I really like my broken toys.

NANNY: Well, I know you like your broken toys, but there's no point in keeping broken toys because we don't want to play with them.

CHILD: [crying] I like to play with them.

MOM: I think that I would probably give them a little more time.

CHILD: [crying] If it's still broken, you can still keep it but never throw it away.

NANNY: They don't know how to handle letting go of any-
        thing.
MOM: It was stressful for me to watch them throw all the
        toys away. Things that I feel mean something to my
        children.
NANNY: This is a *broken crayon*! That is a *broken light bulb*!
MOM: There's no way I will let her do anything that will cause
        any kind of traumatic harm to my children.

Back in the house, Nanny Deb had a stern talk with this mom,
who had a hard time not believing that a broken light bulb
wasn't a valuable family heirloom.

NANNY: You were getting very, very upset out there. This is
        something you have to realize has an effect on your
        children. You are their role model, so they model
        themselves after you. These children are looking to
        you to make sure that it's okay. And you're not okay.
        When you're walking around being anxious, they pick
        up on that anxiety. You know they're different chil-
        dren with their father because he's much more re-
        laxed about these kinds of things.
MOM: I thought they wanted this nurturing mother who
        saved everything.
NANNY: They do need nurturing. These children are very loved.
        That's not what we're talking about here. We're talk-
        ing about getting you to a place where you don't feel
        like you have to hold onto *things* to keep the memory.
MOM: I can't believe I had that kind of effect on my children.
        I would hate for them to spend their life feeling the
        way that I have felt. Because it isn't any fun not to be
        able to let go.

Mom finally began to realize that if she stepped back, her children would naturally step up. As soon as she lessened her anxiety about getting rid of the old junk, the kids pitched right in. Then, they told mom that she had to clean out her room as well. As soon as the closet clearing began, she nearly lost it.

"But these are my babies' Christening outfits," she wailed.

"Then why are they hanging in plastic in your closet?" Nanny Deb asked. "Why aren't they kept somewhere nice?"

Luckily, mom got over her worries, and her kids helped. They brought in the happy face and sad face trash cans, and were thrilled to pitch mom's old stuff in them. They were extremely proud of themselves, and it gave mom a lot of pride as well, especially when she realized that her doing *less* was actually doing *more* for them. It also gave her lots more time to enjoy their childhood.

We encourage pack rat parents to come to grips with this issue, in whatever way they can. We'd never suggest that *everything* get recycled or dumped—only what's broken, unused, nonessential, torn, filthy beyond all cleaning. An easy way to start is to select five special items from each year of each child's life, items that truly are a part of your relationship with your children and your spouse. Make a special life box, decorate it, and place the items inside. Parents can do this with their child's belongings, to keep a sentimental life box, and older children can make a life box too once they've outgrown their toys and things. A cherished blankie or teddy bear means more to children than all the toys in the toy store.

If you have a hard time deciding on the five items, ask yourself what you would take if your house were on fire, or if you had to leave home with only one suitcase. This not only gives you a list, but also helps you realize just how little you do need to have.

Most of all, realize that it's not the *object* that's giving you the memory. Find a photo of your children pushing their little red wagon, put the photo in an adorable frame, and donate the little red wagon to a child who can still fit in it.

Memories are priceless. The stuff that makes the memories is not!

. . . .

HOUSE RULES: OLD TOYS HAVE GOT TO GO

NANNY RULE

Recycling and donating old but still usable toys is a wonderful way to teach the value of objects as well as instill the importance of giving to young children.

Decide upon a House Rule for outgrown toys, and have your children state their piece, as this is a team effort, although the kids are not, as ever, the ultimate arbiters of what will constitute a House Rule. (If they were, they'd keep all their toys forever, among many other things.) Perhaps the rule could be, every time a large new toy arrives, an old, no-longer-played-with toy has to go. When there are too many toys to fit on the shelves, you can also pick two and they have to go.

One rule that has to stick is that if something breaks and is not fixable, out it goes. The only exception would be if the broken toy is a child's primary comfort object or favorite, such as when Teddy gets a broken arm.

When children are under two, it's okay for parents or caregivers to weed through the outgrown or disliked toys and dispose of them when the baby or toddler isn't there, or asleep. For older kids, it can be extremely traumatic when parents take away toys without telling them. Toys shouldn't just disappear. Even discarded toys have value. And you need to show respect for your children's property, even a tiny Tonka truck. We've spoken to many adults who still have traumatic memories of their parents having gotten rid of their toys or other belongings when they were at school one day, or during a move.

Nanny Stella has clear memories of the time she went on a trip with her father and brought back the most amazing dress she'd ever seen, with intricate Austrian embroidery and brocade across the front. She wore it to a ball, outgrew it, and was horrified to see someone else wearing her beloved dress at the same ball the following year. Her parents had given her dress away without her permission. The point of this story is simple: Nanny Stella knew the dress was too small, but she would have enjoyed being given both the responsibility and pleasure of giving it to someone else. Another point is that the toy clear-out is certainly never a time for white lies. Don't say you're giving an old bicycle to cousin Joe in Akron when you've really donated it to the local Salvation Army, and your children may very well see someone riding it a week later.

The best way to work through this is to sit down with the kids when they are not tired or hungry. Explain, if you haven't done so already, that many children do not have as many toys as they do, and the House Rule is that unused toys are donated to help these children be able to play. Say, "What should we give to the children who have no toys?" Listen to what your kids say. Then help them along. Such as, "There are two little blue cars. Let's give one away and then you will still have one." Let the child acknowledge that this is all right. You should soon see the kids being able to do this themselves.

Another easy transition into what should become a habit of toy giving is to do it during the holidays. If your family celebrates Christmas, you can say, "Santa's coming and you are going to get lots of things, so let's go through your things and get rid of some stuff to make room." Even if you don't celebrate Christmas, you can still discuss the spirit of giving during the holiday season. Then go out to the toy store and tell your own children to pick out three things for kids who don't have any toys. We've seen kids who have trouble sharing one toy begging their parents to buy a special Barbie for someone else who may like it.

The entire family should take the toys to the donation site. It makes the concept of giving a very real one. Children are by nature usually very generous. They understand how to give. It's up to you to allow them to do so.

. . . .

CHAPTER 9 HOUSE RULES OF LOVE AND RESPECT: FAMILIES ARE A TEAM

This is one of the shortest chapters in our book, but it's certainly one of the most important.

Families are formed by love. That love is supported by mutual respect. Without either, families fail. House Rules spelling out the need for love and respect are as crucial as House Rules for hitting or cleanup or anything else.

NANNY RULE

HOUSE RULE: FAMILIES ARE A TEAM

Teamwork is what makes families work, which is why designating chores, being organized, and having clear-cut House Rules and expectations make it so much easier for the team to function.

If your kids love sports, then use sports metaphors they'll have heard already at school or at play. Mom and dad and caregivers are the coaches. Siblings are teammates. Some on the team are better at one thing than another, but everyone roots for all their teammates, no matter what.

The goal with the family team isn't about winning or losing a game, of course. The goal is to live a happy, fulfilling, empowering life, one filled with love and trust. That, to us, is the true essence of winning.

HOUSE RULE: SIBLINGS FOR LIFE

NANNY RULE

It's amazing when we call a family meeting, and look at the wary faces of the little ones staring back at us as we unveil their new House Rules. One of the rules that has the strongest effect is brothers for life, sisters for life, or siblings for life. Often, siblings who'd been bashing each other's brains out five minutes before make an astonishing, immediate transformation once they hear this stated.

Siblings for life means they are always going to respect each other, take care of each other, and support each other as they grow older, and for the rest of their lives. There will be no more teasing, making fun of, fighting, arguing, pushing, or whatever else has gone on.

Siblings for life also means they will set an example and help one another, that they will treat each other as they would like to be treated.

And if all the siblings are happy, then mom and dad are happy. And when mom and dad are happy, their children are happy, too.

This is a lesson that they will pass on to their children—it's that powerful.

HOUSE RULE: STATE THE OBVIOUS

When it comes to love, children can never have their fill of hearing you state your feelings. On page 71 in chapter 3, we already discussed how you should tell your children that you love, trust, and believe in them every day. Use the ALL and NEED lists that we've already mentioned to remember what to say to your children. Often it's all they'll need to click right out of a bad mood.

Speaking of love and trust, don't you hate that phrase "quality time?" We do.

It's all "real time" with your children. *Positive* time.

We send our young charges out the door in the morning with a hug, and say, "Do good work today."

Start your day with encouragement and pride in your children. Don't be critical. Do be loving.

HOUSE RULE: FAMILIES RESPECT ONE ANOTHER

A word you've heard quite often on *Nanny 911* is "respect"— and with good reason.

Respect is not a feeling the way love is, something that exists and just is. Respect is a *behavior* that needs to be learned and earned, continuously.

FAMILY RITUALS

One of the nicest way for a family to work as a team is to devise its own unique rituals.

A family ritual doesn't have to cost money or be anything sensationally spectacular. Usually, it just involves time. It can be an individual ritual with each sibling, such as taking a daughter for a smoothie after her karate class, or going to the park with your son for an hour on Saturday. Or it can involve the entire family, where every Sunday night is Chinese restaurant night.

Family rituals can make life easier for families where the parents had tough work schedules, or one parent has to travel a lot, but the children can still count on the special time they know they're going to have with mom or dad or both. And if mom stays at home with the kids, it's equally important for dads to have their own special rituals, not just to spend time alone with the kids, but to give mom a break.

Try setting up game night, which is devoted to board or card games. Make game night a House Rule, if you like, as it makes it a family reality and one that can't be changed without consequences!

Family rituals also make life easier for babysitters and caregivers. As we believe that date night is crucial for mom and dad to have an evening to themselves where they can be a couple and have private time together, setting up a family ritual to do only with babysitters can make this a lot more fun for everyone. Mom and dad will know their kids are enjoying themselves doing something special with the babysitter, and they can relax and in turn do something special with each other.

Many parents whose children are long grown have told us that the one thing they regretted most about their parenting was that hadn't spent enough time having fun with their children. Don' let that be you!

Every family needs to have House Rules about respect. Respect for things and respect for each other. That means mom and dad have to show respect for their children's rooms, property, and, especially as children grow older, their need for privacy.

Equally important is the need to respect what people say. As ever, it all boils down to communication. Say what you mean, and mean what you say. Remember that respect is a two-way street. Children can't respect rules without knowing what they are or seeing them enforced.

As we discussed in chapter 5, House Rules are to be respected whenever playmates or guests come over. No matter if you're allowed to make mud pies in Sammy's kitchen—they're not making mud pies at your home. Parents should post the House Rules in an easily visible place, and simply inform guests, of all ages, what they are. Children who are old enough to articulate the Rules can tell their playmates. Nanny Deb worked for a family whose four-year-old daughter, Kat, just loved telling her friends the rules. "The rule is we have to clean up after we play, okay?" she'd say. Or she'd say, "At your house the rule is you can drink in the family room, but not in my house. The rule is you drink in the kitchen!"

There's no obligation to explain why these are your rules. Suffice to say that these rules are for everyone.

Parents also need to respect their children as individuals. Don't make them be something they're not. Don't constantly compare them to siblings, or friends. Don't have unrealistic expectations. And certainly don't expect them to be your "friends." Hearing a mom gush, "Oh, Jasmine is my best friend" when Jasmine is six, makes us crazy! Are your other friends six years old? We don't think so.

As we discussed on page 77 in chapter 3, the Nanny Rule is, respect is a two-way street. Parents need to respect and validate their children's feelings, opinions, ideas, and personality. But that doesn't mean your children should be given free rein to state these however and whenever they choose. If you don't enforce House Rules of common courtesy, and if you indulge your child's every utterance, this can lead to children talking back, being rude, demanding their way, and mom and dad sitting there saying, "Isn't it cute how assertive little Mikey is?"

Trust us—it isn't cute. And it will create a little diva or a little prince if you allow it to continue.

We had a mom ask us how to handle a painful situation, where her ten-year-old son spoke to her disrespectfully, but was very respectful with dad. Dad would brush off her concerns by saying that boys will be boys. We told her she had to take two steps.

First, she should sit down with her son, and discuss the problem. She could say, "I love you, and I want to be a good parent. I respect you, and I need you to respect me. But I see that you are having a problem respecting me. I want to know what this is about." Then continue the conversation until the truth comes out.

Then, she needed to have a talk in private with dad. With his backup, they needed to tackle this problem as a team. Dad needed to reassess his own behavior, and sit down with their son to make it clear that disrespect is not to be tolerated. And if dad were guilty of indulging in making fun of people, he needed to address his mistake and apologize for it.

Sometimes kids are unintentionally disrespectful when they're trying to be funny. In that case, in a nonaggressive way, simply ask them to repeat the "joke," in your presence, and have a talk about the difference between cutting, hurtful humor, and silly, joshing humor. It's a much-needed lesson, as kids who are allowed to get away with disrespectful behavior at home often find themselves ostracized by their friends when they step out of bounds.

Disrespectful kids live in disrespectful homes. Unfortunately, when mom and dad have no respect for each other, they often make their feelings clear in front of their children, which can inflict incalculable damage over the years. How can a youngster be expected to behave with respect toward his friends, family, teachers, or any living creature when mom and dad don't know how to do it themselves?

It's not enough to say, "I'm your dad and you respect me because I said so!" That will not create respect. It will create an environment of fear, anxiety, and anger in children.

This dad was a former police officer, whose notion of respect was shaped by the misguided notions of the culture in which he worked.

NANNY: This House Rule is respect each other.
CHILD: What's that mean?
DAD: You think that's funny?
CHILD: Yeah.
DAD: Someone telling you that you're not respected by your children, that's like the worst thing a man can hear about. People get killed for that.

We are always upset on behalf of children who live in homes where "respect" is demanded and commanded, often in anger. Yet parents who are brutes when it comes to controlling their tempers are still often surprised and infuriated when their children act out, not realizing that they're simply mimicking mom and dad.

Here, dad spent a day with the kids, and when mom returned, all she did was criticize him in front of the children, who were happily and quietly doing their homework together. Her lack of respect came out in a not-so-subtle undermining of dad's efforts.

MOM: But wait, did your father do the laundry? Did he change the baby's diaper?
DAD: Yes.

CHILD: And he made dinner.

MOM: You cooked? Is it burned? Daddy didn't make enough for me, did he?

DAD: Yeah, there's another whole thing in there.

MOM: Aha, but there's not a fork for mommy available. I got to wash forks.

Nanny told mom to try to be more respectful of dad, and their interaction quickly degenerated into a huge argument, one that had been brewing for quite some time. Notice how they talk *at* each other, not *to* each other.

DAD: Well, it's obvious. My wife and I have issues. When we can't get along and agree on things, the kids pick up on it and that's where they disrespect us. They don't even listen to us. And when I voice my opinion it's counted for nothing. You just give the kids what they want, when they want it. That's the bottom line. You don't want to listen to my opinion any more, what can I do?

MOM: Honestly, there is no respect in this house. And I can't live like that.

NANNY: Then you shouldn't.

DAD: What are you getting bent out of shape for?

MOM: Because you're not talking to me. You're just saying, oh well this marriage is over.

DAD: I never said that.

MOM: Yeah, you did.

DAD: I didn't say that.

MOM: Listen, whatever it is, it is.

DAD: So, then you don't know how to talk to people.

MOM: Neither do you. You're just sitting there rolling your eyes. It's the same deal every night. "Oh, how much money did you spend?"

DAD: I feel like I'm a whipping boy because I was getting blamed for everything that goes on in life. You can't take too much of that when you're trying as best you can.

MOM: I can't take it any more. I have no respect, there's a lack of respect.

DAD: It goes both ways.

MOM: You know, either we work with this marriage or we don't. That's all I'm saying and I'm saying it in front of the kids.

DAD: No, you threw your hands up and walked away.

NANNY: She says to her own kids that she's out of here.

DAD: Right, all the time. She takes them in the car. She calls her mother. Because I'm such a mean guy.

MOM: I never said you were a mean guy. You're always demeaning me.

NANNY: That is something that he is working on. This stuff takes time. It's not going to happen overnight. But I can honestly say to you he has seriously been really working on trying to be positive. He's really making the effort and that's what I want here. I want this effort to be made. But you can't keep constantly just blowing up and threatening to walk out. It's all down to respect. Everything in this house is down to putting your family first and respecting each other.

DAD: But I've been speaking my mind all along. When I'm upset, I tell her where I'm coming from. She doesn't like to hear it. And then she says things in front of the children.

MOM: It's not just me, it's both of us, we both talk in front of the kids.

DAD: If you're that miserable with me, then leave. I don't want to put anybody through that.

NANNY: If he's not feeling the respect that he feels he deserves then he's miserable too. And who wants to raise the kids in a miserable household? You know what, there's a lot of love in this household. I don't care what either of you say, there's love here. I see it.

DAD: I didn't see it a few minutes ago. I saw her walking out the door.

NANNY: There's a lot of resentment, and there's a huge lack of respect. But you get those two things sorted out and there's love here. Find the respect. Find the middle ground.

DAD: You know, it's compromise and that's what marriage and life is. So, I'm willing to accept that.

CHILD: Daddy's actually smiling.

NANNY: Once you guys start to respect each other, the kids will respect you more and more and more.

Mom and dad realized they had to clear the air if they were ever to take control of their house and their lives, and they began working hard on learning to communicate in an honest, open way, and to deal with their problems in private. Once dad became less of a drill sergeant and mom stopped making hurtful threats, the kids could relax, and give their parents the respect they deserved.

. . . .

PARENTING 911
EMERGENCY
GUIDE

10 INSIDE THE HOME

ALLOWANCE

Allowances are designed to give children pocket money to buy the things they want, show them the value of items they want to buy, and help them to learn about the concept of savings.

Every family needs to devise their own House Rules about allowances. You can start with an allowance anywhere from the age of three and up. You need to explain the rules, what money is for, and how to use a bank. Having a fun outing to buy a nice piggy bank may encourage your child to save more.

Some families use the rule of 50 cents per week per age of the child for younger children, so a five-year-old gets $2.50 each week. One way to figure out an allowance is to look at the average prices of the items children most want—such as dolls, trains, or action figures—and think about how long you'd like it to take for your children to be able to save up to buy these. If a six-year-old wants a new Barbie doll, and her allowance is $3.00 each week, it would take her four weeks to save up for a $12.00 Barbie. Properly handled, an allowance teaches both patience and a healthy respect for what it takes to be able to buy a desired item.

It's also interesting to see what kind of "money personality" your child has. Some are hoarders and will save for months to buy a special toy. Others like to spend it every week. Remember, it's their money, and they can do with it what they wish, with your approval of course.

Parents need to specify to their children the chores to be done as a normal part of family living, and which are special chores that deserve either an allowance or a bonus fee, such as washing the car or working in the vegetable garden. There are always jobs around the house that can be done for money if kids want to work, and you should always pay them by the job, not the hour. Parents also need to make it clear which kind of misbehavior may call for a loss of allowance and for how long.

Watch out—there is a huge potential for allowance abuse. Never pay an allowance to children for doing their reading or their homework or for simple household chores. That's called bribery.

Nor should you hand out money as if it grows on trees—especially if you're wealthy and you have it to give. Bratty, spoiled little divas and princes have been given whatever their cunning hearts desired, whether it's toys or money. If that happens, mom and dad should take a good look in the mirror at the real culprits.

Mom and dad, it's up to you to set strict boundaries about what an allowance is for and give your children realistic guidelines for spending it.

APOLOGIES

Sorry is an emotion, not a word. It's meaningless to demand an apology or a "sorry" after every single misdeed. We don't force a child to say "sorry" after a time-out—the discipline was the time-out. "Sorry" isn't some kind of magic eraser that automatically rubs out naughtiness.

Children know when they've done something wrong. When they're still small, give them the words to be able to express themselves. Say, "Sometimes we say things we don't mean, especially when we are angry." Then ask them how they feel about it. Trust us—they'll tell you. They may make excuses at first, but eventually their innate moral sense kicks in, and they apologize.

The point we want to make is that it isn't enough for your daughter to just say she's sorry after she hits her brother and think that's the end of the situation. Children have to understand that what they did—in this case, hitting—is wrong. Sternly telling your child to say sorry (or else) means that your child has not been given a chance to process the emotions and work things out for him or herself.

When parents have good manners and apologize at appropriate times, such as "I'm sorry I misunderstood you," or "I'm sorry I accidentally stepped on your toe," children will quickly learn when they should say sorry.

Trust that your children know when they are wrong.

BABYING

We're not big on baby talk. We talk to newborns the same way we talk to toddlers and bigger kids. That doesn't mean we discuss adult topics or let them watch the six o'clock news. It means we respect their intelligence and ability to grasp new ideas and words and revel in the leaps and bounds they make as they grow.

We're not big on babying, either. Babying is about satisfying the needs of parents who don't want their sweet and adorable little ones to grow up. It also sends conflicting messages to small children. If you're constantly saying, "You're my baby, you're my tiny little baby, my little Jessie-wessie" to three-year-old Jessica, that's how Jessica will act. But twenty minutes later the same mom who does this will say, "Oh, you're such a big girl, Jessica. Why won't you go to sleep?"

If you get into the habit of talking in an adult manner to your babies and small children, it will be much easier to communicate about everything. When Jessica has trouble getting to sleep, mom should come into the room and say to her, "I am getting frustrated because I keep coming in here. Why don't you want to go to sleep?"

Your role as a parent is to be supportive of your children, to encourage their efforts to learn to do things on their own, to prepare them for the world, and to be positive about the fact that they are growing.

Give your children wings. Allow them to fly.

BEDTIME: ROUTINE

Bedtime should be one of the nicest parts of the day, a gentle winding down after a hot bath, with books to read, drooping eyes, and lots of good-night kisses. Spending time curled up with your children in a cozy chair by the bed is one of the loveliest ways to enjoy your children.

On *Nanny 911*, however, bedtime is usually screaming time with kids wound-up from watching a loud and violent show on TV, until we cut down on the chaos and establish a bedtime routine.

Our bedtime routine for babies is the five B's: bath, book, bottle/breast, brush gums/teeth, and bed. This should be modified for toddlers and older kids to the four B's: bath, brush teeth, book, and bed.

After book, it's nice to give a short back rub or extra cuddle. We like to tuck our charges in, then sit in the dark and talk about our day, all the fun things we did, what we ate—it's not so much the content of the talk, but that it becomes something to look forward to. This is one of the most rewarding ways we know to instill trust and love in children, who know they can talk to their parents about everything (and often find it easier to do so under the cover of darkness). It's also a good way to learn about what makes your children tick, and improve their memories.

Children need lots of sleep, and they need to wind down properly so they can drift right off. This means sorting out a routine, with fixed times, and no exceptions during the school week. Sit down with a pad and a pen, and make a reverse timetable. Start with the ideal time for your child to fall asleep, and work backward. If Janette should be asleep at 8:30 P.M., how much time should you allocate to book, then brushing teeth, then bath? The last hour noted in your reverse timetable should be when bath time begins.

Helping your child wind down also means no TV/videos for at least an hour before lights out. It's way too stimulating. (See the TV section on p. 263.) And TVs should never be placed in a child's bedroom, as the children become addicted to falling asleep to the noise from the TV shows. Worse, as seen on *Nanny 911,* kids can wake up at two in the morning to watch an R-rated movie, and mom and dad never knew. Until Nanny Deb made sure dad took those TVs out, there was too much screaming and shoes thrown at her head by the enraged kids.

We also believe that children should stay in bed even if they aren't ready for sleep. You can't force children to fall asleep, but you can insist that bedtime is about being in bed. The routine stays the same, but they can be allowed to read a book or just relax and feel comfortable in their rooms.

Bedtime routines give children much-needed security. They can follow similar routines during trips, or on sleepovers, and still feel safe. And they also make life calmer and more relaxed for parents, who know that bedtime means good night.

BEDTIME: SLEEP ENVIRONMENT

One of the first mistakes parents make when they bring their new-borns home is to place them in cribs filled with all sorts of stuff. Dad hangs the motorized mobile over the crib and wonders why little Patrick won't go to sleep. Mom turns on the light-up crib aquarium, forgets that the batteries need to be replaced, and panics when little Nicole starts screaming as soon as the fishies stop bobbing around in the bubbles.

Mom and dad—cribs don't have to have bumpers. They never need any pillows or soft toys that are potential suffocation hazards. The only thing an older baby needs in a crib is a baby-suitable cloth book. When the babies are old enough, place some cloth books on the side of their bed. This will give them all the amusement they need if they wake up early.

If you give your children crutches to help them sleep, they will soon become dependent if not addicted. Trust us—you don't need sound soothers with rainforest noises. You don't need blackout shades for pitch-dark bedrooms. You don't need music, other than a song or two that are good-night lullabies; after you say good-night, children shouldn't need to continuously listen to music to fall asleep.

For children who need noise to fall asleep, slowly wean them off it. Gradually turn the volume down till it's gone completely. This may take weeks if not months, but once it's done, the children will be freed of the need for a nightly sleep aid.

BEDTIME: LETTING CHILDREN SLEEP IN BED WITH YOU

Some parents love to have their children sleep in bed with them. They have a king-size bed, and everyone gets the rest they need. If both parents agree that this is what they like, and if it works for you, then it's fine. After all, this is the cultural norm in many countries around the world.

But the operative phrase here is if it works for you. That's not what we usually see.

Parents have to make the family sleeping arrangements as a team, and it's not about what just works for the children, or for one parent. If mom wants it and dad is sleeping on the couch, having your kids sleep in bed with you is clearly not working. If mom continues to crawl into bed with a sleeping baby or child, it is about fulfilling her need, not the child's.

We've heard excuses such as, "Oh, but I just love to wake up next to my little ones. They're growing up so fast!" That fine. Make a House Rule that your kids are allowed to crawl into bed at a fixed time in the morning, if that works for both parents. Some of the happiest childhood memories grownups have are from cozy mornings spent cuddled with mom and dad in their bed.

As baby nurses, we've had years of experiences putting young infants on a schedule and having them easily fall asleep alone, in their cribs. We've easily transitioned toddlers starting at about eighteen months this way, too.

1. First, tell your children that they're going to sleep in their own beds from now on, and go to sleep by themselves, and you're going to help them do it.
2. The first night, parents are allowed to put their chairs by the bed and stay in the room until the children fall asleep. But there is no interaction after you say good night. No talking, soothing, patting—nothing. They'll see that you're there, but that you will not respond to them.
3. Move the chair closer to the door each night, until it's in the hallway. Keep doing this until the children can fall

asleep on their own. Do not give in and talk or soothe. You are simply there. If the children get out of bed, put them back in without a word. You may have to do this many times at first.

4. If you stick to this routine, slowly but surely, it will work.

For very young children who are anxious about being on their own, you can bend the rules a bit. Nanny Deb did this with an eighteen-month-old, Amanda. On the first night, they listened to some music. When the music went off, Nanny Deb stayed near the bed. Amanda wanted to hold Nanny Deb's hand, but Nanny Deb wouldn't let her. She just sat close to the bed, softly said, "Night-night" three times and stayed in the room till Amanda was asleep.

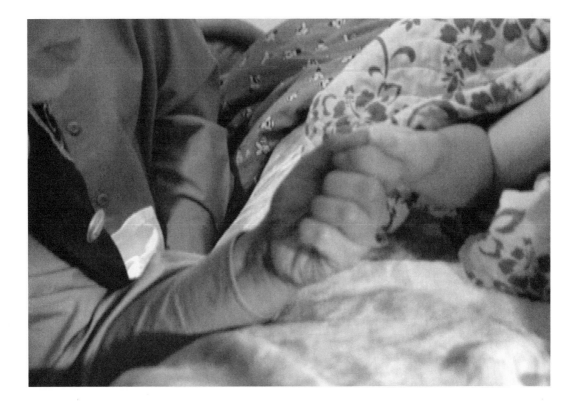

The second night, Nanny Deb moved the chair further away. The third night, she moved the chair even further away, still quietly saying "Night-night." By the fifth night, Nanny Deb's chair was in the hallway and she would just go "Shhh." And by night six, Nanny Deb put Amanda to bed and said, "I'll be in the hallway" and all was well.

For older kids who are used to sleeping in bed with you, try reducing the time without moving the chair. When Nanny Stella worked with two older kids who'd never slept on their own, the first night took an hour. The second night took fifty minutes. The third took thirty. The fourth took five.

And don't make a big deal about it for older kids when you start the process. Simply state the fact—that it's time for Chase and Colette to sleep in their own beds. Put the emphasis on the consequences of what happens when they don't sleep in their own beds without turning this into a negative. Do say, in a calm, bland, matter-of-fact voice, "Tomorrow, I would really like to take you to the park if I'm not too tired. If I could sleep in my bed by myself, then I'm sure I won't be too tired." This will provide positive reinforcement of the "mom needs to sleep in her own bed" concept.

Don't say, "If you don't get in your own bed, we're not going to go to the park." Instead, remove attention from the negative behavior.

If the kids still come into your bed to sleep, when tomorrow comes, you say, "Unfortunately, I didn't get enough sleep last night." Don't be accusatory; just state this as a fact. Your kids will get the message.

Just as parents need date night, they also need the intimacy of their bed to keep their relationship thriving.

BED-WETTING

Some children who are toilet trained during the day still have trouble staying dry at night. Others suddenly begin to have accidents. This is an extremely common problem, but one fraught with worries for the child and aggravation for the parents.

When bed-wetting becomes chronic, such as happening every night, first see the pediatrician to rule out any physical problems, such as a weak bladder or hormonal changes. A very high percentage of bed-wetting is totally out of the child's control due to bladder problems. If everything is in order, though, try restricting liquids after six p.m. You may want also wake a bed-wetter up right before you go to bed to have one last pee. Those who are super-deep sleepers may respond well to bed-wetting alarms that wake the child up in the middle of the night as soon as a sensor detects any urine on the bed.

Whatever you do, never get angry at bed-wetters—tell them it's normal. There is the huge issue of shame for many of these children, and feeling that they're being punished or chastised for something they do in their sleep can produce deep anxiety and even more wetting. Talk to them calmly and without judgment about what's going on. Sometimes kids are afraid of going to the bathroom at school, and they learn to hold it in when they have to go, and this can lead to nighttime problems.

Instead, try using rewards, such as the marble jar, for each dry night. Get the child involved in the clean up process, such as stripping and remaking the bed and helping to launder the wet sheets, to help teach them to accept some responsibility, but not in a negative way.

You may also need to literally retrain your older child as if he or she were a toilet-training toddler again. (See the toilet training section on page 257.) Give them a bathroom schedule, and remind them to go before and after lunch, before class, before and after playing sports, before and after dinner, right before lights out, etc. Using a kitchen timer may help with the reminders. You can also give reminders yourself in a calm voice, so your child knows it's not a big, embarrassing deal. It may take a few weeks, but an easy-to-follow schedule can help get this problem under control.

BITING

Toddlers bite. Sometimes they bite a lot, especially once they realize that biting is sure to get a swift reaction.

Fortunately, most toddlers go on to lots of other charming behavior and leave the biting behind, especially when mom or dad gently remind them that biting is not acceptable and remove them from the person (or cat, or dog) they've been trying to play Dracula with. If they don't want to listen, time-outs work for toddlers close to age two.

We've also given kids teething rings and told them that the only thing they can bite is this ring. That usually cures them of the habit quickly.

If a child bites due to anger or frustration, which is common in toddlers, use your basic talking technique to address the anger. And try to get them to use their words the next time they're angry or frustrated.

BOSSINESS

Bossiness is a very common control issue in children. Some children are by nature more bossy than others, and they often want to play with kids whom they know they can rule with an iron fist. It's important too for bossy kids to learn that they can't always get their way, or they'll soon being to wonder why no one wants to play with them.

Nanny Deb took care of a three-year-old girl who dictated how to do everything, even how to place plates in the dishwasher. While packing the bag to take to the park, she told Nanny Deb, "You put the raisins in the bag before the juice and then the juice and then the crackers and then the wipes."

"What will happen if we do this a different way?" Nanny Deb asked.

She looked a little puzzled, and said, "It doesn't work."

"What doesn't work?"

"The whole thing!"

Nanny Deb paused a minute, then asked, "Can we try it a different way for fun and see if it all works? I like to try new and different things for fun."

"Okay," said the little girl, "but I am still the boss of all the stuff."

Another child of Nanny Deb's, Willa, had a very strong-willed little friend named Maddy. Willa was also strong willed, but she always let Maddy have her way. One day, Nanny Deb heard Willa begging Maddy to play house and let her be a mommy, but Maddy was adamant that Willa be the daddy.

Nanny Deb stepped in and said, "We need to have a talk. Maddy, when we have playmates, we have a rule. Everyone gets to have a turn playing what she wants."

When Maddy had a hard time following the rule, Nanny Deb would help her, but it was now a rule. Maddy agreed and the little dictator disappeared.

BURPING AND PASSING GAS

Oh, how kids love to make noises—especially when coming out of their own bodies. When it comes to burping and passing gas, we've noticed that girls can certainly partake of the "pleasure," but boys usually win in the gross-me-out contests, no doubt about it.

Burping

Most burps are involuntary, but we've overheard plenty of burping contests. Once kids figure out how to create burps, happy hours can be spent making ridiculous burping noises and collapsing in fits of giggles.

Teach your children proper etiquette, however. They should always say either "excuse me" or "pardon me" if they burp in public. And they should not be encouraged to burp in public, no matter how funny it seems (dads are often guilty of egging on their boys). But realize that you won't have any control over the burps that come out when kids get together in school or camp or other play-dates.

Passing Gas

As with real burps, there's no way to eliminate the involuntary passing of gas. It's always going to come out, literally, and always sound funny to kids.

As kids get older, again, deal with the etiquette. When gas slips out, they should say, "excuse me" or "pardon me." As this can be intensely embarrassing when done in front of friends or adults such as teachers, remind kids to get the acknowledgment over with, ignore the teasing, and go about their business. Being embarrassed about gas is a good way to teach children not to mock others who do something embarrassing as well.

When at home, a child who announces that he or she feels something coming should be told to get to the bathroom and praised for letting rip in the appropriate venue.

CELL PHONES

Cell phones have revolutionized how people communicate. They've made life somewhat easier when people are trying to get in touch, and they can be true lifesavers in emergencies. They can also be expensive, annoyingly rude and intrusive, and they have enslaved us to the technology of convenience.

Although giving an older child a cell phone can greatly reassure parents who know that they can instantly reach their child, cell phones should still be thought of as a privilege, not a necessity.

A child who is old enough to be entrusted with a cell phone is also old enough to be responsible for it.

Before a child gets the phone, sit down together and make the House Rules clear about how much you are going to pay for every month. Explain that all calls are itemized, so you'll be tracking who they call and when, so that any cell phone use during school means the phone is automatically taken away for a set period of either days or weeks. Disable the text messaging function if it's abused. Make it clear that if the phone is lost, they may be responsible for helping to pay either the deductible on the insurance, or for a replacement, and the funds will be deducted from the child's allowance.

Setting out crystal-clear House Rules about the phone ought to prevent any abuse. If phone use is out of control, be firm and take the cell phone away. We grew up without cell phones and managed to somehow survive, and we've no doubt that your child can do the same.

CHEATING

Cheating falls into the same category as lying and stealing. It's wrong. It's not justifiable even if everyone else in class is text-messaging math quiz answers to each other, or plagiarizing text from the Internet when they have to do a report. Cheating needs extremely strict consequences, as well as an apology to the person who was cheated—not just a quick sorry. A letter needs to be written, or a sit-down meeting. This can have really tough ramifications, as kids who cheat in school or in sports risk being expelled or being kicked off teams.

Teach your children to stand up for themselves against cheaters. Kids who are afraid to be perceived as tattlers should speak to their teachers in private if they know about classroom cheating. If your son's science partner is cheating, your son should tell the teacher, "I need a new partner because I don't like to cheat."

Be sure to make a House Rule about cheating during game playing, so that the cheater immediately loses playing privileges. And if a checkout clerk gives you too much change, return it. Mom and dad—it's up to you to set the right example. Because ultimately, the cheaters are really only cheating themselves.

CHORES

They need to be a mandatory House Rule. Everyone does chores. Everyone pitches in. This is a family rule. You're in chore land together.

We find it astonishing when parents do everything for their children. Children at preschool are given clean-up tasks to do, and they do them without complaining because the teacher expects them to.

Visitors are often amazed when they see the two-year-olds in the families for whom we are working sorting the colors and the whites in the laundry, or loading their cutlery in the dishwasher. Small children are perfectly capable of doing far more than they're given credit for. Trust us—if they can pull a toy off a shelf, they can put it back!

As ever, if chores are not done, then regular discipline, such as losing marbles from the marble jar, is the consequence. For older kids, not doing chores should result in a more serious consequence. Make sure that the House Rules about these consequences are crystal clear to everyone.

For an alphabetical list of daily chores that should be delegated to different family members, depending on their age and skill level, see page 175.

CLEANUP

As there must be order in the house, the obvious place to start is in the children's rooms. Nanny Stella went to a house where there was so much mess on the floors, there was nowhere to stand. So she took swift action. She informed everyone that there was a new House Rule: Anything left on the floor was going to be put it in a large black trash bag and thrown away. The kids had to get everything up before the timer she set dinged. After the timer went off, anything left on the floor was fair game for her large trash bags, too.

Of course, Nanny Stella didn't throw anything away. At the end of a week, she returned all the possessions from the trash bags she'd stashed away. By then, all the kids were cooperating, and the floors were clean and tidy. She'd taught them to take responsibility for their things, and to understand that actions have consequences. They'd also learned that their house needed to be respected as much as the people in it.

Timers work because kids have been known to dillydally at cleanup without them. We do help children under age three with the picking up, but after age three they can certainly do it by themselves.

As with everything, parents need to be consistent about cleanup and not give in to the inevitable tears or whining.

If you are consistent about the House Rule of daily cleanup, you'll soon find that you won't need a timer, and you won't need to nag. Cleanup will be done because it's expected to be done.

And then you can use the large black trash bags for real trash.

Parents, don't stress about normal mess.

For more information about cleanup and clutter, read chapter 8.

MAKE CLEANUP FUN

When teaching children about responsibility, it's always best to keep the lessons fun.

Turn cleanup into a game. Set the timer and see who can get the most toys put away by the time it dings, and give the winner a reward, such as a marble in the marble jar. Or, make up a story about the toys that are being put away, but it has to be a quick story and finished by the time cleanup is done.

If there is already a toy out and your child gets another one and then another one, we like to say, "Wait, we have puzzles out. We have blocks out. We won't have room to play and I'm going to start tripping over things, so which one would you like to put away?" Let the child decide, and do it.

When you get boxes for storage, let the kids decorate them, with paints or crayons or stickers, coded to the objects inside. Older kids can cut pictures of trains out of a magazine and glue them on their train storage box, for instance.

CLINGING

Clinging doesn't come from kids—it comes from anxious parents who want their children to remain babies. Or from too-busy, inattentive parents whose children learn to cling because it's the only way to get mom or dad to listen and talk to them.

We've seen parents whose children literally seemed glued to them at the hip, including one mom who never put her eight-month-old daughter down all day, even as mom got her older children up, made breakfast, cleaned the house, and took the kids out to play. At least she did put the baby down for diaper changes. Not surprisingly, this baby wanted nothing to do with her dad, as he wasn't about to lug her around all day.

As much as you love and want to cuddle your babies, they need autonomy. They need to learn how to move and crawl on their own, and develop age-appropriate motor skills. They also need to negotiate childhood milestones without mom or dad hovering and

clinging. It's a truly wonderful moment when your toddler first says, "I do it myself"—and does.

We've also seen families where seven-year-old children could not eat at the table without sitting on their parents' lap. Why were they allowed to climb all over mom and dad in the first place? Once behavior likes this becomes a habit, it's going to be extremely hard to break. Tell your children that they don't have to be all over you or pulling at you to get your attention, and stick to it.

As for children who become clingy because they want attention, follow our communication guidelines on page 50 in chapter 3. When children know you're listening, they won't have to cling. Be sure to set up the boundaries, explaining, for example, that you need time alone right now, but you will be happy to hold them after dinner. Suggest that they find something specific to do while they're waiting.

Yes, letting go is hard, and your precious little ones grow up fast, but you must find a way to let go or you will further fuel their separation anxiety.

COMFORT OBJECTS

Many children find great comfort in and become passionately attached to their comfort objects, which we refer to as loveys. Loveys are usually blankets—or blankies, cloth diapers or other pieces of fabric, small pillows, or soft stuffed toys.

We're all for loveys, as they provide comfort and security to babies and toddlers . . . within reason. They are ideally only be used for soothing at naptime and bedtime. When Nanny Deb was working for a family with four very small boys, she found an ideal lovey in the form of a small blanket that was silky on one side and cotton on the other. At naptime and bedtime, the boys were given these blankies, and quickly learned that blankie meant time for sleep. They conk out as soon as they started to rub the blankie. And when they woke up, Nanny Deb took the blankies away. (She bought ten, just in case.)

Realize that loveys can get lost and become filthy, and woe betide any parent who can't find the lovey when your toddler is screaming for it! You may want to think about first giving your baby a lovey that can easily be duplicated, such as a receiving blanket, so a dirty one can be washed and the replacement given in its stead. We'd prefer it that loveys remain indoor objects, as this will save you from having to drive back to Target, like one of Nanny Stella's employers had to do at nine o'clock one night, long after bedtime, to try and find the lovey that had been left in the shopping cart eight hours before. If you're on a trip or your child is going through a particularly stressful time, stash a lovey in your bag, so if a crisis comes up, such as a skinned knee or other upset, your child will be able to calm down that much quicker aided by the lovey. Children used to blankies like the ones Nanny Deb used as sleep-time association will conk out as soon as it's given to them, no matter where you are.

Don't get carried away and indulge your children with multiple loveys. Nanny Deb worked for a little girl, Amanda, who was almost four. She needed a pacifier, three small blankies, the big mama blankie, her large stuffed Bunny, and many other small stuffed animals just to get into the car. Once Nanny Deb had gained Amanda's trust, she said, "If you want to sleep with your animals and blankies, that's fine, but we're not going to take all of them in the car anymore. You pick which ones you'd like to take today." On one memorable outing to the zoo, ten stuffed animals were stuck into the stroller. Gradually, fewer of them were put into the car. Next, Amanda announced that all her stuff could stay on the bed. After about eight weeks, she decided that the mama blanket was too big, so it could stay in the closet, and her pacifier was given to the sick little babies who needed it more.

This process took work, organization, and, most of all, consistency.

COMPUTERS

Computers are amazing. The Internet is a marvel. But for every fantastic advance in technology and learning, there's a downside—child predators trawling for victims, or classmates who've turned into cyber-bullies, or computer games so seductive your son wants to play them for bleary hours on end.

Computer use must be monitored and controlled. You can set time limits so AOL can't be accessed at night, for example, or use parent-controlled account passwords. This may be a very unpopular House Rule at first, particularly with older kids, but there's no other way to supervise what can be a very dangerous thing.

House Rules we suggest are: Family computers should be in family room, where you can see what's on the screen. Games, chat rooms, and instant messaging are forbidden until homework is done, and use is strictly limited during the school week to no more than an hour or whatever you think is feasible. Correct English should be used instead of those ridiculous abbreviations.

Make it clear to your children that you will be monitoring their computers, so they will be aware that you may choose to read their e-mail, instant message logs, or see which websites they've visited. Most of all, any abuse of computer privileges means an automatic loss of access to the computer for a set period of time.

You can also allow computer privileges to be earned through extra chores. Or try giving your children the choice of being given their allowance that week in the form of money or extra hours on the computer that Sunday.

CRYING

Babies cry. Children cry.

It isn't going to kill them. Mom and dad, it isn't going to kill you either.

But although it's understood that babies cry, parents somehow believe that their toddlers shouldn't cry at all.

Children absolutely must learn how to deal with their feelings of anger and frustration—but that's impossible to do if their parents won't let them cry and work out their feelings. This means letting them cry when they're angry or upset.

This is one of the most important issues we tackle on the show. These parents don't teach their children how to deal with anger or frustration, which can become a really serious problem.

Next time your daughter cries, let her do so for a minute. Avoid saying, "Don't be angry. Don't cry. Don't be upset." This both invalidates their feelings, and discourages open channels of communication.

If your child says, "I'm angry," it's your responsibility to not deny the anger, but to calmly ask what's causing it. Then—and this is the crucial part—acknowledge and identify the reason for the crying. Find out what happened. In a calm voice say, "I can see that you're upset," or "I can understand why you are angry."

Then, talk it through. Go back to the feeling that triggered the crying. Help the child calm down.

We are not advocates of letting your child cry for the wrong reasons. We don't let children cry themselves to sleep. What we do is establish a trusting relationship with children. When they know they can trust us and come to us for comfort, they know we will listen to them and validate their feelings when they are crying and upset.

As soon as parents establish this level of trust and comfort with their own children, crying and tantrums will lessen if not disappear altogether.

FEAR OF THE DARK

One of the most common childhood fears is of the dark, of monsters lurking under the bed and in closets. Parents feed into this by saying, "Oh, were you scared of the big green monster?" when their child hasn't yet mentioned the big green monster—but now certainly will.

For children who are truly fearful, acknowledge their fears and never belittle them. Try giving your fearful children walkie-talkies or baby monitors, if their bedroom is upstairs and you go downstairs after you say good-night, so they know you are easily reachable if they become very scared. Make sure the House Rule is no more walkie-talkie if they use it to call you for no good reason.

FREE TIME

We've yet to meet a child who said he'd rather spend every weekend playing sports and going to classes than just hanging out with his family and friends.

What's wrong with doing nothing?

Unstructured free time for play is what encourages creativity. Overstructured, overburdened children, whose every second is scheduled, end up frustrated and exhausted. They have no time to just be.

We've seen too many families where one child takes karate, his sister takes dance, and the third child does both. They come home tired and hungry from classes and school and being shuttled around in traffic jams. They gobble their dinners and collapse in front of the TV before falling into bed.

That is no way to live. That is not our idea of a happy childhood.

Call a family meeting and discuss priorities. One of the priorities must be that children have some time to do as they wish. Another must be that families have rituals they do together. (See page 193 in chapter 9 for more on Family Rituals.)

It's up to all you soccer moms and dads to set limits for the amount of after-school activities, especially in families where the logistics of chauffeuring children around become stressful. Your children can still get into a good college if they don't have five extra classes every week when they're seven.

GETTING DRESSED

Sometimes kids are happy to wear whatever clothes are put in front of them. And then, seemingly overnight, they'll become incredibly fussy and particular about getting dressed. This is actually quite

common for both boys and girls, yet it can quickly degenerate into a real control battle if you let it.

For picky dressers, give a limited amount of choices, controlling them so the child ends up wearing something you approve, such as long sleeves in winter and lightweight shirts in summer. For example, try asking your daughter "Pants or dress?" Then, move on to color. "Pink or purple?" Then, "This shirt or that shirt?" If she insists on a short-sleeved shirt in winter, tell her she can wear it over a long-sleeved shirt. You may also want to seasonally rotate your child's clothes, so all the short-sleeved shirts are boxed up in the basement or attic by the time cold weather hits.

When you do this, your child will feel in control, and be dressed appropriately too. It helps to spend Sunday afternoon or night picking out outfits for the entire school week, and organizing them in a closet or on easy-to-reach shelves. This will free up mornings for getting ready instead of time-wasting battles over clothing.

Nanny Deb had worked with a very strong-willed three-year-old who insisted that she had to wear a dress every day, whether it was snowing, raining, or boiling hot. So Nanny Deb calmly told her that the rule was that she could wear a dress every day, but if it was cold outside, she needed to wear a long-sleeved shirt and pants underneath. And, she would proudly wear a badge that that said I DRESSED MYSELF TODAY to school.

The I DRESSED MYSELF TODAY badge isn't a punishment. Kids love it; it makes them feel secure and competent when they're allowed to put together an outfit that they love—and parents don't have to worry about being embarrassed that other grownups may think they're on the run from the fashion police.

The exception is for religious services or special events which necessitate respectful clothing. Mom and dad, you choose the clothes, or give your children a choice of two outfits.

For children who insist on wearing the same superhero outfit, pajamas, tutu all the time, tell them the House Rule is that clothing must always be clean before it can be worn, and that you are not going to stay up and wash that one item so that they can wear it every day. Help them choose alternates.

HITTING, KICKING, AND PINCHING

The House Rule for hitting, kicking, or pinching is clear. Punching a wall is the same as punching a person as far as we're concerned. There is zero tolerance for any of it. It means an immediate time-out.

Children under four get the usual warning about an imminent

time-out. Children older than four should know better, and it's straight off to time-out with no warning.

Continual hitting, kicking, or pinching means a loss of rewards, too. Make a House Rule about how many marbles are removed from the marble jar for each hit.

Small children need to be taught that it's not okay to hit when they're angry. Tell them: "Let's think of other things we can do when we're angry. What can we do instead?" Give them the words to help them express their feelings and tell you why they are angry.

Try suggesting, "If you need to kick something, you may go outside and kick a ball." Or ask, "What can we kick?" in the same way as you'd say, "What are hands used for?" Praying, clapping, and holding. Not hitting.

Older children also need to come to grips with anger by using words, not fists. Allow them to calm down during the time-out, then have the post-time-out talk. Ask what's going on. Acknowledge the rage. Say, "You were really mad because he took your book. I understand. That would make me angry, too. But the problem isn't your anger, it's your hitting." As soon as your child can get the feeling out that caused the rage that made them hit, the urge to hit will go away.

If a child is having severe hitting problems due to an unusual amount of stress such as coping with a move or a family loss, try giving them a "hitting pillow" as a temporary means to deal with the rage. This should only be an emergency measure, as children should never be encouraged to hit, unless they're in a martial arts class.

Nanny Deb worked for a family with two children, age seven and eight. Their dad had died the year before, and their grief and loss had turned to rage. It was so bad that the kids were pummeling each other on a daily basis. The little girl, Jacqueline, would retreat to her bedroom, stating that she needed her privacy and time to think, and when she'd come out, Nanny Deb would gently steer the conversation.

NANNY: Are you ready to talk?

CHILD: Not really.

NANNY: You know, we have to talk about this hitting and punching problem. It's something that we're going to do. Let's find a way.

CHILD: I want to play with you instead.

NANNY: If you want to play with me, we're going to have to talk, so let's find a way.

CHILD: I want to play ball.

NANNY: That's great, here's the plan. When I throw the ball, I ask a question. You throw the ball back, and you answer the question.

Once Jacqueline was able to funnel her aggression into a game of ball, she was able to talk about her hitting and come to grips with her feelings. Nanny Deb had gotten to the root of the problem that was causing the hitting, not just doling out discipline for the hitting itself.

Children lash out for a reason. It's up to you to find out why.

HOMEWORK

We agree with parents that schools sometimes give out too much homework, even to kindergartners. Regardless, it is your child's responsibility to take care of his or her homework, not yours. You can help your children, but you can't do it for them.

One of the biggest problems with homework is kids finding the time to do it. Make a House Rule about when and where homework is done. It has to be part of your routine. Your kids should come home, have a snack, and do their homework within a fixed range of time at a dedicated space—whether it's at the kitchen table or at desks in their rooms. If they are in after-school care, homework should be done there. No TV, no computer, no video games, no books, etc., until the homework is done—and done properly. Perhaps you could set a time for homework to be done. If the deadline is five o'clock, say, "If you are finished with your homework by five, you can watch something on TV, or you can call your friend and ask her to come over." That should be enough incentive. The sooner homework time becomes a routine, the sooner the homework will get done.

If your kids play sports, then set up a homework time for after dinner, and enforce the rule about doing it then, too.

If your kids come home with friends from school, the House Rule remains the same; it doesn't change for guests. First snack time, then homework time, which means playmates do their homework as well. Never mind the protests from playmates, along the lines of, "Well, my mom will help me with my homework later." You can reply, "If you need help from your mom later, that's fine, but it's my job to sit here and make sure everyone does their homework. After homework is done, you can go and play." You may be amazed at how quickly homework gets done.

HYGIENE

Hygiene must become a habitual part of a daily routine. It's very easy to do this with babies, when you're following the five B's of bedtime (see page 206). Starting early means babies and toddlers accept the fact that teeth must be brushed, hands and faces cleaned, and hair combed and brushed. It isn't an option.

Toys played with outside should be cleaned before they're played with inside. When they're big enough, have your children help. Fill the kitchen sink with soapy water and dirty toys while you're cooking. You can also set a small pot full of soapy water on a large tray on the floor, with a waterproof mat underneath, and let toddlers splash away. And with hand-washing, there are lots of child-friendly, fruit scented liquid soaps in pump bottles, so there's no excuse. You can even make your own colored soap by adding in a few drops of food coloring.

Baths

Kids love dirt, but they go through phases where they don't like washing it off. The House Rule is bath or shower every night, unless it's winter and their skin is very dry. No excuses. Babies and toddlers sometimes suddenly act afraid of water, and they may scream hysterically. Stay calm and don't make a fuss. Try again the next night. With most little ones, this phase disappears as quickly as it arrives. Wash their hair anyway, with tear-free shampoo despite protests or screaming. Use bath toys to make bath time as much fun as possible. As your children become adolescents they can start to get smelly, so this is the time to have a discreet conversation about body odor and deodorant, and enforce the rule about daily baths or showers.

Teeth

Baby gums should be wiped with a clean washcloth, and teeth brushed with a soft finger brush and fluoride-free toothpaste. Add a pea-sized dab of fluoride toothpaste after age two, and help your little ones with brushing until they are competent, usually age five to six. We both like to play the sugar bug tooth game—we tell children that sugar bugs will chomp their teeth if they don't brush, and then shut off the light for a minute to "look" for bugs. Children love playing this game.

Toilet

For hygiene after toilet use, encourage children to wipe themselves as soon as they're trained. By age four to five, children should be able to wipe their bottoms without adult aid. A few marks in underpants are no cause for concern while they're learning. If necessary use disposable toddler wipes, which are soft and wet, to make it easier. Show them how to flush. And set the right example for your children—always wash your hands after using the toilet.

IMAGINARY FRIENDS

One of the most common childhood flights of fancy is the invention of imaginary friends. This is usually a short-lived phase, starting at about age three, and perfectly normal. Never scold a child for having an imaginary friend.

Our technique for coping with imaginary friends is to treat them as members of the family and kill them with kindness. Treat "Pandora" as if she really exists. So Pandora needs to follow all the House Rules. When Pandora misbehaves—and she will, if only for a child to test mom and dad's limits—then Pandora receives exactly the same discipline as her owner. This will quickly stop Pandora from taking over the household and driving you crazy with her antics.

LYING

Honesty is the best policy. Lying cannot be tolerated. However a child has misbehaved, the consequences should never be as severe when the truth is told. Make this House Rule clear, as children are often afraid to tell the truth for fear of getting into trouble. Use this model: "If you tell me the truth, even if it is bad, I am not going to get mad at you. There will be consequences for what you did, but I am not going to get angry. If you lie to me, there will be much more serious consequences." Children are so relieved to not be judged that the truth will come spilling out.

If you suspect lying, be creative. Here are some suggestions.

- "I understand what you're telling me. If I check with so and so, is he going to tell me the same thing?"
- "I already know the answer, but I want to hear it from you."
- "I will give you the benefit of the doubt because I know you want to tell me what happened."
- "I know you are smart and I want you to think about it and then tell me."

This will empower children to confess without shaming them. Once they accept responsibility for whatever happened, you can calmly discuss the consequences and any loss of privileges, if the deed was serious enough to warrant them.

MANNERS

Manners aren't just about "please" and "thank you." Manners give us a moral code to live by.

Children learn what they live, and need to be taught early on what manners are—you can start with concepts as simple as please, thank you, and "May I?" when babies are just beginning to talk.

Mom and dad need to learn their manners, too. Parents often tell us that their children have wonderful manners in school. That's because the teachers brook no nonsense, and use their own good manners to teach their students how to behave.

Instilling good manners can be tough for children when their own parents are rude and thoughtless at home and scream at other drivers when they're behind the wheel. And turn off the TV so that the rudeness currently popular in sitcom families doesn't invade your own living room every night.

Nanny Stella worked for a family whose eldest daughter said, "If you don't do what I say, I'm gonna get you fired." Stella's calm response was, "I don't work for you. I work for your parents." This child soon learned to curb her rudeness, too.

On one of the *Nanny 911* episodes, nine-year-old Joseph was hitting his sister. Mom and dad were not only equally rude, but also rewarded him with ice cream despite his appalling behavior.

DAD: Stop! Shut up! Joseph, get off her! You don't get it, do you?

CHILD: It's fun to beat up my sister.

MOM: He won't listen to me. I can't control him. You go tell your sister you're sorry.

CHILD: First they pick on me or call me names. And yell at me, so I just kill them.

MOM: Don't you say anything like that.

CHILD: I didn't say it.

MOM: You don't even think it.

CHILD: I didn't think that. La, la, la, la.

DAD Shut up! Okay, all right, you want some ice cream? Stop it. Act your age. How old are you?

CHILD: Ice cream.

DAD: How old are you?

CHILD: Ice cream.

DAD: He doesn't listen.

CHILD: Ice cream.

DAD: You're not listening to me. You're not going to get anything.

CHILD: Ice cream.

MOM: Joseph, just listen if you want ice cream.

CHILD: I want it, now!

MOM: I know you do.

DAD: You're not listening.

CHILD: I want ice cream before I die!

Once Nanny Stella established House Rules of no yelling and families respect one another, Joseph stopping hitting, starting asking properly for ice cream, and mom and dad learned to stop yelling and curb their own rudeness.

Manners are universal. They don't change, whether you're at home or going out. You can hardly expect children to be polite in public when they are allowed to be rude at home. As you do to prevent tantrums, prepare your children prior to going out. Tell them what kind of behavior is acceptable, and what the consequences will be if they act up.

At the Table

Once you sit down, it's time for manners. You use a napkin. Children eat with a fork or spoon. You keep your mouth closed when you chew. You never have the TV on. You never eat standing up. You never wolf down your food. You ask politely for someone to pass the salt.

If someone wishes to leave the table, he asks, "May I please be excused?" And he shouldn't expect that the answer is going to be yes, either, even if he's finished his food first.

Manners in restaurants are exactly the same as at home.

Thank-you Notes

"Thank you" isn't just a couple of words. It's part of the concept of graciousness. A thank you is an acknowledgement for a gift, a kind deed, or any similar behavior. Thank-you notes aren't about telling Grandma how much you liked your present. They're about understanding key concepts of gratitude, giving, and graciousness.

Thank yous are not so much about how you do them, but that they're done. If you're brutally honest and know you can't get around to thank-you notes, have to courtesy to say a special thank you. An email will do, but a handwritten letter is much nicer.

Make thank yous fun. Parents often have piles of their children's art work stashed away, so, with your child's permission and help, cut a painting into a heart, have the child write on the back. If they're learning to write, have them sign their name or initial, with a few words from you saying thank you. If they are too young to write, they can still color a note.

Thank yous are small gestures that always generate huge results—priceless feelings of happiness and acknowledgment.

MEDICINE TAKING

Few children like to take medicine, but it has to be done.

Medicine syringes assure that the proper dose gets inside, so use them whenever possible, instead of droppers or spoons for babies and toddlers.

For older kids, try putting medicine in a cup, then set it down and say, "I don't think you could possibly take that medicine when I'm not looking." If your children have seen *Mary Poppins* (where the medicine magically changes color), trying coloring the medicine and putting it in a special bottle. Many pharmacists have multiple flavors for prescription medicine, so let the child pick out the flavor.

But if you have to force a little mouth open and squirt the medicine down the hatch, so be it. Acknowledge that it tastes awful. Have a small candy or cup of favorite juice nearby and give it to the child immediately after the medicine to help cut the taste.

MONEY

As we said in the allowance section, money is to be earned, not given freely or used as bribes. Children should be taught the value of earning a dollar when they are small. Kids love to "pay," so let them help you give bills and coins to cashiers. This will teach counting as well as responsibility.

When you go toy shopping, determine a limit before you leave the house. If you tell your son that you have $20 to spend, don't buy a toy that's $21.95. He can make up the difference himself with money from his allowance next time.

Please note that some money conversations are not appropriate around children, and worrying about the bills is one of them. Keep money worries private, or you can create undue anxiety in children who'll start to fear that their electricity or phones will be shut off.

NOSE PICKING

Kids love to pick. Some love to eat the result. There's only one word for that: Yuck!

Next time someone starts digging for buried treasure, hand over two tissues. Say: "It's time to go fishing. Here's your rod and net. Use the rod to find the fish. Then put it in the net. When you're done, throw it in the ocean [the toilet or garbage can]."

Turning nose picking into a game makes it more fun for the child, less disgusting for you, and it won't escalate into a control issue with children sitting with fingers up their noses just to drive you crazy.

PACIFIERS

In England, we call pacifiers "dummies." No doubt because the parents who allow pacifier use to continue realize that they are the real dummies for creating little addicts in the first place.

Newborns are naturally orally fixated, which is why pacifiers are comforting to them. After six months, though, they should be less orally fixated, and pacifiers go from being comfort objects to being crying plugs.

We would prefer parents to not give babies pacifiers at all, but if you've started, try your best to take it away at the six-month mark. Babies who are starting to teethe will suck on fingers. Or you can give them teething rings or thick, rough washcloths to chomp on, anything but that dreadful piece of rubber.

We can't stand seeing pacifiers in public places. If you do let your babies continue with pacifier use, teach them to associate it only with naptime and bedtime, as Nanny Deb did with the loveys described on page 224. Take the pacifier away as soon as the babies wake up.

Taking pacifiers away from older children can go surprisingly smoothly, though, especially if they're prepared in advance—and especially if you do not project your own anxieties about the process onto your children. Discuss the fact that pacifiers are for babies, that there are babies who need them more, and you are giving the pacifiers to these babies on such and such a date. Then do it cold turkey. You can make a ceremony of it if your children like that sort of thing. One three-year-old we know announced that he wanted to throw his pacifiers in the ocean for the baby fish, so that's what he did. Another gave hers away to the Binkie Fairy.

Nanny Stella worked for a family where the three-year-old Seersha and four-year-old Theron were still addicted to their pacifiers. She explained to mom and dad that cold turkey would be the only possible method to deal with this problem, and that she would tell the children that the pacifiers had to go to the babies who needed them. She also told the parents that the first night was going to be tough, and they would have to stay strong.

NANNY: Okay, I'm going to give the pacifiers to the babies now.

DAD: You're a big boy.

CHILD: I don't want to be a big boy!

Theron had a total meltdown, and started coughing so much his parents feared he would throw up. Mom and dad both got upset.

NANNY: But what if you don't do anything for another five years, and then he still makes himself sick? If you don't take that pacifier away now, he's not going to be able to do that until he's seventeen. I honestly believe that he can do this and you can do it.

MOM: This is so harsh.

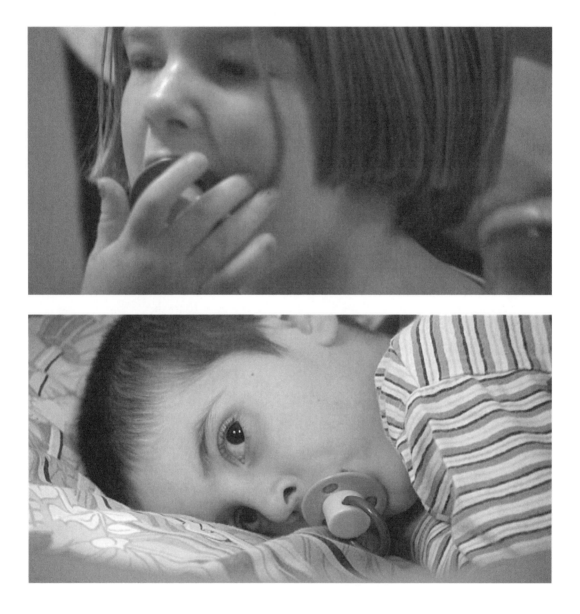

NANNY: What are you going to achieve if you give it back to him?

MOM: I'm just trying to find if there's a nicer way to do it.

DAD: There's no nicer way to do it.

MOM: I'm not putting my kids through this again.

NANNY   Honestly, this is nothing. But if you don't take them away, they are going to be there for a much longer timeframe.

The kids were up most of the night, begging for their pacifiers. And their parents kept saying, "They're with the babies. They're not here." It was very hard to hear Seersha and Theron crying, saying between sobs, "We're babies. We need them." The situation didn't improve much the next day.

MOM: Theron is the way he's been all night—angry, upset. And he has every right to be mad.

NANNY: But you two are the parents and you are in control. As upsetting as this is and as tired as you all are today, and as tired as the children are going to be, the end result is going to be no pacifiers. It will be easier tonight. If you're patient, you ultimately will succeed. You have to decide on the value of what you're looking for, and the price you are going to pay.

MOM: I know, but from my point of view, you came across really harsh last night. You haven't been in the situation that we're in right now.

NANNY: That's not true. And I think it's important for you to stop making excuses.

The second night was worse. Seersha was screaming for her pacifier and hitting her mother. But mom stayed firm. If she didn't, she'd fail herself and her family.

MOM: It's really hard emotionally. It pulls on my heart and I want to go in, but I know the right thing to do is stay out of the room.

Mom didn't give in, and instead took advantage of this chance to grow as a parent. And then, the kids went to sleep. The next night, they didn't ask for their pacifiers. They didn't cry or make a fuss. They just went to sleep.

When you realize cold turkey is the only way to go, you'll find the strength as this mom did to be firm and consistent, and soon pacifiers will be nothing more than a bad memory.

PICKY EATERS

Your toddlers may exist on the air diet—it seems that's all he or she will eat. Adventurous eaters can seemingly morph overnight into picky eaters, especially as toddlers or preschoolers. Their actual caloric needs are actually quite small at this age, so parents often unduly worry. If you are worried, or your child is losing weight, consult your pediatrician.

Make balanced, nutritious meals, and keep offering a healthy variety of foods. There should protein, carbohydrate, fruit, and vegetable on the plate. If they don't eat it, it's their choice, but it's got to be on the plate. At every meal. If your child doesn't eat much at all, just keep offering. Don't look at it as a waste if Melanie has turned her nose up at broccoli for the fifteenth time. She may like it on the sixteenth.

Here are a few tips.

- Do not offer multiple food choices. If you don't want to hear the answer, don't ask the question. You devise the menus, and children who say they won't eat pancakes because they want eggs can be told that eggs are on the menu for tomorrow, and today is pancake day.
- Feel free to involve older children in menu planning and cooking, if they have distinct preferences. Or set up a routine where Mondays you eat pancakes and Tuesdays you make a cheese

omelet. Let the kids help devise this routine and they'll be more likely to be pleased with it.

- Make what's on the plate look enticing. Use cookie cutters for fun shapes, or cut-up veggies for faces. Turn a broccoli spear into a forest, and so on. Food has to be eaten within a fixed time limit. If kids want to pick, fine. The plate is going to be cleared when dinner is over. No child ever died from starvation from missing one meal.
- Soda is not a food group. It should be banned from the house—for everyone. Decide if it can be a restaurant treat, then ask your server to water it down by half.
- Keep your own food preferences to yourself. Saying you hate cabbage is not going to entice anyone to try it.
- Try to keep fast foods and processed foods to a minimum. They're full of fat and salt and junk calories, and hardly encourage healthy eating.

PLAYMATES

Parents often worry when their children suddenly claim to hate their best friends. Try to stay out of it because what usually happens is that the kids are best friends again two days later. Allow your children to process their own feelings about friendships, and encourage them to talk to your about it.

Teach them how to deal with what they may perceive as rejection. If your son says, "Hi, I'm Phillip. Would you like to play?" to another boy who says no, tell Phillip, "Oh, he must be busy."

As children grow older, they can have a very hard time understanding how once-beloved friends can turn catty and clique-y, and shut them out completely. As with every tough emotion, let your child talk, acknowledge their hurt, and come up with alternatives that suit your child's personality, such as getting involved in other activities or spending time with new friends.

POTTY MOUTH, SWEARING, AND TALKING BACK

When they are little, kids find it incredibly hilarious to say charming things like, "You wiener-head, you poopy noopy, you doo-doo-face, peepee caca-doody!"

Resist the impulse to laugh. Children use potty talk and swear words to get a reaction and attention from their parents, or to feel grown up, or to keep up with their peers who get away with it and think it's cool.

Potty mouth can quickly escalate into swearing, talking back, and disrespect. Nanny Stella worked for a family where their four-year-old daughter called her mother a "fat f**k." So Nanny Stella handed this girl some toilet paper and told her that the House Rule was that swearing could only be done in the bathroom. By the time this girl climbed up the stairs to the bathroom, she was too tired to want to swear. Swearing at the toilet wasn't anywhere as much fun as swearing at mom.

Although you can't protect your children from hearing foul language in school or in public, you can protect them from what comes out of your mouth by stopping your own swearing. If you swear, and most parents do, apologize and give yourself the same consequence as your children—the loss of a marble from your marble jar. Come up with better words than your habitual cussing, such as "Fudge-ripple ice cream cone" instead "F**k." Use a dictionary to come up with some real zingers to replace the bad words—this will not only improve everyone's vocabulary, but also give you a private family joke to enjoy instead of swearing when your temper gets the best of you. You can learn to censor yourself and your children can, too.

If the use of bad words or talking back continues, make a House Rule about the consequences. Say, "We really need to stop using that word or there's going to be a consequence."

POUTING

Some parents put children in time-out for pouting, but we think that's a bit too harsh.

Children pout when they feel upset, resentful, or frustrated. Don't ignore the pout. Say, "You seem like you are upset," then sit down and talk to them about it. If they want to sulk, allow them to do so in a private place, such as their room, and tell them to take all the time they want to do so, then come back to talk to you when they're ready. You'll be happy to listen to them.

RESPECT

A word you've heard quite often on *Nanny 911* is "respect"—and with good reason.

Respect is not a feeling the way love is, something that exists and just is. Respect is a behavior that needs to be learned and earned, continuously.

Every family needs to have House Rules about respect. Respect for things and respect for each other. That means mom and dad have to show respect for their children's rooms, property, and, especially as children grow older, their need for privacy.

Equally important is the need to respect what people say. As ever, it all boils down to communication. Say what you mean, and mean what you say. Please realize that children can't respect rules without knowing what they are, or seeing them enforced, so do communicate the rules to your kids, and use them.

House Rules are to be respected whenever playmates or guests come over. Parents should post the House Rules in an easily visible place, and simply inform guests, of all ages, what they are. Children who are old enough to articulate the rules can tell their playmates.

There's no obligation to explain why these are your rules. Suffice to say that these Rules are for everyone.

Parents, you also need to respect their children as individuals. Don't make them be something they're not. Don't constantly compare them with siblings, or friends. Don't have unrealistic expectations. And certainly don't expect them to be your "friends."

As we discussed on page 77 in chapter 3, the Nanny Rule is respect is a two-way street. If you don't enforce House Rules of common courtesy, and if you indulge your child's every utterance, this can lead to children talking back, being rude, and demanding their own way.

Sometimes kids are unintentionally disrespectful when they're trying to be funny. In that case, in a non-aggressive way, simply ask them to repeat the "joke" in your presence. This may lead to a talk about the difference between cutting, hurtful humor, and silly, joshing humor. It's a much-needed lesson, as kids who are allowed to get away with disrespectful behavior at home often find themselves ostracized by their friends when they step out of bounds away from the house.

Disrespectful kids live in disrespectful homes. Unfortunately, when mom and dad have no respect for each other, they often make their feelings clear in front of their children, which can inflict incalculable damage over the years. How can a youngster be expected to behave with respect toward his friends, family, teachers, or any living creature when mom and dad don't know how to do it themselves?

It's not enough to say, "I'm your dad and you respect me because I said so!" That will not create respect. It will create an environment of fear, anxiety, and anger in children.

ROUGHHOUSING

Nanny Stella knew a family who once became entangled with an eight-year-old named Gideon. Gideon became famous in this family as the only child ever banned from their house. He didn't seem to understand that the back screen was a sliding door, and insisted on pushing each time he went through it. He thought nothing of leaving the gate open and couldn't imagine why we wanted the dog to stay in the yard. He picked the cat up off the table and pitched him across the kitchen. He tossed the couch cushions at another child one afternoon. Please and thank you were not in his vocabulary, even as he helped himself from the fridge.

Gideon's mom made excuses. "He is a boy, you know," she said, as his brother sailed down the stairway on a saucer sled and hit an already large dent in the wall. "This is the way boys are supposed to behave."

She supposed wrong.

We've seen plenty of kids who put the rough in roughhousing. Most of them were boys. Their pretend play would quickly escalate into knock-down, drag-out fights where kids could really get banged up. To be fair, parents and teachers who are used to more prim, stereotypically "girlie" behavior may not understand that boys are hard-wired for more exuberant physical play than girls may be. Boys who are never allowed to play with guns, for example, will still use their fingers to mock-shoot.

We're not doing any favors to boys if excuses make roughhousing acceptable, however. All children need to have limits about what constitutes rough play, and how to respect siblings or friends who do not want to wrestle on the couch with them. House Rules for roughhousing need to be explicit. If someone says, "Ow!" or "Get off!" the game ends. Explain the difference between roughhousing and hurting, and discuss limits on what can take place during wrestling sessions before they take place.

Roughhousing often gets out of control when kids are bored, or don't have enough outlets for their energy. If you can't get them outside to play—perhaps it's pouring rain, or you can't leave the house for other reasons—there are plenty of physical activities that are safe for both kids and furniture—jumping jacks, setting up an "obstacle" course with large boxes, dancing, exercise videos. Or try giving rewards such as marbles for the marble jar when you ask your rambunctious children to wash the floor or dust the shelves. That will give them something to do and help with the cleaning.

SHARING

What are a toddler's favorite words? "No!" and "Mine!"

Sharing is a tough concept for small children to learn, and we can't blame them. You certainly don't want to share your shiny new car or zippy new laptop with your best friends, and kids don't want to share their possessions, either, especially their special possessions. And isn't it amazing how all toys become special when a playmate is coming over?

One way to ease children into less-fraught sharing is to prepare them before a playdate. Say, "Jules is coming over today, so if there is something that you don't want to share, let's put it away now. You don't have to share your special toy, but anything else is for sharing." This shows your children that you respect their property and their special things, but that sharing is part of playtime, too.

Another important point to make clear is that a child's possessions are not going to leave with the playmate. Say, "Everything that is in our house does belong to you. When your friends come over, you share, but when your friends leave, it all stays here. School property stays in school. Mom and dad's desks and things stay at work." This will help lessen worries that toys may disappear.

Also try saying "We take turns in this house" instead of "You must share your toys." Taking turns often seems fairer to young children.

For siblings who always seem to want to play with certain toys at the same time, buying multiples can lessen the fighting. Have your kids choose their favorite color so sharing won't become an issue.

Set up a House Rule about respect for sibling property, too. Toddlers can certainly learn to keep hands off of a sibling's toys, no matter how tempting. Each child's toys should be off-limits to siblings, unless permission has been granted.

SIPPY CUPS

Sippy cups are great for transitioning or traveling, but when it comes to an everyday replacement for regular cups, we can't stand them. They may be convenient for mom and dad who don't want to clean up spills, but kids old enough to hold them can start drinking out of regular cups.

For parents worried about cleaning up spilled juice, make a House Rule about where cups are to be used. Why should children be able to drink all over the house? They can drink in the kitchen or dining room.

Children also can learn to start using glasses and yes, china plates, when they're dexterous enough to handle them. They can't use plastic forever.

We also worry about rampant juice consumption, which provides junk calories and can rot teeth. If your kids clamor for juice, wean them of the habit by gradually watering the juice down to a mixture of at least half juice and half water.

SNACKS

Nanny Deb worked in a house where the children were allowed to eat whatever and whenever they liked, helping themselves from the fridge and pantry, resulting in sugar-fueled rampages and tantrums.

She sat down with the boys and said, "Today we're going to have a big lesson about what's healthy for our bodies to eat, and what's not healthy for our bodies to eat.

"So this is what we're going to do. We're going to clean out the pantry and we're going to make a special place for the things that are not super-good for our bodies."

Then she put a lock on the pantry, much to the boys' shock.

Once the only snacks in the house were healthy ones, the boys gobbled them instead of junk, and their behavior improved immediately.

Keep healthy snacks on hand at all times, in places easily accessible to your kids. The cookie jar and stashes of candy should be out of reach.

Snacks we like are: Cut-up veggies, like carrots, peppers, broccoli, cherry tomatoes; fresh fruit; dried fruit (don't allow too much at once, as it may cause diarrhea); whole-grain crackers; peanut butter on whole-grain bread or crackers; string cheese; whole-grain graham crackers; or nonsugar whole-grain cereal.

Snacks to avoid: Anything with sugar as the primary ingredient, especially high fructose corn syrup; anything with white flour as the primary ingredient; juice; anything with trans-fats.

SORE LOSERS

The old cliché "It's how you play the game that counts" holds true. Teach children that playing the game is what's important, not winning or losing.

When you're playing a game—whether it's Go Fish, Monopoly,

or chess, don't let your child always win. Many parents do this, thinking that it will help build their child's self-esteem and teach the rule of the game. Children need to know how to lose.

Show them how to be a gracious loser. The easiest way to do this is to let them win a few times so they can see how you lose. Be a good sport and don't make a fuss. Say you sure had fun anyway, and maybe you'll win next time.

Families who have regular game night and play a lot of board games and card games tend to have the fewest sore losers.

SPANKING

Never spank! Spanking, or any other form of corporal punishment, or any form of threatening a child with violent bodily harm, is a major parental problem. We've seen parents smack beds with belts in a rage, or put hot red pepper flakes in their children's mouths. It's all about parents losing control. We certainly understand the overwhelming desire to smack a child who's been really, really naughty. But spanking merely reinforces that anger, and teaches children that violence is an acceptable solution to problems. Although you may have been spanked as a child, that does not mean that it's okay for you to spank your children.

Nanny Stella worked for a family where six-year-old Will liked to spank his three-year-old brother, with his parents' blessing yet. But why did a six-year-old feel compelled to discipline his brother? Where was mom? Vacuuming. Where was dad? Out in the back yard, tending to his pigeons. Will was acting like a parent out of desperation because his own parents had abdicated all responsibility for discipline in their home.

Once Nanny Stella told dad he had to become a more involved parent, and established House Rules for discipline, Will's need to spank his little brother stopped immediately.

What do you do if you slip? Put yourself in time-out. (See page

28 in chapter 2.) Then apologize. Set a good example even when you're not happy with your own behavior.

SPITTING

Spitting at people, things or on the floor is never allowed, and consequences need to be enforced.

It is okay, of course, for children to spit in the sink when they are brushing their teeth. Children who seem to be in a sudden want-to-spit phase can be encouraged to brush after every meal, to get it out of their system. That usually works like a charm. They can also spit out food—discreetly—into a napkin, if something tastes bad or unusual to them, for instance, or they've taken big a mouthful. Show them how to do it, and have lots of napkins handy.

STEALING

Stealing is like cheating: absolutely forbidden, with strictly enforced consequences. Plus, money to pay for any stolen item is an automatic allowance deduction.

Still, nearly every child pinches something at some point in their young lives. The impulse is nearly irresistible.

Children who steal should be taken back to the store (or whatever the location) with the stolen item, and apologize. For children over ten, if stealing continues, they should be taken to the police station for a stern talk. That may sound drastic, but it's better to scare children straight while their still young and impressionable than to see them arrested a year later.

Inadvertent stealing only requires a returned item with an apology (and no discipline). This is common in children who may not know that items on a counter near a cash register aren't giveaways. Nanny Deb once went shopping with a five-year-old, and he took a lollipop out of the store, and assumed she'd paid for it. When she saw him licking it, she informed him that it hadn't been paid for. He told her he was sorry, and they went back inside. She told the clerk that she hadn't paid for the lollipop, and wanted to pay for it now. It was the right example to set.

TATTLETALES

Tattling can be a huge problem, as kids by nature develop a code where they don't like to play with children who are perceived as tattletales. So children who have been taught to tell the truth find themselves caught between being truthful and being thought of as a snitch.

Preschoolers often come home with a daily litany of who did what to whom. If four-year-old Toby says, "Oliver hit me today and he pushed Randall and he pulled Lily's hair, too," say, "Thank you for telling me. Now how are you going to deal with this when someone hits you? Or do you want to figure it out together?"

You can also try, "That's interesting, but what about you? What did you do today?" Don't feed into the story and say, "Oh, poor Toby, Oliver hit you? What a naughty thing to do. Let me see your boo-boo." That will merely encourage tattling.

For older children who come running over and say, "Jackson just kicked me," say, "Thank you for telling me. Now go find a way to handle it." Then let them handle it.

If Jackson had been kicking the kids at school, say, "Jackson pushed you? Well, what did you do?" After you hear the answer, say, "What do you think you could do next time that could be better?"

This technique will enable your children to cope with tough situations, and show them that you trust their judgment.

If a child is being bullied, reporting it to you is not tattling.

Make that differentiation clear. For more about Bullying, see page 292 in chapter 12.

TELEPHONES

We've worked as baby nurses for new moms who were so used to always answering the phones that they pass us crying babies—or asked us to hold the phone to their ears while they nursed.

Parents will always face situations where the phone must be answered. Don't make this a habit, however. Use an answering machine or voice mail so you can screen calls. In most cases, your children's needs take precedence over answering the phone. Try making a House Rule that the phone is never answered during homework and dinner times. This is especially important if your time with your children is limited due to hectic work schedules.

By the way, we don't think it's appropriate for toddlers and preschoolers to answer the telephone, unless they are expecting a call from their friends, or you have given them permission to answer.

TERRIBLE TWOS . . . AND THREES . . . AND FOURS . . .

The same genius who came up with the term "quality time" doubtless came up with "terrible twos" too.

We don't think of any age is terrible, because if you follow our techniques and are consistent, it won't be. Instead of thinking as behavior as terrible or bad, look at the positives—your children are establishing their independence, learning to communicate, and testing boundaries. When you set appropriate boundaries that make children feel safe, what had been terrible behavior will stop.

Parents also refer to the terrible twos as an excuse for kids having a tantrum or public meltdown, instead of dealing with whatever caused the meltdown in the first place. The CRAB list will help you remember what toddlers need:

THE CRAB LIST

Consistency
Routine
Attention
Boundaries

Another technique that works well with toddlers is redirection. If a child is drawing on the table, say, "We don't draw on the table, use paper, please" and then give the child paper. Pushing the buttons on the DVD player? Push the buttons on this toy instead.

Don't forget that children who constantly hear you saying, "Oh it's just the terrible twos," will start to believe they are terrible. And act out to prove it.

TOILET TRAINING

Nanny Stella memorably worked for a family where the three-year-old, Jack, could only pee in the shower stall, or outside. He claimed the toilet was too scary, so his mom dutifully followed him out to the lawn and the garden.

"Look how you're watering the plants!" Mom exclaimed in delight, as Nanny Stella watched in appalled amazement. Later, mom confessed that she'd tried blackmail, bribery, yelling, and pleading, but nothing had worked. Nanny Stella explained that Jack had an extreme control issue, and was literally crying for attention. And his horrific outside peeing certainly got him a lot of attention.

Toilet/potty training is perceived as a tough issue, but it

shouldn't be. It's a natural process, one that will give children a huge sense of accomplishment. But it can only be done when both children and parents are ready—the children physically ready to understand how their bodies work, and their parents emotionally ready to stop taking responsibility for their children's need to go. More than anything, parents must absolutely be consistent with potty training methods, be patient and relaxed, have cleanser nearby to deal with accidents, and never force training on a child who isn't yet ready. (The average age for training is from two to three.)

When training is forced, or children aren't ready, these children soon figure out that the only two things they can control in their young lives are what they eat, and when and where they pee/poop. When they are getting enough attention from their parents, they also quickly learn that attention will be paid when they refuse to do what mom or dad says to do on the toilet.

Nanny Deb had a family where little Lauren was nearly four, and her mom was so desperate she resorted to the military approach—to scare the pee out of her daughter. Mom sat in the bathroom and yelled at Lauren until she went. Here, mom lit into Lauren during another hapless toilet session.

Mom: You're going to go for me this time, right? You've been saying that for a year. If you go in your pants, I'll make you sit in it for a while. Sit there and go. Are you going? Come on. Concentrate on the task at hand.

Child: No. I want to go poo-poo.

Mom: Well, it's not a matter of what you want to do—it's a matter of what you need to do. Could you even sit there and give it a chance?

Child: I can't do it.

Instead of nagging, Nanny Deb brought out the nanny pants, nice white panties for Lauren to try.

NANNY: Lauren, you get to wear the nanny panties. And nanny does not want to get pee-pee on her. So there's no pee-peeing on nanny.

Then Nanny Deb told Lauren she would get a marble for her marble jar for the first time she tried, even if nothing came out, and that she was in charge of when she went pee-pee. It was time to focus on positive, not negative, reinforcement. That was enhanced by the pee-pee dance.

NANNY: Okay. Let's go. Take off your diaper. You got your nanny panties. Say, pee-pee, we want to do the pee-pee dance.

CHILD: We want to do the pee-pee dance. I'm not ready.

NANNY: You're not ready? Okay. Good try. Yay!

CHILD: Do I get a marble?

NANNY You can get a marble because you had a good try. Remember, don't pee-pee on nanny, right?

CHILD: Right.

NANNY: And after you do pee-pee in the potty, you do the pee-pee dance. You go, Oh, I gotta go pee-pee. I got to go pee-pee. I got to go pee-pee, oh! Then you run to the toilet. Then, after you're through, you do the pee-pee dance. *I did pee-pee on the potty. I did pee-pee on the potty. I did pee-pee on the potty. Whoo!*

When Lauren soon went on the toilet, Nanny Deb gathered the family around.

NANNY: Okay, everybody, come on out to the hallway. Lauren did a poo-poo in the potty, a poo-poo in the potty!

After that, Lauren was trained. Here are some more potty training tips.

- Tell children that it's their choice. That you know they are big girls or big boys. That you know they can do it. But don't say in a way that's perceived as pressure or threatening, as in "Come on, just do it already, I know you can, or I'm not going to play with you." Positive reinforcement, please!
- Toilet training involves having accidents. Kids must have accidents to know what the sensation feels like, and to not like it. For this reason, avoid using pull-ups for daytime training. They hold a lot of water and make it too easy to get lazy.
- Never shame a child after an accident. Simply clean it up and give them new clothes to put on.
- Nor should children be afraid to have an accident. They don't want to pee on their nanny pants, or on Scooby Doo or Strawberry Shortcake, but if they do, have them help you put the underpants in the washing machine and don't make a fuss.
- Make training fun. Get boys a stool and have them aim at Cheerios or Fruit Loops floating in the toilet as a target.
- Involve your child in picking out the potty chair. Many kids are afraid of the toilet, and prefer to train on a chair until they're comfortable sitting on a potty ring inserted into the toilet seat. One mom we know bought her two-year-old son a potty chair painted to resemble a throne. He loved playing Prince Potty and was trained a week after the chair arrived.
- Reward a child, even if he or she has only tried and nothing came out. Have them get used to the feeling of sitting on a potty or a toilet, with no pressure to do anything.

- Watch for signs that the kids have to go—girls holding their legs together or boys holding their penises. Kids deeply engrossed in play often forget, and have accidents.
- During training, increase fluids to help them pee more frequently.
- We're not usually fans of character clothing, but if your son loves Superman, he'll be less likely to pee on his Superman underpants. Take your children on a special shopping expedition to buy their favorite character underpants. For boys, you can buy plain boxers or briefs and call them "daddy pants"; for girls, buy adorable panties and call them "mommy panties."
- Many parents like to train during warm weather where kids can run around naked. That's fine, but don't allow them to pee anywhere just because they're outside. Always try to find a bathroom. If there's not one nearby, use a drain or a private a spot in the woods or garden as you can find, and make sure your child knows this is a special exception to the rule. You can also find small portable toilets with disposable liners that will prevent accidents during outings when a child has first gotten trained.
- Pull-ups are fine at first for nights. After a few weeks of being trained during the day, start transitioning to pull-up free nights. You may want to wake your child to pee before you go to bed during this stage.
- Toddler boys learn more quickly when they can watch an older boy or dad do their thing (don't forget to shake those last few drops). Single moms of boys should try to find a trusted older boy to help their son with the basics.
- Children need to feel comfortable during training, and need undivided attention—in the house—to do so. There's no easy way around this. If you have to take vacation time to train your kid, that's what you'll have to do. It'll be worth it when training is mission accomplished.

TOYS

One new mom joked to us that her baby should have come home from the hospital with a lifetime supply of AA batteries and a small Philips screwdriver, to help with the battery compartments in the ridiculous amount of toys she'd been given.

No child needs expensive toys, or tons of toys, or six blue cars when one will do. Most would rather play with the box that a toy came in than the toy itself, or pots and pans and Tupperware. Generic toys such as blocks and boxes stimulate imaginative play. Battery-powered toys that only do one thing over and over do not.

If you do have an overwhelming amount of toys, try rotating them. Hide some of the toys in a childproofed closet, and bring them out when your child needs redirection. Don't bring out more than three toys at once when they're playing, as it's too much for them to focus on.

Some families like to make a House Rule that every time a new toy arrives, an old one has to go. Whatever you decide, make sure your children don't come to expect a toy every time you go to the mall. And never use toys to bribe children to behave.

TV

Television has become the world's most popular, consistent babysitter. As it is a passive activity, it turns people into inactive couch potatoes with weight problems and attention-span problems. It plants ideas in little kids' heads that fast-food meals are great because they come with toys . . . and that they simply must have that new ammo-blaster-super-soaker-mega-gun or Suzette-the-Super-Model doll or Cavity Crunchies cereal because they've seen the commercials fifty times in one week.

There's nothing wrong with a little TV. Some children's programming is fantastic. But as the saying goes, too much of a good thing . . . starting with multiple television sets in the house. Televisions should never be turned on simply for the sake of having it on as background noise. We don't think children under the age of twelve should be allowed to have a TV in their own room, where its use can't be monitored, and where disturbing images from the news can cause anxiety and nightmares (make a House Rule about when older children are allowed to watch the news, depending on their maturity).

Nor should TV ever be used as a means to lull children to sleep. Children need to learn how to calm themselves unaided by a machine. When it's bedtime, the TV goes off. Give your child the responsibility of saying, "I know it's eight-thirty and the TV has to go off."

Nanny Deb worked for a family that was addicted to TV, and it had become far too important to the children. That wasn't surprising, as their mom confessed, "Some people would think you would be overstimulated with the TV. But it kind of has a soothing effect on the children, I think, because they've become accustomed to it."

The House Rule about TV should be that it is a privilege, not a given. Time for watching TV needs to be earned. It is a reward for doing chores and behaving well. Dole out thirty minutes of TV at a time.

We wish TV could be banned altogether during the school week, but we know that isn't realistic. Sometimes parents simply have to get things done and let their children watch cartoons or a video. A short time is fine. Five hours is not. Our ideal after-school program would be homework, reading, playing, chores, and interacting with your siblings and family. We never allow the TV to be on in the morning, as it becomes impossible to get the kids to the breakfast table and out the door to school on time. If you simply must have a few minutes to yourself in the morning, restrict TV use to the few minutes after breakfast, when the children are set and ready to go.

Once you start to restrict TV watching, you may be surprised at how much more time you have to spend with your family, playing together and having fun. Let your children come up with some creative ideas to replace TV shows with games of their own devising.

VIDEO GAMES

We've been around kids who can't have a conversation with us because they're so deeply engrossed in their Gameboy. Or who couldn't tie their shoelaces, but had phenomenal manual dexterity on video-game joysticks. Our preference would be for no video games, but that's not realistic, especially in homes where older siblings play games, or mom or dad love to play with their children. And hand-held video games can be sanity savers for mom and dad on long trips.

As with TV, video games must be monitored and restricted. Their use is an earned privilege, not a given. This is especially important for older kids, as some of the games are extremely violent, racist, and offensive.

Decide upon a House Rule for the earning of video game playing time. During the school week, once your children have earned their time, give them the choice of a half-hour of video games or TV, not both.

WEANING

We often wean babies and toddlers off their bedtime bottles around age one only to find that parents have given them back. One family Nanny Stella worked for went away on a trip, came home, and announced, "There's bad news, he's back on the bottle."

She said, "He's back on the bottle with you. He's not back on the bottle with me."

Never use bottles or sippy cups as comfort objects. (See sippy cups on page 251.) Kids dragging their bottles or cups around, sipping juice all day or milk all night, fills their tummies with junk calories and can seriously damage their teeth. We know small children who've had to have baby teeth root canals under general anesthesia due to bottle rot. It is a very real problem, one that should never start in the first place.

For more about pacifiers, see the section on page 240.

WHINING

Why do kids whine? Because their needs aren't being met. Once you give your children the comfort, respect, and acknowledgment of what they're looking for, whining and tantrums will stop. Once you make it safe for your children to use their words and talk about their feelings, they aren't going to repress these feelings and then blow up later over something that's seemingly inconsequential.

The children we look after learn very, very quickly that whining will not work with us. We teach them how to use their words to express themselves. And if they don't use their words, they don't get what they want.

For more on whining, see chapter 4, page 114.

YELLING

As we mention in chapter 2, Nanny Stella worked for a family where dad came up with this zinger: "To me it's not yelling. It's talking loud."

Children learn what they live. They don't yell unless they hear yelling. Plus they learn to yell when it becomes the only way to get your attention.

Obviously they'll pick it up on the playground and in school, areas where you can't control other children's behavior, but your House Rule is no yelling, and we talk nicely to each other without shouting.

Teach the difference between an inside voice and an outside voice. Children naturally shout when they're playing. That's fine— it isn't the same as yelling in your face to get you to listen.

11 CHAPTER OUTSIDE THE HOME

CAR TRIPS

Most states have mandated that children be restrained in back-seat car seats and booster seats until they reach eight years of age or eighty pounds. Newborns and babies less than twenty pounds should be in rear-facing car seats in the back seat.

Children traveling in cars without proper car seats or sitting in the front seats aren't just matters of breaking the law. Parents who allow this are risking their children's lives, both from accidents and the car's air bags, which can save an adult's life but prove fatal to children.

On one memorable *Nanny 911* episode, a family of rambunctious boys refused to stay in their seats on a trip to the store. Nanny Stella suggested that dad bring the car seats into the house, so that the boys could play in them, get used to them, and "claim" them. Their mom scoffed, but the boys were in their proper seats in a flash.

Make your child's car seat *his or her own*. When they're old enough, have your kids help you clean the inside of the car, using a hand-held vacuum, including their car seats. Let them be responsible for the seats.

In addition, make the inside of the car a friendly environment,

so kids know there's always something to play with. Stash a selection of toys near the car seats—make them special toys that they can play with only when they sit in the car seat.

If your baby or child isn't that used to a car seat (perhaps you live in a large city and don't own a car), have them get used to one gradually. A long car trip with a child unused to being restrained is a recipe for disaster.

CLASSES

In moderation, classes can be fantastic opportunities for children to grow, learn, use their bodies, and make new friends outside of school. They can also have horrific consequences, as we've seen many families where the children's social lives take more scheduling than the parents. Too many classes can become overwhelming. Kids are so busy running to classes that everyone becomes seriously stressed. Homework, which should have priority, doesn't get done. Mom and dad spend more time stuck in traffic than they do playing with the kids. Taking four different children to four different classes on four different nights and still trying to make a healthy dinner isn't feasible. No one's happy.

The scheduling of after-school activities has to work for the entire family, not just the kids clamoring for tae kwan do or gymnastics. If mom becomes chauffeur, who's going to properly look after the toddler, who's stuck in the car for hours? What if money is tight and it's hard to pay for the classes?

Mom and dad need to reevaluate priorities. First, you've got to be bluntly honest with yourself. Is this about you or about your child? Is it beneficial for this child? Does the five-year-old really want to piano lessons or do you? Are your kids set on acting or do you want them to be in commercials? If the class really is right, what about logistics? How will the class fit into the family schedule?

For older children who say they really, really want to go to ballet, take them to a sample class and see what it's like. Then have this conversation: "If you want to go, there are twelve classes, which means you will be coming here for twelve weeks, and I will pay for it. But you are going to have to follow through, and you won't be changing your mind after four classes and telling me you really don't want to do this anymore." Children are capable of taking responsibility for finishing what they started.

Sometimes, of course, children become disenchanted with a particular class and don't want to go anymore. Perhaps they feel as if they aren't good at what they're learning, or they have missed a class or two and feel like they can't catch up. Talk to the teacher in private and make sure nothing untoward is happening, such as bullying from a classmate, or shame about a body during a sports class. And talk to your child, asking gently what the problem is. If your child is genuinely upset, not just bored, say, "This class costs a lot of money, and you made a commitment to go. If you still don't want to go back it's really going to take a lot for me to sign you up for something else. So here's what we're going to do. We'll go in and sit together and watch the class for ten minutes. Once you feel like you're ready, you can go to your regular place. After the class, if you still don't like it, I promise you that you won't have to go back."

This technique will alleviate the stress and worry about having to keep going, and many kids end up liking the class again and finishing the course.

Children over the age of eight or so should also be responsible for telling the teacher why they aren't coming back to class, either in person or in a letter. Again, this teaches responsibility for decisions, as well as courtesy for a teacher's work.

As for joining a team such as little league baseball or youth soccer, which often means a tougher schedule, we suggest that children know exactly what's involved physically and mentally. Will they be able to follow through? Unless they are sick, they're going to have to show up on Saturday mornings and be on a team. Even if they don't fully play, they still must show up. Being part of a team means supporting your teammates and not letting them down.

DAWDLING

Children just love to dawdle. Trailing a toddler exploring every nook and cranny on the street is exhilarating—at first. It's no joy when you're late or dawdling becomes an easy way to get negative attention from mom or dad.

Nanny Deb once took care of Erik, a three-year-old boy, and they used to walk on a bumpy road to the local subway station the mornings to catch the train to preschool. He was a dillydallying little boy, so to speed things up, she used to sing him songs. When she saw a bump ahead, she'd tell Erik to run, and as soon as they got closer to the bump, they'd sing "The Grand Old Duke of York." As they walked over the bump, they'd stop and sing "At the top of the hill," then keep going. Erik never knew he was being hurried along; there was no whining; and they were always on time for school. (To this day, his nickname is "Grand Old Duke"—and he's twenty-four.)

Use your imagination to help speed your kids along without blowing your cool. Try having a running race. Say "Betcha can't catch me," then let your child "catch" you after jogging just out of reach halfway down the block.

It is often a struggle to diminish the dawdling at home, however. Children can become so wrapped up in what they're doing that they're unable or unwilling to shift gears and move on to the next thing, especially if they have to stop one activity and leave the house.

Make your warnings specific, and be sure your child has actually heard them. This means giving the warning right next to them, at their level, and waiting for an acknowledgment. Say, "We have to leave in ten minutes, so, in five minutes I will give you a warning. When I come in with my coat and hat it will be time for you to start getting ready."

For older children who love to read, it's hard to discourage that activity, but sometimes a book needs to be put down. Try saying: "You can read the rest of the chapter now, then two more after dinner." With fantasy play, what works is, "You can dress up all your dolls now, then leave them on your bed so when we come back you can finish your game."

DOCTOR AND DENTIST VISITS

No one likes to go to the doctor or the dentist, especially kids. Many pediatricians have waiting rooms full of toys and books, but they're also full of sick kids. Worse, the exam rooms are often full of crying kids. Try taking your children along on your own visits to the doctor or dentist during routine exams. It's a good lesson for all of you—parents must hide their own anxieties in front of their children, not project them, and demonstrate how everyone needs to go to the doctor or dentist, in order to keep our bodies healthy.

Focus on the positive. Take a beloved stuffed animal in the exam room, and have the doctor examine it first. Then you can say, "Bear was very brave, and it didn't hurt at all when the doctor looked in his ears. He loves his new Band-Aid." If your child ask why the baby started screaming, tell the truth. Say, "Maybe she needed to get a shot, and she doesn't have to words to say she didn't like the pinch, and that's why she cried." Try to focus on what you're going to do and where you're going to go after the doctor visit.

Never lie about shots. As much as it might start a bout of crying, it is still better to prepare children when you know shots might be required.

When medicine is required, try to make taking it a game, but make your children aware that they have to take it to get better, in the correct dosage etc. No is never an option when it comes to medicine. (See medicine taking on page 239 in chapter 10.)

HIDING

Hide and seek is fine outside, as long as you know where your children might be hiding at all times. Teach your children that hiding from you on purpose is dangerous, and that it has consequences, and will not be tolerated. If you are calling their name and need to know where they are, they have to answer. Demonstrate beforehand what your answer-me-now voice is, and let them know you mean business.

OUTINGS

We've all seen children have complete and total meltdowns in public, their parents beet-red and furious. Most likely, you've said to yourself, "Thank goodness that isn't me and mine."

There's no reason to dread outings once you've established basic House Rules. Your children should understand that actions have consequences, and spell out what the consequences will be during outings. They will also understand how to control yelling and screaming, that whining doesn't work, and know that misbehavior will result in a public time-out, or them being taken outside if they don't calm down. They will use their manners. They will know that *I want* does not mean *I need*.

Always prepare your children before the outing, no matter where you're going, whether the trip is two hours or two weeks. Never leave the house without preparing *yourself* with a nanny bag (see sidebar), fully stocked with snacks, little toys, books, and a change of clothes for the kids.

Make outings interesting, so your children will always look forward to them. Listen to audio books or music. Sing songs together, especially rounds such as "Row, Row, Row Your Boat." We love to play games, especially those that improve visual skills, memory, and storytelling imagination. Some are as follows:

- I wonder where they're going. Invent an entire story around people you see.

- Let's find an animal. The first person to see a horse, for example, gets a marble for the marble jar.
- I Spy
- Nonsense stories. Start with "I see a hippo walking down the street, and he was carrying an umbrella. . . ." The next person has to keep the story going.
- Ghost stories, for older kids.

Travel and being away from routine is tough on kids, even on long-awaited vacations. Parents underestimate how tough it is, so in this case we relax the rules and let kids have more time than usual with toys that are usually restricted. A candy bar won't hurt either. For longer outings and vacations, bring new toys or toys rotated from the stash in the closet so they seem new, as well as sticker books, crayons and drawing pads (Magnadoodles are great because there's no paper), or new paperbacks. Kids old enough to use hand-held game players or watch DVDs on a portable player can have unlimited use on train, plane, and car rides, although we still don't allow *constant* use. Get new mini travel games and movies to watch, with a separate headset for each child. Stash them in new, small, travel-size child backpacks to make everything easier to find. With new toys and games to occupy them, kids will see outings as a treat, not an endurance marathon, even if it feels like that to you.

Be sure to feed your kids during outings, too. It's very easy to forget that they can't go as long as you between meals—or between rest-stops. Whining and fighting can start when kids are hungrier than they are tired.

Try to keep your routine as close to your regular schedule as possible. Use the same drawers for clothes in the hotel dresser. Bring a small pillow from home, as well as the all-important loveys. If feasible, schedule long flights or rides for nap time or overnight, or try to skip a nap so that children readjust to time changes more easily.

The more organized you are, and the more you have planned ahead for all the kids' needs, the more enjoyable your outing will be. But even if rules are relaxed and vacations are far more flexible than usual household routines, it doesn't mean that you should avoid *any* routine. Bedtime should still be treated the same way. This makes children feel safe even when they're far from home.

THE NANNY BAG

Nannies always have snacks in their bags. We've gone many places where we end up feeding other hungry children because the other parents have forgotten the snacks.

We always like a change of clothes, no matter the child's age, just in case. Stash them in large labeled garbage sacks with handles. We keep baskets in the back of our cars with clothes, snacks, and other supplies.

For babies, in a smaller insert bag, pack a bottle, formula (if needed), four diapers, wipes, pacifiers (if used), diaper cream, disposable bags for soiled diapers, antibacterial hand sanitizer, powder, one full extra outfit plus one shirt for spit-up, two cloth diapers for over the shoulder, burp cloths, bibs just in case, and empty Ziploc bags.

For older babies, add jars of baby food, toys, cloth books, teething ring, wet wipes, hand sanitizer, and empty Ziploc bags.

For toddlers, add diapers or pull-ups if not toilet trained, disposable bags for soiled diapers, wipes, diaper cream, full change of clothes, healthy snacks such as cereal, raisins, string cheese, mini-bottles of water, wet wipes, and hand sanitizer. You can even add tiny toilet rolls and seat covers (available at drugstores). Wet washcloths are nice for the beach or in hot weather.

Always refill the bag as part of your daily routine *before* you go to bed.

PLAYGROUNDS

When your children's friends come to your house for playdates, they follow your House Rules. But this is hard to enforce when children are playing outside in a public or school playground. Especially as it's not appropriate to discipline other people's kids, no matter how bratty they're behaving.

You can still make other House Rules that apply to outdoor play. One rule should be that children do not touch other people's toys until they find out whom they belong to. One they know, they can ask permission to play with it. Likewise, teach your children to tell others that their permission must be asked for and given before one of their toys can be played with or shared.

For grabbers, take the toy back gently, and try to offer an alternative. Try saying, "I'm sorry you can't play with it now because Harry's playing with his tractor, but if you'd like to play with his bucket and spade you can." We recommend that you bring more toys than your children can play with, so sharing doesn't become an issue. It's hardly the children's fault if they've been taken to the playground without any toys.

Although it's not polite to reprimand or scold someone else's children no matter how gently you do so—or how badly you want to scream at their parents after Spoiled Sam grabs your son's truck for the umpteenth time—it is always appropriate to say, "I'm sorry, you can't have that," and take it back. Often, children who are assertive and confident at home or school freeze when strange children are rude in playgrounds, and they don't know what to do except get upset.

When older kids are running around being aggressive towards your younger kids, it's okay to say, "I know I am not your parent, but I am an adult and I want to keep you safe, so I am going to take away that stick and ask you to play carefully." We often do this at playgrounds when older children start interacting with our younger charges after we ask the older kids where their parent or caregiver was, and they didn't know. This is not a reprimand—it's a safety issue for all the children involved.

For children old enough to do this, help them confront other children who have taken toys or pushed them, etc. Tell them to go back and say, "It wasn't okay that you pushed me." For children who are too scared to do so, we help them. We'll take them by the hand, go back to the offending child, and say to our children, "Did you tell him that wasn't okay? It was my body and you pushed me." This is highly empowering for small children who need to learn to assert themselves in a non-threatening, matter-of-fact manner as they grow.

If someone else's child is totally out of control, we've stood up and asked who the person in charge of this child is, and calmly informed them of what happened. Don't be too embarrassed to report a violent incident. If it continues, however, without any correction from the parent or caregiver, it's better to hover a bit closer so the violent child gets the message that you will not allow any harm to come to your child.

RESTAURANTS

You can hardly expect young children to sit still in a nice restaurant for an hour while you eat, yet parents do this all the time—then wonder why patrons, whose plans for a lovely, quiet evening have been ruined, are glaring at them with murder in their eyes as you leave with your fussing children in tow.

As with all outings, prepare children for where you're going and how you're going to expect them to behave. Don't take children with short attention spans to elegant restaurants with slow service. Be fair to your children and to other diners and don't expect a child who's never sat at the table at home for more than twenty minutes to last for more than an hour in a restaurant. Choose child-friendly restaurants. If you aren't sure, make a quick call to find out.

Order food and drinks for them as quickly as you can. If possible, take a little walk around the restaurant, even if only to the bathroom, before the food arrives. When they've finished, give them crayons or markers and coloring or dot-to-dot books, or small toys for quiet play, to occupy them while you eat. If you're strict about no toys at the table as a House Rule at home, either make a new Rule for restaurants, or allow only crayons and markers, and books. Or supply the children with special toys only for play in restaurants, similar to the kind of toys you keep in the car for play while in car seats. As soon as the food arrives, all play materials are put away until the meal is finished.

Manners in restaurants are the same as at home.

Nanny Deb once took a two-year-old girl, Eva, to a restaurant. Eva was very rude to the server when she was given milk, and she wanted lemonade. "I want lemonade." she shouted, and her yelling soon escalated into a near-tantrum. Nanny Deb told her, "We do not speak to the servers like that. That is very rude. You need to stop and listen to me." She took Eva outside, and told her that she needed to calm down, and when she was calm enough to listen, Nanny Deb was ready to talk.

After two minutes, Eva said, "Okay." Nanny Deb said, "You shouted at our server, and that was rude, so if you want lemonade I need you to walk back with me into the restaurant. I need you to sit at the table and I need you to apologize to the server and tell her that you did not like milk and you would really like some lemonade."

Back in went Eva and Nanny Deb. Eva apologized, and they had a fine meal together.

Don't ruin your dinner merely to placate a child. If a child wants to leave before everyone is ready, say, "I know you're ready to leave and you've been very patient. You can play with your crayons for another ten minutes while we finish, or you can join in the conversation." If they act up, try to get a chair from another table, and tell them that they are being distracting, and to sit there for a few minutes.

If frustration or upset escalates into a tantrum, tell the child that you are not going to tolerate this behavior, but always start with a time-out first, in a place where the child can try to calm down. Follow these steps.

1. Tell the child that if he or she doesn't calm down, he or she is going to have a time-out. Then count to five as your warning.
2. Take the child to a quiet spot for one minute per year of age.
3. Ask if the child is ready to discuss the matter calmly.
4. Listen to the child, and then thank him or her for talking. Take him or her back to the table.
5. Go back to what you were doing.

Only if the child is unable to calm down do you tell him or her that you are leaving, and then follow through, with your tantruming child in tow. We've walked out of restaurants before the meal has been served, with six siblings in tow, when one child is acting impossible, and then gone back in to eat when the child has calmed down. Be sure to inform your server that you are taking a break for a few minutes, and you'll be back soon. With other children around, the tantrum usually ends quickly.

RUNNING OFF

Thinking your child is lost is cause for heart-stopping panic. It's our job to keep the children in our care safe, especially when we go out in public.

Toddlers love to run off—there's so much to see and explore, and they're too young to understand possible dangers. Older kids might be aware of dangers, but they too can easily get distracted. They certainly can understand that they're not to get out of the car until you've told them it's safe.

Get in the habit of playing games, starting with toddlers, to reinforce the House Rule that running away is not acceptable, and that mom or dad or the caregiver needs to know where the children are at all times. If they do run away, the consequences must be immediate. *You must leave and go home.* If toddlers don't listen, leave and tell them you won't be coming back.

Among the running-off games that children love are Red light, Green light. Give the kids some leeway with distance. Let them start a few steps away from you. Red means stop, green means go. Or try Stop, Look, and Listen, and Statue Freeze. Little kids just love to "freeze" at whatever they're doing, and if you play this game whenever you go out, it will help teach them how to stop at dangerous street corners or in parking lots. One mom we know gives her kids imaginary "speeding tickets" if her kids run too far ahead of her when they're out for a walk. The "speeding tickets" brings the focus back to mom and helps the kids to come back and walk together as a family.

Toddlers need to be trained not to run off in stores. We've often used what's called a harness in England, and a leash here. It goes over the child's chest, and we hold onto a handle or strap. The child has plenty of slack to move around and explore within arm's reach. Sometimes we've been criticized for "putting a child on a leash," but that's usually from someone who's never had a child—and certainly hasn't had a child try to run off. We simply reply to critics that trying to keep our children safe is at least as important as our dogs.

For older children, decide upon a family meeting place before getting out of the car in case you accidentally get separated. This could be in front of McDonald's on the second level at the mall. Do not set a family meeting place near an outside door. If your children panic, tell them to find a mother with children and ask her for help. (For more information, see stranger danger, on page 303 in chapter 12.)

For trips to places where it's easy for older kids to get separated, such as malls or amusement parks, we like to use long-range walkie-talkies or two-way radios. If parents can't see their children, they can use the radios to find them and touch base. Two-way radios also work well for parents who split up and each take some of the children. Even big kids are thrilled to have their own radios, and use them responsibly. They can easily hook on belts so they won't get lost. And then your children won't get lost, either.

SHOPPING

As with restaurants, you need to prepare your children before going shopping. This is especially crucial when shopping will be in any area close to a toy store. Children somehow have built-in homing devices leading them straight into temptation.

If you have prepared your children, you will prevent the whining, pleading, and begging that happen when they see toys. Before you leave the house, state what is being bought that day. Say, "Today we are not buying any toys." Children will doubtless ask anyway, but that's what children do. Don't give in.

If there are toys in a large store and passing by them is inevitable, you can say, "Today we are not buying any toys. But you can look for five minutes. If you see something you really like, let's put it on your holiday/birthday Wish List." Adding an item to a Wish List today is a good way to distract children, as it keeps them occupied with thinking about the toy while knowing that receiving it may be a possibility in the future. Older children can keep an actual Wish List and take it with them during shopping expeditions.

Don't get into the habit of buying children something every time you go shopping, even if it's only a piece of bubble gum, or this will become a very hard habit to break.

When you go grocery shopping, ask the children to help you. Tell them what's on the list. Ask toddlers to tell you when they see the milk, or the apples. Have them count as you put items in the basket. Give older kids their own lists so they can comparison-price different items, and this will teach math skills, too. Stick to your list, as well, to set a good example.

Be sure to take snacks with you when shopping (See The Nanny Bag sidebar on page 277). Many shopping meltdowns are caused by simple hunger, especially once kids start smelling food. Never take a child to the supermarket right before lunch or dinner. It's okay to snack on a healthy boxed item you are buying if you've forgotten a snack, and this will make demands for checkout candy less likely, too.

Most of all, plan shopping expeditions for times when the kids aren't exhausted. It's not fair to expect a tired child to trail you around. If there's a tantrum, follow the steps in the restaurant section, on page 279.

Be organized. Always use a list. Try to go off-hours if at all possible. Better yet, try to avoid taking the kids with you if you know it triggers tantrums. Buy their clothes yourself, have the kids try them on at home, and return them if they don't fit or the kids hate them. The more you plan before you leave the house, the less of a hassle shopping will be.

VISITS TO FAMILY AND FRIENDS

When in Rome do as the Romans do, as the saying goes—with preparation. Although you can't expect friends and relatives to childproof their homes before your visit and explain that other people have their own House Rules. If Auntie Ruth collects bone china teapots, and her rule is no touching the teapots, then inform your children in advance. Parents should improvise if at all possible. A child will be less likely to touch (and break) Auntie Ruth's adored teapots if they can bring their own plastic tea set to play with at Auntie Ruth's house. And Aunt Ruth won't be offended if you call her beforehand and ask that anything especially dangerous or breakable be removed from the reach of little hands before you get there.

It can often be difficult for children to visit relatives when there is underlying family tension; or when relatives may be unpleasant, rude, or thoughtless. We believe in Families for Life, but it is tough when families are having serious problems. You're stuck with your family even when you're not getting along with other family members. Our general rule is that if parents are uncomfortable visiting relatives, for whatever reason, certainly do not bring your children along. Children should never become privy to adult problems in family disputes.

For visits such as birthday parties, do the same thing: set the boundaries before leaving. When taking your two-year-old Carlton to a birthday party, it is perfectly normal for Carlton to want to open all of the birthday boy's presents. Tell Carlton in advance that it is not his birthday, and he will only be allowed to open presents if he's asked for help. If you don't allow your kids to eat cake, remove them from the party before cake time; if your child has a nut allergy, remember to bring safe snacks and treats from home.

This dad sat down with his boys before going to a neighbor's barbeque, and stated his expectations.

DAD: I want to talk to you. When we go to that party, we're going to remember our manners. All that things that Nanny Deb taught us. Remember: please, and thank you, brothers for life, communication, okay? Those are all going to be very, very important today. And I know you guys can do it because you've been doing great.

His formerly out-of-control boys were thrilled to make their dad proud, and to live up to the expectations. They behaved so well, that his neighbors began to wonder if their own children could use a little bit of the *Nanny 911* techniques on their kids, too.

12 TOUGH ISSUES

ACCIDENTS

Accidents happen, even to the most cautious children and parents. Parents and caregivers should be CPR-trained so that they can click into emergency mode and deal with a serious accident as quickly as possible, *without* panicking. Although your child being hurt is one of the most terrifying situations a parent may have to cope with, it is imperative that *you* remain calm. A hurt child can panic and go into potentially lethal shock if a parent is unable to cope.

Keep a first-aid kit in an easily accessible spot in the house and make sure everyone in the family knows where it is. A list of emergency numbers, such as local poison control, should be prominently posted, either on the refrigerator or near a phone. If you're not sure how bad an injury is or what to do, never move a child. Call 911 first, then follow instructions. It's better to be safe and ask for help than to worry about "bothering" your pediatrician or paramedics.

If you have to take your child to the emergency room, tell your children that you are going to a good place with a lot of doctors who are there to fix accidents and make people feel better. If at all possible, try to take a bag of toys to keep children occupied whenever possible, especially if there is going to be a wait to see a doctor.

Children should be taught to call 911 as soon as they're old enough to understand what an emergency is.

ADOPTION

Adoption is a marvelous way to build a family. Most adoptees grow up to be well-adjusted and secure, with positive attitudes about their early circumstances. Several older adoptees we know always celebrated their adoption day with their families, so that's something we like to do with the adopted children we look after, as well.

As with all topics dealing with love and security, you need to talk to your children honestly, and make it clear to them that you will always be there for them if they need you. As adoptees grow older, they can struggle with their losses, and mourn for biological relatives they never had a chance to know.

Adopted children should be told the truth, in age-appropriate language. When younger adoptees ask about babies growing in tummies, you can say, "You didn't grow in my tummy, but you grew in my heart," which is certainly true!

Some adoptive parents say, "Your birth mother loved you so much she gave you up to have a better life." If the birth mother is known, as in an open adoption, that may be true. If the birth mother's circumstances are not known, we don't advocate lying to spare your child the painful truth—whether about adoption, or any topic. You can just as easily say, "I am sorry I don't know exactly what happened, but I feel in my heart that you were loved."

We also believe that the "she loved you so much" scenario often plants fear in adoptees. Adoptive parents and siblings, who are also "loved so much," could just as easily not want to or not be able to keep the adoptees any more, either.

Adoptees also have to deal with intrusive and painful comments. Children are naturally curious about those who are "different," and they can taunt and tease. One of the best resources is the *W.I.S.E. Up! Powerbook* by Marilyn Schoettle, which teaches children how to walk away with dignity, as well as talk about their adoption in a format that encourages parents to read along, and play-act different scenarios.

Remember, adoption is not your story. It belongs to your adopted child, and it's his or her decision to make about when to share this information. Children will model their responses after yours. For parents who've adopted transracially, such as Caucasians adopting from China, racial differences are obvious, inviting comments from strangers—some well-meaning and some just plain rude.

If a question has crossed the line, such as "Where's she from?" or "Are they real sisters?" try not to answer rudeness with more rudeness, as hard as that may be. Throw the question back at whoever asked it by saying, "Why do you ask?" Or ignore it politely by saying, "I'm sorry, but that's a very personal question. Have a good day!" Or, "Excuse me, but we do not discuss our family with total strangers. Goodbye!" This will empower your children to deal with intrusive questions about any topic as they grow older, too.

We suggest that adoptive parents familiarize themselves with the unique attachment issues of adoption, and incorporate the adoptee's culture, if transracially adopted, as best you can into new family traditions. There are many books available on attachment, and there are excellent resources on the Internet, especially support groups on Yahoo! and other search engines.

BABYSITTERS AND NANNIES

We've met plenty of families who've rarely if ever used babysitters for their children. While such parental devotion certainly is ad-

mirable, it's equally cause for pity. Parents need to go out for date night to keep their marriage strong. Children need to be exposed to a wide range of other grownups—teenage babysitters, grandparents, other relatives, older babysitters, nannies, au pairs, mothers' helpers, or neighbors—to expose them to other personalities. We'd hate to be the sheltered four-year-old taken to preschool for the first time, and left to fend for him or herself in a room full of other children who've already had far more exposure to other adults.

For parents who've had trouble using babysitters, start slowly. Years ago, Nanny Stella met a mom who'd never left her child with anyone, not even a family member. Nanny Stella told her to do it in five-minute increments. The first day that grandma comes over, step out of the room for five minutes. The next time, do ten. Gradually get to the point where you can not only leave the room, but the house as well. Parents must get over their own anxieties about leaving their children. We know it's hard, but your children will thank you for it!

We've also seen the other extreme, and have been hired, through an agency, by families where the parents have literally left us alone with their children after only spending a few minutes with us. This is equally difficult for children. They need to be prepared when new faces are coming over.

Take the time to prepare your kids that this is a babysitting night, and they're going to have a good time with whomever. Ask them to assist you in giving the babysitter the House Rules, which is a must. Leave some room for an adjustment time—don't run out the door the minute the babysitter arrives. Tell the babysitter if there are any special exceptions to the House Rules that night, such as extra ice cream, a video, or extra playtime. That helps make the adjustment go a lot smoother, and makes babysitting night more exciting.

The easiest way to introduce a new sitter is to spend some extra money, if possible, and have the sitter come over and stay with the children on an afternoon or night when you're home. Then the children know this person is safe, can get used to his or her personality, do fun things, and not be scared the next time.

It also helps to use regular sitters. If your Date Night is on Fridays, make it a ritual where mom and dad go out, and Babysitter Betsy comes over. Everyone gets to stay up for an extra hour and eat popcorn in the living room. Then your kids will look forward to mom and dad leaving as babysitter night will be treat night, and you can relax knowing that they're in capable hands.

Parents often spend more time researching what new car or computer to buy than they do researching what nanny or babysitter or daycare to choose. Be a savvy consumer. Use reputable agencies, and always check several references to make sure that stories match. But although references are crucial, so is your instinct. If you don't feel comfortable with someone, no matter how glowing the references, find someone else. It may be a simple personality clash. It doesn't matter. If a new person doesn't feel right, he or she isn't right for you . . . or your children.

For those on a tight budget, see if you can swap babysitting with a trusted friend or neighbor. Or you could barter with a sitter; perhaps a handy dad could do some handyman work in the house of the family down the street in exchange for that mom babysitting her children and yours.

BULLYING

We were both bullied as kids. Nanny Stella was stuck with a pin to see if she would pop because she was a few pounds overweight. Bullying can create terrible, terrible feelings of shame, mortification, and vulnerability in children.

Bullying is an epidemic. Children who are hurt and angry lash out. Children whose actions have no consequences continue to bully unabated. And children who bully are often bullied themselves.

If you suspect bullying—your child suddenly announces he doesn't want to take the bus to school anymore, or grades start plummeting, or he or she is acting out in self-destructive ways, for example—keep gently probing until the truth comes out. You have to establish trust with your child. Kids will take a lot of abuse before they tell you things, too, and they're expert at hiding shameful information from parents. Make sure that your children know from an early age that talking about anyone who hurts them in any way, with words or with bodies, is a special problem, and it is *not* tattling.

Teach your children to be assertive and confront bullies as soon as you can, such as with toddlers at the playground. Tell them that it is never okay for someone else to make you feel bad about yourself. Show them how to say, "What you did hurt my feelings."

If your children report that they're being bullied at school or on the way to school, have them follow these steps.

- Say to their teachers: "X is always bothering me. I've told my parents/caregiver about it, and he's still bothering me."

- See what their teachers' response is, then have your children report it to you or the caregiver.
- If their teachers don't handle it, your children should report exactly what was not done to you or the caregiver that night.
- You or the caregiver should set up a meeting with your children's teachers to make them aware of the severity of the situation. Document everything that is discussed. Teachers will be less defensive and children less embarrassed—or fearful about more taunting—if parents do this after school hours.
- If the teachers don't take prompt action, make an appointment with school administrators. Document everything. Schools are legally mandated to intervene.
- If the bullying is racial in nature, this may constitute a hate crime. Parents may have to resort to going to the school board and/or getting legal advice for racial bullying that is denied or denigrated by teachers and administrators.

Parents must be proactive to stand up to schools and that allow bullying to continue despite parental warnings about it. Your children also need to know that you are willing to fight on their behalf.

If your children are being bullied through instant messaging (IM), which is often untraceable, set controls on their computers so that they can only IM people they know. Monitor computer use. Have your child inform you the instant IM bullying begins.

If your child is being bullied by another child on the playground, or by a playmate whose parents you know, go to those parents and tell them what is going on. Some parents will dispute the bullying, and perhaps say that your child is a "baby" and "should learn to take it," or give the excuse the "boys will be boys," or some such. Simply reply: "Let's agree to differ about that point. Our children aren't playing together now." Then leave, or if the playdate is in your house, it's now over and the bully must leave.

Some parents enroll their children in martial arts classes, not to encourage striking back at a bully, but for the opposite reaction, as good martial arts classes give a core of respect and discipline. They also strengthen bodies and make children feel self-confident, which can help a child being bullied to regain confidence in his or her own body.

Sometimes your own children can bully, especially if they're being picked on, and feel the need to make someone even more vulnerable than they are feel as bad as they do. Obviously, bullying has serious consequences. Ask, "What about you do you feel is missing and that you have to treat the other person badly?" Then add, "I am disappointed in that choice of behavior, but it doesn't take away from the fact that I still love you. Now, what are you going to do to apologize to the person you bullied?"

The earlier you start empowering your children to stick up for themselves, the less likely they'll be to allow bullies to continue their hurtful ways.

DESTRUCTIVE FRIENDS

Destructive friends are similar to bullies. When sweet and loving friends suddenly turn on each other, the results can be devastating.

This kind of behavior often starts in preschool, and it can escalate to the point where it's out of control. One week, children are friends, and then they aren't. It's extremely confusing for young children who take statements like "I'm not your friend anymore" literally.

If your child has been hurt by a friend, give him or her time and space to calm down. Then have a comforting talk, saying that you understand how painful this is. Do not be judgmental or say things like "I never liked that Pamela anyway. She was always mean to you," even if it's true.

Explain that sometimes people say mean things when they are

angry or upset. Have your child say, "Well, you may not be my friend anymore but I'm still going to be your friend."

Children are often cruel simply because they want their own way, such as "I'm not playing with you anymore and I hate you unless you give me the truck" For those situations, have your child say, "Fine, I know you're angry but it isn't going to work."

Play-act these scenarios. You can even use dolls to stand in for the children. It may help your child feel better.

Sometimes you may have to do damage control because of the lack of parenting skills in someone else's home. Explain that some families don't have House Rules like ours, and the children haven't learned to be nice, and that they probably don't mean what they say, and that you'll be having a talk with the offending child's parents to explain what House Rules are.

MOVING

Moving is one of the most stressful things any family can endure, and it's easy for overwhelmed parents to forget just how much it can affect their children, particularly if a move will take the family far from all that is known and loved.

If you're moving in the same community, don't take the children house-hunting, as it can be overwhelming. When you do find the right house or apartment, however, take them there and show them their new rooms. Have them help choose the paint colors and décor for their rooms, and ask them where they want the furniture to be placed. Involve them in packing—it's a great time to get rid of clutter, and teach children about donating unused toys and things. Get them excited and try to treat the move as an adventure, not a chore, even if you really have to fake it. When children are participants in the move, it becomes far less stressful for them.

If you're moving far from home and can't physically visit the house, use photographs. Kids can still choose paint colors and make decisions about their new rooms without seeing them in person.

Once you've moved, unpack the children's rooms first. Place the furniture where the children have decided it should go, or in the exact same spot it was in the old room. Keep your daily routine, and especially bedtime routine, as close to the old one as possible.

Take the time to meet your neighbors. Ask who has children. Bake or buy cookies and go visiting, if feasible. Try to become active participants in your community. The sooner you feel at home and the kids make new friends, the easier the transition will be.

PEER PRESSURE

There are two kinds of peer pressure: pressure for things, and pressure to behave a certain way.

Children naturally want to fit in and be popular, and this can lead to some very bad choices by children too inexperienced to make them.

Peer pressure to buy things starts as soon as kids figure out what commercials are—which is another reason to keep the TV off. But you'll find that when your House Rules about allowance and disposable income are realistic, and your children have learned respect for money and how it has to be earned, they'll have an easier time understanding that some people are rich and others are not.

Tell them that their clothes or designer items don't define them, that there is no shame in not being able to afford something. And, most of all, that what truly means something in life—namely love, happiness, and respect—can never be bought. Only freely given or earned.

Children with good values about money will still want what their peers have, however. Have them use their allowance to earn coveted items. Give them a choice of extra chores that will earn money. You may consider telling them you will match what they've earned after they've gotten to a certain amount.

There are also many ways to be creative with limited income, if you decide that your children can have some of the things they want. Larger cities often have consignment shops, where people can sell their outgrown clothes and buy different ones, often brand-new. Go to flea markets. Sell unwanted toys in garage sales or sidewalk sales or on ebay.com. A great way to have kids become more responsible for their toys is to explain their potential for "growth." When Nanny Deb's brother was a kid he loved his Legos, and had set up a large board with a complicated train system. When he wanted a bike, he sold his Lego train set and was able to get the bike of his dreams.

If your children want something you *can* afford, but you don't want them to have it, such as designer sneakers they'll outgrow in three months, tell them the truth. Explain why. Peer pressure for things is very much about the values of your family. You can't wear designer clothes and then tell your children that the designer clothes aren't important!

Peer pressure to behave is much more complicated, as even the nicest of kids will do terrible things in order to be liked or to keep up with the more popular classmates. House Rules about behavior with friends need to be explicit from preschool age on up, although it becomes increasingly difficult to monitor behavior as your kids approach adolescence.

Your children are often struggling to make good choices, and it can be excruciating if not impossible for them to say to their friends or peers, "I can't hang around with you because you are a bad influence."

Keep channels of communication open. Involve your children in activities where they can excel, and where their values are cherished. Peer pressure at school can lessen when your kids find something that they're good at, and this can open up a new world of less judgmental or selfish friends and accomplishments.

SIBLING RIVALRY AND NEW BABIES

Sibling rivalry can start while mom is still pregnant (think Cain and Abel), and that's when mom and dad should start preparing siblings for the baby's arrival. To all the wives and mothers reading this book, imagine your husband walking in and announcing that he's brought home a new wife, and he just knows that you're going to be best friends forever. That's exactly how children can feel about a sibling.

Although preparation is key when you're pregnant or have a known adoption date, don't tell a two-year-old when you're only six weeks pregnant. Tell them when you're showing. We like to make big sister/brother T-shirts, and spend an afternoon decorating them. We also make a large calendar before the due date and mark off the days. Give older kids token gifts during the baby shower, too.

When the baby is born, take siblings to the hospital and say, "The baby brought you a big brother/sister present," and have it be something the older children have really wanted. When the baby comes home, stick to your routine. You can still read a book to your toddler while feeding the baby. No child wants to feel as if the new baby has taken his or her place in the house as well as in mom and dad's affection. Older siblings usually love to help with babies, so ask them to do little chores like fetching diapers or burp cloths which are things that children eighteen months old can do. Let them help bathe the new baby, which is usually a relaxed and fun time. Verbal kids should be encouraged to sing songs to the baby, while school aged kids can read to the baby. You needn't constantly say "Shhh, the baby is sleeping" or "Be careful"—but you can create an atmosphere that makes them want to join in and help. Provide reassurance that you love them as much as ever, if not more, for being such a loving and wonderful big sister/brother.

The concept of siblings for life is key to minimizing competitiveness and jealousy as children grow older. One family we know took their children out to the backyard, and had them grasp hands around a tree to prove their togetherness. Nanny Deb told a family of squabbling boys, "You lose your friends, but you are stuck with your family. You have to work it out. You are brothers for life." Then she gave them brothers for life T-shirts, and they finally began to realize just how much they loved each other. Parents must enforce the fact that siblings are the people children should be getting along with most in the world.

Don't label them as "the shy one" or "the ringleader" either—children take those labels to heart.

It's next to impossible to do, but parents should try their utmost not to compare children. We hear things like, "If Jason was potty trained when he was two and a half, what's wrong with Jacob? He's three already." Recognize that every child is different. Some will be toilet trained at two. Some will be smart or gorgeous, others less so.

Focus on who your child is, his or her unique strengths, and what he or she does well. Try not to nag, especially the your-brother-already-did-it-so-you-go-and-do-it-too type of comparison. Positive reinforcement, such as, "Well, Jason may be good at math, but you are good at spelling," will go a lot further than "Why can't you get an A in math like your brother?"

Make your expectations clear, realistic, and consistent for all siblings. Problems often escalate when parents indulge the younger children's misbehavior at the older children's expense. Be fair with your discipline and deal with the child who did the crime. If three-year-old Brianna took six-year-old Joanna's toy, don't say, "Oh,

Jo, let her play with it." Give Brianna solutions for the problem, such as, "This is Jo's toy and you need to give it back to her." If that doesn't work, say, "You're not respecting your sister's possessions. This is her room and you need to leave. It is not okay to just come into your sister's room and touch her things unless she says it is okay to come in."

A big problem we see is favoritism. It's human nature to favor a child who is most like you, or who may be cuter or smarter than the rest of your brood. Children always know when there's a favorite, whether it's stated or not, and this can create intense jealousy, rage, and lifelong hurts. Nanny Stella worked for a mom who had twin boys, and immediately favored one of them, despite protesting that she didn't. Nanny Stella explained that it was quite common to bond separately with multiples, especially if one is smaller and more fragile and seems to need more help.

It's very, very hard for parents to acknowledge that they play favorites. What we say is "It isn't that mommy or daddy loves that child more than they love you, it's just that they love them differently. It's a *different* love, not a better one. You will always be *someone's* favorite." This helps. As does mom and dad making an effort with the less-favored child, and getting to know him or her better.

Grandparents often inadvertently play favorites too, and it's up to parents to have a quiet word with them about this. Nanny Deb was lucky to have grandparents who always bought a little something for all the siblings, no matter whose birthday it was, and we like to do that, too.

In a large family, it's tough to give each child the attention he or she needs. But it's not tough to say that no one person is more important than the other—and say it aloud so that all the children know it.

All families should set aside special time for each child. Give each child special mom time and dad time, ideally each day, where that child is guaranteed your undivided attention. The longer the time you can spare, the better. This can be during going to school time, or bath time, or reading time, or even potty time. Make sure that the House Rule is no interrupting during mom or dad time unless it is an emergency, and certainly not because the phone is ringing. Knowing that there will be uninterrupted alone time with parents goes a very long way to soothing nerves and enhancing conversation.

Also set up date nights for kids, which are special outings with only one child and one parent. Families with a large brood can try kid date night once a week. Let the child pick the activity that can be done in the time you have, whether it's a movie, or shopping, or a manicure, or a trip to the park.

Every child will need extra attention at some point—and with a bit of luck, not all of them need it on the same day! School may be harder than usual, or your daughter's best friend said something awful, or your son just needs you. Temporarily giving extra attention to a child who's made his or her needs clear is not favoritism. It's providing comfort—and that's just good parenting.

Families who encourage teamwork and the notion of siblings for life will be raising children who can get along with everyone, not only their family members. They'll be the sort of kids who, at their birthday party, open a present and say, "Look, we can *all* play with it." And then they all will.

SINGLE PARENTS

For single-parent households, obviously there is only one page, and no arguments or undermining about who does what, and why.

All our techniques and House Rules are the same for single parents. The problems single parents face are that they're both the good cop and bad cop by default, and they have no live-in backup to help with the tough chores of parenting. It can become overwhelming, especially when finances are tight. On the other hand, when you must play good cop/bad cop, at least you are only arguing with yourself!

When Nanny Deb was a baby, her parents divorced, and she was raised by her mother. Nanny Deb had a very vivid imagination, and as she was the only child in school with no dad, she invented one—and six siblings, too! Well, her teacher bumped into Nanny Deb's mother in town one day and said, "Oh, Mrs. Carroll, I don't know how you do it." Needless to say Nanny Deb got in serious trouble for lying. The point is, If you're a single parent, talk to your children, and explain that there are many kinds of families and not all have two parents, and each family has pluses and minuses.

Nanny Deb also knew a mom who had twins by artificial insemination. When the twins were six, they were asked where their dad was, and were told they didn't have one. When pressed, they would say, "Well, our mom wanted kids but she needed a man to help so she went to a place and asked them and there was a nice man who wanted to help so he had given the place sperm so a lady who wanted a baby could have one and that guy is our dad." That usually put an end to the questioning! Of course, if you feel your parenting situation is a private matter, follow our suggestions in the Adoption section on page 288 for talking about personal information.

Single parents should try their utmost to accept all the help they can get, and not be afraid or embarrassed to admit to fatigue. Everyone who's a parent knows how hard it is to be consistent and on top of things all the time.

It's extremely important for children to know that *you* are the parent and that *you* are in charge. You're not their best friend, and you're not using them as a replacement for a partner. Try to establish an extended family, whether of relatives or friends. Find good, reliable, older role models, such as a brother, cousin, trusted friend, or colleague, big brother/big sister organizations, and support groups, especially for single moms raising boys or dads raising girls.

STRANGER DANGER

Whenever a child is abducted or sexually abused, shivers of fear go through parents, dreading that it may happen to their own beloved offspring. While the overwhelming majority of abductions and abuse are committed by family members, that horrific fact provides little reassurance to anxious parents.

We grew up in communities where most children walked to and from school, played outside on the street, in yards, or in friends' houses, with no advance scheduling, with no cell phones or call waiting, and certainly with no parents hovering anxiously to see where we were.

Times have unfortunately changed for the worse where it comes to children being allowed to go off on their own. It's just not possible or realistic to be trusting and open with strangers anymore, even those who may live nearby. Which is even more reason to get involved in your community, meet your neighbors, and have a communication system in place so you know where your children are. Cell phones, for all their annoying intrusiveness, are an absolute lifesaver in this regard.

Teach your children that they must *never* go off with anyone at all without mommy or daddy knowing about it, even if that person says a little puppy is hurt and needs that child's help. Predators know exactly how to entrap children, and they often do it with pets, or by donning a fake uniform and pretending to be an official.

The *only* person who can pick them up will be someone who is approved and talked about in advance. The easiest way to do this is by using a password. An approved person will *always* know the secret password that means it's safe to be with him or her. This can come in handy in case of emergencies, such as a friend having to pick up a child when a sibling broke her leg and is in the hospital, etc.

Also teach your children to say or shout, "Don't touch me!' if they don't want to be touched. Instead of shouting "Help!" children should shout, "Fire!" as this is more likely to attract attention.

Model appropriate behavior for dealing with strangers, so your children learn that an invasion of personal space is not acceptable. If a stranger makes what you feel are inappropriate comments, simply say, without rancor, "We don't discuss our family with strangers" and walk away.

If strangers touch your children, say, "Please don't touch my daughter/son. We're learning about not talking to strangers." Then walk away.

When going on outings where you're worried about getting lost, write their name on their torso with a marker along with your cell phone number, or put a card in one of their pockets with your name and cell phone number.

One of the hardest things to do is have faith that your children know what's safe and what isn't. Your being afraid isn't going to provide any additional protection, and can create undue anxiety. Take a deep breath, believe that you have taught your children well, and trust that they will be safe.

ACKNOWLEDGMENTS

· ·

NANNY DEB

This book is due to a lifetime of experience, so there are many people to thank!

I want to thank all of the families I have worked for—you know who you are, and I could not have done this without you. Thank you for welcoming me into your homes; you have all captured my heart. To Linda and Johnny Wachsmann, my first family, who hired me as an eighteen-year-old from Wales, thank you for believing in me. Thank you to David Olson and Mary Lawson, who inspired me to move to the United States and spread my wings. Thanks to Marina Claessens—you encouraged me to follow my dreams and become a better person. Thanks to the Foote family—without you I probably would not have made it to the U.S.A. Also a big thank you to Kevin and Anne Beall, with whom I survived my first brutal New York snowstorm. To Michaela Van Caneghem, thank you for everything. To Shelley Curtis and Dr. Frank Litvack, for always welcoming me with open arms and hearts. Thank you to Corbin Bernsen and Amanda Pays, you really are my family, I love you! To Mr. and Mrs. S., thank you for all of your kindness and generosity, words cannot say enough, you are forever in my heart. To Mama D and her girls, you taught me a lot about strength of character, and for that I will always love you and be forever grateful. To Amy P. and Bernie Weinraub, thank you again for everything. To the Grecos, thank you for the ride and for sharing your amazing boys with me for so long—you are always in my heart. And to the Sonnenfelds, thank you for letting me do the show and for trying to make it all work.

Thank you to my mother for giving me the freedom to fly, even though it was hard. Your strength continues to inspire me. I love you. Thank you to my brother Howell for letting me practice my nanny skills on you when you were just a baby. Also thank you to my cousins, Chris, Nigel, and Mark for letting me be a "mother hen" to them. Thanks to my Uncle "Nunkie." He knows why! And thank you to both my grandmothers, Nana Carroll in heaven, who watches over me and who I know has a hand in all this—you were a true light in my life; and to Nana Jones, thank you for all the times you played dolls with me; some of my funniest childhood memories are with you "Mrs. Winterbottom."

Thank you to Julie Swales, without you I would never have auditioned for *Nanny 911,* and to Gar Lester, for helping her convince me I needed to do it!

And lastly, to all of my wonderful friends, thank you for supporting me along this journey. We have seen the best of times and the worst. Janet, Julie, Geraldine, Lorri, Kelly, Marianne, Lindy, Dessi, Karen, and Edith—you are amazing women! And to Stella, without you there would be no book and no *Nanny 911.* Meeting you has changed my life. Your generosity is endless, your laughter contagious, and your heart enormous. You are one in a million!

NANNY STELLA

I would like to thank my family and friends, who always encouraged me to be who I am, and for putting up with me, especially the Duxbury Clan and The Doney Gang.

To my mother Anne, who instilled in me "Weebles wobble, but

they don't fall down." To my Dad Jim and my Grandma Lizzie, who look down on me from above. I know that you are taking care of me and I know you are both very proud. To my sister Jessica, for letting me be her sister. To my brother Billy, for constantly reminding me where we come from, and to his fiancée Julie for always geeing me along.

To Kizz for always knowing that "I could do it." I miss you, my friend.

To Claudia Khan from the Help Company, who gave me some amazing placements over the years and was the one who put my name forward for the *Nanny 911* casting process. Thanks, Claudia!

To Ara Keshishian, my agent at CAA for handling all that red tape.

To all the families who have played a huge part in the evolution of Nanny Stella, without them I would not have the experience I have. I cannot mention them all, but some require a definite nod. To Cindy Quane, Greg, Bryan and Jimmy Breen, words cannot express the gift you gave me. To J and K, for giving me the job of my career and encouraging me to pursue the chance of a lifetime, but most of all for sharing with me Max, who is without doubt one of the loves of my life. To Jennifer, Jason, and Jarret Sturtz, without their support I could not have participated in *Nanny 911* as I did.

To Deb Carroll, Deb, you really are the modern day "Pied Piper" simply because when you speak, children follow, especially with your infamous "whoo whoo!" You inspire me. And if you weren't at the end of the telephone on many an occasion I would have committed hara-kiri. Thank you for the laughter and the tears. You have an amazing spirit and presence; I am honored to call you my friend.

To my stepson Justin and his brother Jai, what an incredible lesson in life you have taught me.

To my husband Mike, you are the most amazing man, especially because when I am losing my head you keep me grounded. Kissing those frogs was well worth it. "I found all I waited for; I could not ask for more." Please know I love you ten!

FROM NANNY DEB AND NANNY STELLA

Wow! Who would have thought it possible for two British nannies to be starring in a hit TV show . . . not us!

We would like to thank the people who made this dream a reality. Paul Jackson of Granada USA, you truly are an English gentleman! Bruce Toms, who joined us on this roller coaster ride, pretended not to listen when we asked to get off, and thankfully still returns our calls. Special thanks to both of you, who liked what you saw and who subjected the rest of the world to it.

To all the wonderful crew, staff, and everyone behind the scenes at *Nanny 911*, Granada America, and the Fox network, thank you for all the moral support and for helping us on this amazing ride. To Michael Shevloff, who joins us in the field for a cup of tea; Gerry McKean, who we're hoping won't need this book; Michael Gretza, who keeps everyone grounded; Karen Benckendorffer, for always trying to make our journey a smooth ride; and Kevin Lillestol who invented the word budget (thanks for the hobnobs!). We would also like to thank Mike Darnell for liking what he saw in us and Jill Hudson for all her great public relations efforts.

Most of all, thank you to the *Nanny 911* families for opening up their homes and hearts to us. Keep up the good work! A special mention must be made to the Silcock boys, who humbled us with their extraordinary spirit. Go, Team Silcock!

Love, Nanny Deb and Nanny Stella

KAREN MOLINE

This book would not exist without the phenomenal knowledge and skills from two of the most loving, compassionate, and generous women on this planet: Nanny Deb and Nanny Stella. I know I will forevermore be a much better parent thanks to their wisdom and kindness, whether my son believe it or not!

Many thanks as well to Suzanne Gluck and Jonathan Pecarsky, my marvelous agents at William Morris; the exemplary Paul Jackson and Deborah Nash at Granada America and Karen Beckendorffer at *Nanny 911*, for help when it was most needed.

Much gratitude goes to our passionate and peerless editor, Doug Grad, who is not only smart and sanguine but also a great dad. And to Judith Regan, Tracy Carns, Kim Hadney, Mandy Kain, Paul Crichton, Michelle Ishay, Larry Pekarek, Vivian Gomez, Cassie Jones, Jim Geraghty, and Daniel Nayeri at Regan-Books, for all their sterling assistance.

And heartfelt thanks to my own nanny, Sithar Dolma, for her patience, love, and calm; my sister, Julie, for help above and beyond; and most of all to my son, Emmanuel Thanh Sang, who fills my heart with joy and delight even when he doesn't want to listen to the House Rules.

GET ALL THE **411 . . .** ON **NANNY 911!**

Sign up for the exclusive mobile phone service from Nanny Central, and be the first to hear about *NANNY 911* news, advice, tips, contests, and more!

Is your family out of control?

Don't delay—sign up today!

To subscribe to the service:

Send a text message with the word "JOIN" to the shortcode 62669 (NANNY)

You will then receive a text message from *NANNY 911* with full details about the latest service and how to participate.

For further information about how to send a text from your specific phone and details on *NANNY 911* mobile see www.nanny911.tv

This service is supported by all major U.S. carriers. Standard carrier messaging charges may apply. (U.S. customers only)

NANNY 911

ARE YOUR KIDS OUT OF CONTROL?
If so, GIVE YOURSELF A BREAK
and contact NANNY 911!

Let our incredible "Nanny Specialists"
work their magic!

For casting information and to apply:

Go to www.nanny911.tv and download
the application. Send in along with your videotape
and family photos to the casting address provided.